BRAND AID

(BRAND AID)

Shopping Well to Save the World

Lisa Ann Richey and Stefano Ponte

A Quadrant Book

UNIVERSITY OF MINNESOTA PRESS

Minneapolis

London

Quadrant, a joint initiative of the University of Minnesota Press and the Institute for Advanced Study at the University of Minnesota, provides support for interdisciplinary scholarship within a new collaborative model of research and publication.

QUADRANT   http://quadrant.umn.edu

Sponsored by the Quadrant Health and Society Group (advisory board: Susan Craddock, Jennifer Gunn, Alex Rothman, and Karen-Sue Taussig) and by the Center for Bioethics.

Quadrant is generously funded by the Andrew W. Mellon Foundation.

Portions of chapter 1 previously appeared as "Better (Red)™ Than Dead? Celebrities, Consumption, and International Aid," *Third World Quarterly* 29, no. 4 (2008): 711–29; reprinted by permission of Taylor and Francis Ltd. Portions of chapter 4 were previously published as "Bono's Product (RED) Initiative: Corporate Social Responsibility That Solves the Problems of 'Distant Others,'" *Third World Quarterly* 30, no. 2 (2009): 301–17; reprinted by permission of Taylor and Francis Ltd., http://www.tandf.co.uk/journals.

Published by the University of Minnesota Press
111 Third Avenue South, Suite 290
Minneapolis, MN 55401-2520
http://www.upress.umn.edu

Library of Congress Cataloging-in-Publication Data

Richey, Lisa Ann.
    Brand aid : shopping well to save the world / Lisa Ann Richey and Stefano Ponte.
        p.   cm.
    A Quadrant Book.
    Includes bibliographical references and index.
    ISBN 978-0-8166-6545-7 (hc : alk. paper) — ISBN 978-0-8166-6546-4 (pb : alk. paper)
    1. Economic assistance—Developing countries. 2. Celebrities—Political activity.
3. Social entrepreneurship. 4. Social responsibility of business. 5. Branding (Marketing)—
Social aspects. 6. Consumption (Economics)—Social aspects. I. Ponte, Stefano. II. Title.
    HC60.R482 2011
    361.2′6—dc22

                                                                            2010044990

Printed in the United States of America on acid-free paper

The University of Minnesota is an equal-opportunity educator and employer.

18 17 16 15 14 13 12 11   10 9 8 7 6 5 4 3 2

In memory of Nereo Ponte

The **RED** pill makes you larger. Just say yes. You buy a **RED** product over here, the **RED** company buys life-saving drugs for someone who can't afford them over there. That's it. So why not shop 'til it stops. Why not try some off-the-rack enlightenment. We can spend and destroy. We can wear our inside out. You will be a good-looking Samaritan because, and this is very good news for some of us, sinners make the best saints.

—Product **(RED)** video,
Emporio Armani "One Night Only"

CONTENTS

PREFACE

If you read the advertisements for the RED American Express card, you will find that "you can feel great about spending, whether you are buying cappuccinos or cashmere." American Express asks readers to ponder what we consider to be one of the more perverse outcomes of the HIV/AIDS pandemic in Africa—"Has there ever been a better reason to shop?"[1]

Both of us have done field-based research in Africa since the early 1990s. When the first RED products were launched at Davos, we had recently returned from working over the previous year on separate research projects in South Africa. Part of Lisa's research involved months as a participant-observer in an AIDS treatment clinic in the oldest township of the Western Cape. Part of Stefano's research dealt with how corporations were changing their ways of running a business in postapartheid South Africa.

Our own personal responses to the things we have seen and heard in the field have been diverse, and certainly not always completely thoughtful or constructive. Spending hours listening to negotiations between AIDS patients, their healthcare providers, and their virus is always emotional and difficult. Making sense of "Black Economic Empowerment" initiatives in the context of rampant unemployment and continued labor exploitation in South Africa is not straightforward either. Inadequacy and frustration is what we have both experienced with our own understandings. For example, it was difficult to maintain analytical distance when an eight-year-old girl dressed in a school uniform—the African mirror image of one of our own daughters—walked into the clinic to get medicine to manage the disease passed to her by a sexually violent relative. Yet never, in response to the complexity and frustration, the hope or gratitude of understanding the impact of HIV and AIDS in Africa, did we ever imagine that this might provide "a reason to shop." What could one possibly expect to buy that might get us out of such a predicament?

The Product RED initiative and its public uptake fascinated us in its portrayal of both AIDS and trade in Africa. Thus, this book stems from a critical theory impulse and a moral dissatisfaction with Product RED. The complex scripts of race, gender, and global economic inequality are ignored with justifications that "AIDS is an emergency" (see Calhoun 2008) and, thus, normal rules do not apply. At the same time, the "normality" of consumption and the social and environmental relations of trade and production that underpin poverty, inequality, and disease are not questioned. It is also essential for Product RED that the beneficiaries are strangers, reduced to bare lives, which can be counted in the calculation of "lives saved" as easily as pill counts or merchandise inventory. Africans with AIDS are presented in smooth, virtual representations in which "global politics" is reduced to style.

Both of us have been conducting research projects with extensive fieldwork in Tanzania, Uganda, and South Africa, and shorter stints in other African countries. Lisa's other books look at issues of health, gender, and international development in Africa (Vavrus and Richey 2003; Richey 2008). Since 2005, she has been working in South Africa and Uganda on the politics of access to antiretroviral (ARV) treatment for HIV/AIDS. Stefano's other books are on market liberalization in African agriculture, the changing role of Africa in the global economy, and commodity trade (Ponte 2002; Gibbon and Ponte 2005; Daviron and Ponte 2005). Since 2005, he has been working on the political economy of food-safety standards, environmental and social labels, and corporate codes of conduct.

Methodologically, this book is an intermediary study, so we are not researching the motivations of the people who give aid (either the consumers or the corporations) or the perceptions of those who receive it (the beneficiaries of Global Fund–supported initiatives in Rwanda, Lesotho, Swaziland, or Ghana). The point of our book on Brand Aid, like branding in general, is to demonstrate the privileged role of this intermediary realm—where value is created.

This is a book based on an analysis of academic, popular, and practical business literature and on the plethora of publicly available information from the RED campaign. We have spent countless hours researching the frequently updated RED Web site, are Facebook fans who receive RED news and marketing, and are members of the "joinred.com" community. We have also engaged in participant observation in various shopping venues with RED products in the United States and UK.

Early along in the project, we attempted to conduct interviews with the companies involved in RED on their corporate social responsibility (CSR) and RED-specific activities. These were largely unsuccessful (with the exception of Armani). We did not conduct fieldwork, so there were no independent site visits of the RED companies' suppliers' factories in developing countries, nor did we interview the African women and children with AIDS who were "saved" by RED, at least not specifically for this book.

The disconnect between the RED treatment virtualism (in which "saving AIDS victims" is reduced to buying them pills) and witnessing the daily negotiations of AIDS patients with chronic illness and poverty—how their supporters, their doctors and counselors, and patients themselves were struggling and living in a context where ARV drugs are available—has resulted in this book. As a response to such a vast chasm between a global initiative and how Africans with AIDS are saving each other and saving themselves, it is meager. This book is not engaging in academic regret, mourning the loss of authenticity in development, manifest in the example of RED, but instead is trying to understand the nature and conditions of what RED means and what it does. Product RED is an innovative modality of international development financing, and one that is likely to spawn a variety of similar Brand Aid interventions. It provides an easy solution to current crises in international development—one that enables corporations to raise their CSR profile without substantially changing their normal business

practices while consumers engage in low-cost heroism without meaningfully increasing their awareness of global production–consumption
relations or the struggles of living with HIV/AIDS. In this form of
Brand Aid, the problems and the people who experience them are
branded and marketed to Western consumers just as effectively as the
products that will "save" them.

The Product RED initiative is variously referred to in the media,
the Web sites of RED companies, and its own Web site www.joinred
.com as RED, Product(RED), Product RED, (RED)™, plus permuta-
tions of the RED theme combined with the RED companies' names
and products. In the rest of the book, we use only the term "RED" to
avoid confusion, except when a different form is included in a quotation
or when a specific RED product is mentioned.

As we worked on this book, friends and colleagues sent us encour-
agement in the form of scholarly articles, links to Web sites, celebrity gossip, a RED t-shirt, and the opinions of their own friends, colleagues, and children on Product RED. It is a pleasure to thank them
here. We benefited from many thoughtful readers and supporters of
this work, to whom we owe a great debt. Thanks to Rita Abrahamsen,
Ann Anagnost, Melanie Bielefeld, Simon Bolwig, Dan Brockington,
Alexandra Budabin, Padraig Carmody, Sylvia Chant, Amal Fadlalla,
Didier Fassin, Peter Gibbon, Margaret Gifford, Daniele Giovannucci,
Andrea Goldstein, Lene Hansen, Graham Harrison, Jim Igoe, Steven
Jensen, Sam Jones, Ippolytos Kalofonos, Peter Kragelund, Christian
Lund, Peter Lund-Thomsen, Henrik Secher Marcussen, Claire Mercer,
Vinh-Kim Nguyen, Elina Oinas, Colleen O'Manique, Jim Pletcher,
Lone Riisgaard, Hakan Sechinelgin, Morten Sigsgaard, Dan Smith,
Howard Stein, Grahame Thompson, and Lindsay Whitfield.

We had the opportunity to present parts of this work to audiences
of scholars and students at the University of Toronto, the University of
Michigan, the London School of Economics and Political Science,
the School for International Studies at the University of Toronto,
the Center for Advanced Security Theory and the Department of
Geography at the University of Copenhagen, the Communication for
Development Program at Malmö University, the Centre for African
Studies at the University of Edinburgh, and the Center for Gender,

Power, and Diversity at Roskilde University. We benefited from comments on our presentations as part of the "Social and Political Aspects of AIDS" working group at Makerere University in Kampala, the "Cultural Production and Experience Strategies, Design, and Everyday Life" conference and the "Politics at the Margins of the State" seminar and Roskilde University Development Day in Roskilde, the UNESCO-SSRC–organized conference on Gender and HIV/AIDS in Paris, the "International Network on Religion and AIDS in Africa" conference in Copenhagen, and the "Branding AIDS" conference in Toronto (special thanks to Yuvraj Joshi, who organized this inspiring event).

Thanks to our colleagues who participated in the panels we organized on this work at the "Nordic Africa Days" conference (Cissy Kityo Mutuluuza, Louise Rasmussen, and Danai Mupotsa) and those at the International Studies Association panel (Craig Calhoun, Andy Cooper, and Johanna Hood). We are also indebted to audiences at the meetings of the African Studies Association (U.S.), the International Studies Association, the Association of American Geographers, the African Studies Association of the United Kingdom, the Association of European Centres of African Studies, and the Nordic Media Association. Lisa gratefully acknowledges research support from the Danish Development Research Council. The book benefited from the attentive work of three anonymous reviewers and our editor, Richard Morrison. Finally, very special thanks to our research assistants Mike Baab, Ekaterina Bang-Andersen, and Anna Maria Escobar Fibla.

We appreciate the patience of Sasha, Arianna, and Zeno William.

INTRODUCTION
RED and the Reinvention of International Aid

RED

Bono's launch of RED at Davos in 2006 opened a new frontier for financing development aid. The Irish singer from the world-famous rock band U2 is the front man for the first attempt to fund one of the largest providers of global AIDS treatment through the purchasing power of Western consumers. RED is "a business model to raise awareness and money for the Global Fund by teaming up with the world's most iconic brands to produce RED-branded products."[1] Consumption, trade, and aid wed dying Africans with designer goods. With the engagement of American Express, Apple, Converse, Gap, Emporio Armani, Hallmark, Motorola, and now Dell, Microsoft, Starbucks, and many others, consumers can save HIV/AIDS patients in Africa. They can do so simply by shopping, as a percentage of profits from RED lines goes directly to support the Global Fund to Fight AIDS, Tuberculosis and Malaria.

According to RED's official Web site, "RED is the color of emergency and the color of blood, which is life, and our soil, which feeds us."[2] From an Emporio Armani RED watch to a RED iPod™ and from Converse (RED) sneakers to a (RED)GAP sundress, a percentage of the profits from the sale of all RED co-branded products is contributed by the "iconic" partners directly to the Global Fund. Companies pay a licensing fee to RED and commit to a five-year partnership. In its first five years of operation, RED donated over $160 million to the Global Fund. RED grants are made through the Fund's standard disbursement processes and have been dedicated to the Fund's best-performing programs for AIDS in Africa—initially to Ghana, Lesotho, Rwanda, and Swaziland, and more recently to South Africa and Zambia.[3]

RED products include laptop computers, Frappuccinos, tennis shoes, greeting cards, skateboards, and a cashmere bikini. RED goods have been heavily marketed and made widely available in the UK and the United States. Selected RED products have been released in many other countries, including Japan, Switzerland, France, Canada, and Singapore.

RED has received extensive media attention, including promotions on CNN's *Larry King Live,* two RED issues of *The Independent* (edited by Bono and Giorgio Armani), Trafalgar Square's MOTO(RED) concert featuring the Scissor Sisters, and a massive $25 million marketing campaign by Gap. This campaign included stars photographed by Annie Leibowitz and wrapping Chicago's three-story Michigan Avenue Gap flagship store in red vinyl.[4]

The launch of the U.S. RED campaign was the feature topic of a whole episode of the *Oprah Winfrey* television show. The *Oprah* episode opened in its usual studio, with a duet sung by Bono and Alicia Keys. Oprah wore a Gap RED "INSPI(RED)" t-shirt that she credited with the power to save the world. Oprah explained:

> You know clothes are usually not important or significant. They usually just cover your body, but I'm wearing the most important t-shirt I've ever worn in my life. I love this so much, I've bought one for every person in this audience. The t-shirts that we are all wearing today are from the Gap's new RED line, and the Gap gives half of the profits of their RED products to fight AIDS in Africa and that means that just the t-shirts that this audience is wearing today will provide enough medication to prevent transmission of HIV from mother to child [the camera cuts to two young, white, concerned women in the audience] for over fourteen thousand pregnant women [audience cheers]. This show today is about getting the medicine to the people who need it. So by just

buying a t-shirt, a pair of jeans, even a cell phone, you can actually begin to save lives.[5]

Then Oprah and Bono jumped in a red Ford Thunderbird and sped over to Chicago's Michigan Avenue. They alighted onto a red carpet in front of the Gap flagship store to begin their "fashion spree." Inside the shop, there was a fashion show of RED clothes with Christy Turlington, Penélope Cruz, and Kanye West as models. They talked and bought at the Gap and then continued up Michigan Avenue to Apple, Armani, and Motorola shops as well. This RED launch was covered by over three hundred broadcast media outlets in the United States. On a television spot, Bobby Shriver of the famous American Kennedy clan and cofounder of RED stated that after the *Oprah* show there had been a run on Gap RED products, which would continue to be sold for the next five years.

Oprah interviewed Christy Turlington (also sporting an "INSPI(RED)" t-shirt), who identified not as a supermodel, but as a "mother of two." Turlington gave a concise summary of the RED initiative: "It doesn't get any more simple or bigger than that."

As of December 2010, RED had contributed $160 million to the Global Fund, less than 1 percent of the total (public and private) $18.2 billion disbursed by donors to the Global Fund since its inception. Ninety-five percent of disbursed funds came from "traditional" bilateral donors. The rest came from private sources. Within private sources, "traditional" philanthropy provided the bulk (the Gates Foundation provided 69 percent of all private funding alone). RED is actually the second largest source of private funding. So, from one point of view, RED is a small drop in the Global Fund's large bucket. From another point of view, it is an important source of funding within the private sector, and it is being taken seriously as a potential funding modality by the Global Fund itself.

In the popular media, criticisms of RED for having a limited impact on AIDS in Africa, given its great expenditure in product marketing, have been quickly and skillfully rebutted by RED supporters, including regular media appearances by Bono.[6] RED promoters argue that because the product mobilizes a previously untapped constituency to contribute to aid for AIDS in Africa, this constitutes "new money" going to fight the disease. Marketing money would have been spent anyway by major corporations. Thus, any contribution made by RED is better than the contribution that would have been made without it—nothing.

But, as we will discuss in the book, corporate social responsibility (CSR) is becoming increasingly popular, and there is no reason why one can assume that RED budgets would not have been invested by these companies into other ethically oriented initiatives. One cannot take for granted that consumers' RED choices simply replace their previously "unethical" ones, thus leading to a more positive outcome. However, we can observe that the framing of the impact of RED as measurable and concrete (comparable only to nothing at all) is part of the construction of the initiative itself. RED promotes itself as if it were in a vacuum, not part of the many different kinds of consumption choices that individuals can make every day that actually affect the lives of women and children with AIDS in Africa.

But the point of our inquiry is not to adjudicate the "success" of the RED initiative in raising funds, nor is it to compare RED as a modality of aid financing with other types of existing interventions. Our investigation demonstrates how RED functions using the guarantee of celebrity together with the negotiated representation of a distant "Africa" to meet competing, and incommensurable, objectives. We demonstrate how RED solves the contradictions between shopping and helping within its own modality, and how in doing so, it creates surprising relationships entwining compassion with consumption.

Aid Celebrities and Hard Commerce

Aid celebrities—Bono, Jeffrey Sachs, and Paul Farmer—guarantee the "cool quotient," the management, and the target of the RED modality of aid financing. Bono is the rock star who led his fans to believe that they could solve Africa's problems of AIDS and poverty. Jeffrey Sachs is the economist behind the Millennium Development Goals (MDGs) and the Global Fund. And Paul Farmer is the physician who convinced the world that treatment of AIDS was possible in even the poorest communities. Thus, these aid celebrities guarantee that RED can be taken seriously as a practical step that Western shoppers can take to help solve important global problems. By claiming to be linked to commerce, and not philanthropy, RED reconfigures international development around aid celebrities and consumer-citizens united to do good by dressing well.

The RED genesis story as popularized through mass-media coverage depicts RED as the creative fruit resulting from many seasons of labor by the aid celebrity extraordinaire, Bono.[7] RED is described as the outcome of Bono's having thought that his ideas for helping the poor needed to be marketed in a less "misty-eyed, bleeding-heart way."[8] And in fact, according to popular media buzz on the initiative, "the real surprise is that Bono turns out to be a card-carrying capitalist. He wants companies selling RED products to make a profit by helping the poor—doing well by doing good."[9] In the words of the American Express RED launch representative at the Davos meeting, it is "conscientious commerce"—good for business, good for all.[10] Product RED provides a new mechanism for development finance that weds "hard commerce" with help, consumers with celebrities, and doctors with rockers.

Giorgio Armani was most explicit in his recognition of the capitalist bottom line with his speech launching the RED Emporio Armani product line at Davos: "The new formula is that this is charity to the world of course, but particularly it is the fact that commerce will no longer have a negative connotation."[11] Bono explicitly rejected that he was being used by companies to restore their reputations.[12] "We are not endorsing their products, these products endorse us," Bono claimed.[13] RED consumers are encouraged to "upgrade their choice" in the products they buy as one would upgrade an airline ticket or a portable computer model. In RED, moral choice-making is framed within logics of market rationality and individual entrepreneurship: in other words, "profitability *is* the moral framework" (Banet-Weiser and Lapsansky 2008, 1255; emphasis in the original).

RED as "Best Practice"

RED is a quintessential concoction of current understandings of "best practice" in corporate strategy, aid, and trade. In relation to corporate strategies, it promotes the concept that CSR is good for societies, environments, and profit. Two decades of civil society action against corporations' labor practices, environmental mismanagement, predatory extraction of natural resources, unfair trade practices, and high prices for HIV/AIDS drugs have pushed CSR onto the agenda of many mainstream corporations. Often, corporate responses to CSR concerns have been reactive, rather than proactive.

In contrast, RED proactively seeks to engage businesses in its version of CSR that marries co-branding and help to Africa. The fact that such successful brands participate in this exercise implies for others that it meets their financial, social, and environmental objectives (the so-called triple bottom line). Also, RED's architecture takes its inspiration from the currently favored form of corporate organization, the "network" company—flexible, organized by projects, lean, and generally better able to plug into several other networks (Boltanski and Chiapello 1999).

In relation to international development assistance, RED fits the sought-after model of aid efficiency. It is a private initiative providing funds to a public-private organization (the Global Fund), which channels them to successful applicants who are responsible for local implementation. RED is an initiative that is not burdened by additional bureaucracy. All the elements are present already: the Global Fund, which prides itself of having overhead costs of only 3 percent;[14] DATA (Debt, AIDS, Trade, Africa)/ONE, Bono's own lean organization from which RED emerges;[15] and the flexible and efficient corporations that produce the fashionable goods (or rather, they market them). The Global Fund notes explicitly that "the agreements with RED and its partner companies do not add significant administrative work for the Global Fund or its recipients, ensuring that the funds raised go to where they are needed most."[16]

Finally, RED fits a recently consolidated paradigm that both aid *and* trade are central to development. RED is removed from both the old days of leftist tirades against trade (aid, not trade) and from the opposing stance against aid (trade, not aid).

RED, the Global Fund, and "Worthy Recipients" of Aid

RED is a new modality of aid *financing*, not aid delivery per se. The Global Fund acts as a regranting intermediary between local applicant organizations who will implement the activities and funders, most of which are traditional bilateral and multilateral donors. RED is the only Global Fund contributor thus far to determine where its monies will go: RED funds are allocated to the best performing programs on HIV/AIDS in Africa.

Significant changes in the past decade involving increasing access to antiretroviral (ARV) drugs for treating AIDS in Africa have reconfigured the landscape of aid for global AIDS. The recipients of RED funds, "women and children with AIDS in Africa," are quite different from the more controversial target groups of AIDS interventions elsewhere, or those of the pretreatment era. As we describe in chapter 2, RED profits go to "good AIDS," and to deserving recipients. In many ways, the distant others helped by RED resemble more closely the proximate others helped by the "pink ribbon" corporate campaigns to support breast cancer in the West. King documents how breast cancer funding is dependent on its easy fit with "corporate values" with its focus on "mothers, daughters, sisters and friends" and the common cultural perception that "among people with breast cancer, there are, thankfully, no men, no gays or lesbians, no IV drug users, and no sex workers" (2006, 77–78). In both campaigns, beneficiaries are people who are not directly associated with sexual deviance or substance abuse. The particularly heterosexual transmission pattern of African AIDS combined with the recent opportunity to treat the disease with ARVs makes it possible to save women and children with AIDS in ways that appear ethically and politically uncomplicated.

AIDS provides the quintessential cause as the outlet for RED's hard-commerce approach to doing good also because, like fashion, rock music, or celebrity, it is about money, power, and sex. As described in the *Sunday Times*, "the sex appeal of red" comes also from stars like Scarlett Johansson, "the sizzling face of Bono's new ethical brand." "Johansson is peeling off her clothes in a photographic studio in LA, in preparation for becoming the pin-up for Bono's new plan."[17] Johansson's interpretation of why the product is called RED is that "It's a sexy, hot color that's vibrant and attention-grabbing. It has been since the 1940s, such a time of high glamour and red lipstick and red nails. That's probably why they chose it for this campaign—glamour!"[18] The sexy messages promoted by RED are unrealistic and contradictory to the "Abstain, Be faithful, or use Condoms" (ABC) approach to sex in the HIV/AIDS era. Consumers are encouraged to express their sexuality, their attractiveness, and their desire through consumer choices, with no recognition that sexual exchange is often part and parcel of successful consumption patterns in the societies most affected by AIDS (see chapter 2).

Taking RED Seriously

While RED may seem far removed from conventional aid, we argue that it would be a mistake to dismiss it. RED is not simply media glitz aimed at mainstream consumers of midrange products. The 5 August 2006 issue of the internationally prestigious medical journal the *Lancet* was a co-branded product: *(The Lancet)*[RED]. This was the first time the journal had included advertisements, as RED product ads covered its pages in between cutting-edge articles on medicine. The *Lancet* wrote a compelling editorial blurb in favor of RED and also contributed $30,000 "in support of this important project."[19]

Product RED is listed, together with the Global Fund, in a recent list of "new networks mobilizing citizens, voters, and consumers to take personal action against poverty" (Nelson 2008, 156–57). Also, the Global Fund takes RED seriously, and its internal documentation suggests that RED is viewed as the precursor to other attempts to fund the organization through consumer campaigns (see chapter 3).

The impact of RED is important on two related fronts: the material and the representational. On the material front, as we will show in chapter 4, RED is a "disengaged" form of CSR—mostly separated from the operations in which the RED corporations are involved. RED does not attempt to change or improve the normal functioning of business and trade. At the same time, RED's beneficiaries are distant—Africa, AIDS victims—constructed as "over there" and not likely to be part of the RED companies' core consumer group. RED does not attempt to implement better work, social, or environmental conditions of production. In other words, RED is focused on the welfare of Africans with AIDS in its beneficiary countries, not on the welfare of workers in factories producing RED products. RED seeks to support a social cause that is removed from the everyday lives of most of its consumers. Yet

RED's use of media presents these sufferers as if they were close and known by consumers who are led to believe that they can be meaningfully involved in the scene of suffering. Within the emerging realm of "causumerism" (or shopping for a better world), we argue that RED facilitates a shift from "conscious consumption" to "compassionate consumption" and deflects attention from addressing the causes of problems to solving their manifestations.

But the power of RED is not simply a material power that stems from the way that the initiative engages corporations and consumers. RED's impact is also based in its images, its pictures of the world (see chapter 2). AIDS is a sexually transmitted disease for which there is currently no cure. Yet Western shoppers are animated by a confident Bono who speaks from American television screens claiming: "We can be the generation that ends extreme poverty. This is our moment to show what we're about." As Arabella Lyon argues in her own work analyzing the bloated and exploitative nature of pity, "Long before globalization and mass media, emotion was understood as useful for political manipulation" (2005, 175).

RED shifts focus from the product it is selling to the people with the problem it is solving. This dislocation results in depoliticizing both trade and AIDS in Africa as RED works on solving the manifestations of a problem without considering its causes. "As 'infotainment' on the nightly news, images of victims are commercialized, they are taken up into processes of global marketing and business competition. . . . Suffering, 'though at a distance,' as Boltanski (1993) tellingly expresses it, is routinely appropriated in American popular culture, which is a leading edge of global popular culture" (Kleinman and Kleinman 1996, 1–2). As explained by Susan Sontag: "The imaginary proximity to the suffering inflicted on others that is granted by images suggests a link between the faraway sufferer—seen close-up on the television screen—and the privileged viewer that is simply untrue, that is yet one more mystification of our real relations to power" (2003, 102). Thus, RED is a poignant example of the global appropriations of suffering, one that sells both their suffering and our power to ameliorate it as effectively as it sells computers, greeting cards, or lattes.

A close examination of RED will demonstrate how relations of inequality are inherent in donor-recipient exchanges, and that RED is a new player operating within the context of a long and contentious debate on international development aid to Africa. Negotiating the terms of giving speaks as much about the donors—or in this case, the consumers—who give, as about the needy Africans with AIDS, who receive. Product RED relies on the mutual coexistence of proximity and distance, or empathy and separation, between the shopper/helpers and the producer/sufferers. RED is manufacturing a certain kind of awareness through its representations of Africans with AIDS and the international interventions that can save them. It is also modelling a form of CSR that privileges moving away from tackling the normal functioning of production and trade toward solving the problems of distant others. In RED, consumers can be good, companies can do good, and Africans who need some good done for them can get it.

In sum, RED should be given serious analysis as a manifestation of (1) the impact of aid celebrities on policy making, (2) the legitimacy of consumption as a vector for helping, (3) the shift away from businesses' emphasis on "engaged CSR" to helping "distant others," and (4) the construction of Africans with AIDS as worthy recipients of profits generated from heroic shopping.

BRAND + AID CELEBRITY + CAUSE = BRAND AID

In this book, we argue that RED is to date the most advanced manifestation of the rise of what we call "Brand Aid." Brand Aid is the combined meaning of "aid to brands" and "brands that provide aid." It is "aid to brands" because it helps sell branded products and improve a brand's ethical profile and value. It is "brands that provide aid" because, like other cause-related marketing initiatives, a portion of the profit or sales is devoted to helping others. As a response to the crisis of legitimacy in international aid to Africa, Brand Aid also helps to rebrand aid itself and aid to Africa in particular (see chapter 3). At the same time, it legitimizes a corporate involvement in "doing good" that is not related to corporations' own actions and operations, and in which beneficiaries are distant others.

Brand

Brand Aid (as the heading above suggests) is based on three pillars: a brand, one or more aid celebrities, and a cause. The first pillar of Brand Aid, branding, is about conveying a mark to consumers. It is a commitment to consistently delivering a material and symbolic experience of a certain quality. Brands, as we will see in chapter 5, have a monetary value of their own, with many of the most successful ones representing more than 40 percent of the owning company's total market value. But as brands can become valuable assets with proper management, they can also turn into liabilities. They are vulnerable to negative media exposure, which in turn can affect consumers' brand perception and shopping choices. Managing the ethical profile of a brand is therefore a key issue for companies. This can be done by adhering to codes of conduct, labeling, and certification schemes on labor, environmental, and social issues related to production and trade. It can also be achieved by building an "iconic profile" for a brand, a profile built on culture rather than the product itself (Holt 2004). Brand Aid can be an attractive vector for building the ethical component of brand reputation and for turning brands into icons. It does not question the fundamentals of "hard commerce" and at the same time can help increase sales, visibility, and brand equity. In the case of RED, Brand Aid also helps to shift attention from the product to a cause by enacting the myth of "just capitalism," a capitalism that is good for all, a win-win solution to the world's most pressing problems.[20] The fact that RED is a co-branding exercise helps in managing individual brand risk by spreading the risk of failure or of negative repercussions among several brands and by externalizing it to the nonproduct brand, RED itself.

Aid Celebrities

The second pillar of Brand Aid is the aid celebrity. As we will discuss in chapter 1, aid celebrities transport the modalities of the celebrity into the realm of international development. They embody a manufactured consensus, let simple moral truths substitute for rational debate, and thus manage the affect of those who would solve the world's problems. There is a "felt need" for grounding the impulse to "do good." We are not critiquing the impulse to do good globally, for Africa or elsewhere, but suggest that this is where the power of Brand Aid exists beyond the material realm of stylish clothes and smart gadgetry: it exists through the mobilization of affect to produce certain kinds of donors who care.

Within Brand Aid there is no expertise outside of the celebrity modality. We make a distinction in our analysis of RED between the celebrities who are brought in as a supporting cast for various products, performances, and the brand itself and the "aid celebrities" who are fundamental to the social contract on which RED is founded.

Famous faces abound in all aspects of the RED campaign; celebrity models like Gisele Bündchen and Christy Turlington, actresses like Penélope Cruz and Scarlett Johansson, singers like Joss Stone, and artists like Damien Hirst engage in highly publicized activities in support of RED and its products. The use of celebrities to sell products is of course nothing new, but RED moves beyond mere celebrity endorsement by relying on the appeal of aid celebrities for the brand's credibility. In Product RED, Paul Farmer provides the ethical guarantee that AIDS is an important problem that can be solved in poor countries, Jeffrey Sachs provides the efficiency guarantee that the RED brand and the Global Fund are effective means for solving this problem, and Bono provides the attention guarantee that exposure and access will come from linking aid celebrities to other famous celebrities to insure the cool quotient of the initiative. Bono may seem less "expert" than the other aid celebrities, but in fact, he has the broadest scope and carries surprising legitimacy in practitioner and academic circles. Bono gave the 350th commencement address for graduates of Harvard University in 2001, in which he praises Jeffrey Sachs, Bobby Shriver, and the pope for their work on debt relief—"A rock star, a Kennedy, and a Noted Economist crisscrossing the globe, like the Partridge Family on psychotropic drugs, with the POPE acting as our . . . well . . . agent."[21]

The aid celebrities are there to guarantee that the consumers' desire to help save distant others will be fulfilled through the correct product choices. Brand Aid brings modernization theory into postmodern times: consumption becomes the mechanism for compassion and creates new forms of value. Celebrities are the lubricant for this political-economic formation, acting as emotional sovereigns, mitigating the threat to capitalist accumulation posed by the need to display corporate social responsibility.

Celebrities are fundamental in selling products to the masses, and with Brand Aid, international development assistance becomes another marketable product. Brand Aid promises resolution to a myriad of historical conflicts about the possibilities of being a donor and of confining the most intrinsic problems of development within a geographical demarcation that can be kept separate from the Western self.

When the RED Web site advertises that "There are hundreds of ways to support the elimination of AIDS in Africa,"[22] they are not referring to the provision of condoms or legal reforms to uphold women's rights, nor are they referring to improving communication between spouses or one-stop shopping for all kinds of reproductive health services; they are not referring to effective microbicides or reducing socio-economic inequality. The "hundreds of ways," represented by small, colorful pictures that move onto the screen of the RED Web site one after the other, are consumer products—greeting cards, take-away lattes, fancy computers, and stylish sunglasses. Product promotion and aid fund-raising are united in RED. We are accustomed to celebrities who sell cars and songs; aid celebrities who sell development interventions are both familiar and new. In RED we see celebrities who sell the possibility of saving someone else's life. Saturating RED communications with celebrity content normalizes the celebrity modality. Even members of the corporate elite share common attributes with celebrities like Angelina Jolie (Cooper 2008c). Thus it becomes not simply acceptable, but expected to find a photograph of Bono accompanying any major piece of news on African development in the media.[23] The popular assumption that international development is a field populated by experts who tour exotic places in the company of supermodels helping grateful masses is a powerful virtualism. As we discuss in chapter 2, our use of virtualism draws on its political-economy manifestation articulated by Carrier and Miller (1998) who are, notably, ethnographers. Virtualism is based on a profound degree of abstraction, disengagement with the embodied, lived experience, and a decontextualization of the highest form (see Miller 1998, 205–13). AIDS treatment as represented in RED is a pragmatic abstraction of a complex experience, that is, not the opposite of "reality" but a making of reality that produces particular effects. This virtualism of AIDS in Africa, limited to ARV pills, is an example of how "reality" becomes performed more and more like it was imagined in the first place.

Cause

The third pillar of Brand Aid is the cause. A spate of recent books examines the possibilities of whether a form of capitalism that is more creative and to scale, termed "philanthrocapitalism," can solve both global and local problems that historically were subjected to political debate in democratic societies (Bishop and Green 2008; Edwards 2008; Kinsley 2008). A growing number of analysts and leaders, such as former U.S. president Bill Clinton,[24] see potential in what the rich and large corporations, assisted by professional intermediaries and celebrities, can do in solving the world's problems. Such potential stems not only from the money they can spend, but from the leverage they can apply on others (NGOs, governments) to use resources more innovatively, efficiently, and in a "business-like" manner. As Bill Gates put it, "the challenge is not to identify the right problems but to identify the right solutions" (cited in Bishop and Green 2008, 152).

Yet others, such as many of the contributors to Kinsley (2008), argue that business should focus on what it does best: provide goods and services to consumers and maximize profits. Edwards (2008) is critical of philanthrocapitalism, but from another standpoint. He argues that it is a symptom of an unequal world, rather than being its cure. He also highlights that the involvement of business and markets to bring about changes that traditionally rely on social movements has had quite mixed results, typically stemming from the differing perceptions on redistribution and social justice. Still, Brand Aid is predicated upon the notion that business can work effectively to promote international causes.

Philanthrocapitalism, "creative capitalism" (as termed by Bill Gates), social entrepreneurship, and Brand Aid all work on solving existing problems—how "we" (in the West) mobilize resources to solve a problem instead of asking questions about how the problem came to be. In chapter 5, we argue that RED, as a form of Brand Aid, enacts the myth of "just capitalism" to reconcile the contradictions of global wealth and poverty. It does so by portraying the idea that capitalism can be fixed to rein in its excesses and target its creativity and resources to help groups of "deserving others" (Africans suffering from AIDS). And in a period of economic crisis and financial insecurity, RED can still exploit the myth of just capitalism by portraying itself as a workable alternative to "casino capitalism" and as a modality where consumption and cool can be channelled toward a good cause.

Brand Aid and other forms of creative capitalism may be useful for solving existing problems when these are not acknowledged to be explicitly linked to the normal functioning of capitalism or the companies themselves. These sorts of initiatives will not be able to tackle problems to which businesses are closely linked. And the more resources go to ameliorating the symptoms, the less likely resources will go to examining the root causes of existing problems. Problems are created and understood only in the way that allows them to be solved by these interventions. Thus, in the RED example, AIDS can be thought of in no other way outside of the primacy of drugs.

Brand Aid: Precursors, Contemporaries, and Prospects

Brand Aid, as epitomized by RED, does not come out of nowhere. It is a form of cause-related marketing, increasingly used by companies to build up their brand image, sell products, and in the process, help a cause. Many examples of linking product sales with donation and celebrities have been seen over the past two decades—among many others, we find MAC lipsticks sold to fund the MAC AIDS foundation, Kenneth Cole's "Awearness" line of clothing and accessories to support various charities, and a special edition C350 Mercedes to support breast cancer causes.[25]

Other RED-like initiatives that use shopping as a means for solving global concerns are becoming increasingly popular. For example, in February 2008, Benetton launched its "Africa Works" campaign, promoting the Birima microcredit program in Senegal, a cooperative credit society founded by the Senegalese singer Youssou N'Dour. Images on billboards and in the press throughout the world featured photogenic West Africans as "everyday people" who are "depicted with the tools of their trade against a neutral background."[26] When shoppers buy an "Africa Works" clothing item from Benetton, an unspecified percentage of the profit supports the Birima project. However, these sorts of initiatives also differ from RED in a number of important ways that we will discuss in chapter 4.

Brand Aid is a form of corporate philanthropy as well. But in traditional philanthropy (as in the examples of the Ford, Carnegie, Rockefeller, and Gates foundations), the act of giving is formally independent from the act of profit accumulation: normal business practice leads to accumulation of profits, assets, and capital that are then later used for purposes that have little to do with the operations in which the company is involved.[27] In contrast, Brand Aid allows the making of profit and donation at the same time. Companies use "doing good" to sell a particular set of products.

Finally, Brand Aid draws upon the awareness created by the fair trade movement and other social movements that have increased consumer knowledge of companies and products and stimulated consumers to assess products vis-à-vis their impact on societies and environments. But there are major differences between Brand Aid and its fair trade precursors. For example, RED is based on "celebrity validation," which relies on personal capacity, while "ethical and sustainable" trade and CSR are usually based on certifications, labels, and codes of conduct to form "impersonal" and systemic solutions to problems of quality, food safety, environmental impact, and social conditions of production (see chapter 4). Although to consumers, both celebrities and labels are "shortcuts" for very complex socioeconomic and environmental processes, the informational depth of the message carried through is quite different. Codes of conduct and ethical trade initiatives are ultimately about improving the conditions of production for laborers and/or small farmers. RED is about accepting the status quo, maximizing sales and profit, and donating a portion of sales of products (no matter how or where they have been produced) to help "distant others" in Africa.

As with all other corporate philanthropy and cause-related marketing, RED is vulnerable to economic downturns, which puts its long-term viability in doubt. The vulnerability of RED to lower sales (of all products of partner companies, and of RED products in particular) translates into the vulnerability of the beneficiaries of RED contributions. Public aid and philanthropic giving from private foundations (based on endowments) are also vulnerable to economic crises (lower income from taxation, lower value of endowments if stock markets fall), but both are less vulnerable to market fluctuations than corporate philanthropy.

Perhaps ironically, the value of brands, including the RED ethical co-brand will become even more important as consumers try to buy more with less. Individuals may stop donating, but they will continue purchasing products. Thus, instead of mobilizing in response to economic crisis or engaging in some other form of citizen participation, consumers may continue to try to change the world through shopping, with RED leading the revolution. "Instead of making the center marginal, the marginal is diluted and re-invented so that it seamlessly blends with and validates the center. Brand culture, then, provides a context in which consumers enjoy and enact a kind of agency—one that is precisely anticipated by the brand itself, and thus works to perpetuate the seeming inevitability of brand culture" (Banet-Weiser and Lapsanksy 2008, 1254). Brands appear inevitable and business seems the obvious solution to solving global problems in a context in which it can be the only solution. Yet, as Patton argues, "AIDS is not a fixed thing, a natural phenomenon that necessarily engenders one response or another" (2002, 25). However, RED produces a virtualism of AIDS treatment in which "lives saved" is sold as a commodity as much as the t-shirts, bracelets, or computers. In doing so, Brand Aid has found a way to generate capitalist value from those persons whose physical and economic abjection places them completely outside of capitalist reproduction.

SCOPE AND STRUCTURE OF THE BOOK

In this book, we argue that RED is the quintessential manifestation of a phenomenon we call "Brand Aid" that brings consumers and branded corporations into international development through celebrity mediation. We also discuss the specific forms that contemporary capitalism is taking as the context for the operations of RED companies. We have chosen not to frame our arguments explicitly as part of the massive, and increasingly popularized, critique of neoliberalism. This is because we hold some discomfort with the abuse of "neoliberalism" in current political-economy debates, which has drained the term of much of its analytical force (see also Ferguson 2009). Also, we fear that the weight of connecting the diverse strands of our critique into the existing arguments of neoliberalism would flatten the complexity of the dynamics we are elucidating. We do draw on some of the specific examples of grounded critique within this literature (such as the contributions to Collins, di Leonardo, and Williams 2008) in our arguments. And we believe that many of our critiques in this book are, of course, compatible with and supportive of some contemporary criticisms of neoliberalism, and readers for whom this is a meaningful category of analysis are welcome to consider it in those terms. However, we propose Brand Aid as a disruption to what has become an overgeneralized critique of neoliberalism through a focus on an empirical case study.

Greater resonance exists between Brand Aid and the notion of how affective, immaterial but never nonmaterial, labor constitutes the way in which the "value of labor and production is determined deep in the viscera of life" (Hardt and Negri 2000, 365). "Immaterial labor" is the kind of work that takes place within the post-Fordist context, or "the epoch in which information and communication play an essential role in each stage of the process of production" (Lazzarato and Negri 1991, 86). The link between the material and cultural is epitomized by the concept of brand, which we develop in chapter 5. "Immaterial labor might thus be conceived as the labor that produces the informational, cultural, or affective element of the commodity" (Virno and Hardt 1996, 262). The affective laboring process is done simultaneously in RED by celebrities and by "suffering strangers" with AIDS. Together—and not without the critical elements of material, bodily, labor (see Dyer-Witheford 2001)—the interplay of these two sides of the virtualism of AIDS treatment produces valuable commodities. In the archetypical example of the Product RED virtualism (see chapter 2), the lives of people with AIDS in Africa that are "saved" are being sold as commodities to Western consumers in whom compassion, a most unstable emotion (see Sontag 2003), has been aroused, and shopping, with the guarantee of the emotional sovereign of the celebrity, produces the translation of affect into action.

But describing AIDS treatment in Africa as a virtualism does not mean that we believe that ARVs do not work to save the lives of women, children, and men with AIDS in Africa. ARV drugs are indeed an essential part of AIDS treatment for patients all over the world whose HIV virus has become advanced enough to diminish their immune system and to prevent vertical transmission of the virus. However, drugs are not the only significant components of a system of AIDS treatment. Saving lives in Africa begins with the actions and beliefs of the people whose lives are to be saved, and interacts with social, spiritual, medical, and political relationships. These power relationships involve local and global points of both solidarity and conflict. RED's depiction of ARVs as sufficient for saving lives produces a virtualism in which treatment becomes understood only in terms of providing the necessary drugs, and thus, interventions are put into place only to provide drugs. This neglects many of the other important aspects of AIDS prevention, care, and treatment, of overall healthcare for Africans who may or may not have AIDS, and of nonmedical needs for maintaining the social as well as the biological life of a human being.

This book develops a two-pronged perspective toward understanding the political economy of culture as exemplified by Brand Aid through our case study of RED. In doing so, the following chapters aim to balance what are in fact two perspectives that are not easily wed: cultural analysis (interrogating the images of Africa, AIDS, gender, and celebrity that make RED so appealing) and political economy (a materialist analysis of the companies involved and the playing of Brand Aid vis-à-vis ethical standards). Chapters 1 and 2 are most explicitly cultural in their approach, while chapters 3 and 4 are material analyses. Chapter 5 on brands combines the cultural and material in roughly equal proportion. Our conceptual "tool" for weaving together a political economy of culture comes from "Brand Aid," which links together the consumption of products and images (branding) and justifies calls for consumption on the basis of contributing to international development aid.

The first chapter, "Band Aid to Brand Aid: Celebrity Experts and Expert Celebrities," examines the celebrity modality that is constitutive of Brand Aid. We argue that celebrities are playing a significant role in the global economy, acting as emotional sovereigns and guarantors of accountability and social justice. First, we define the meaning of celebrity and aid celebrity, and then place the involvement of celebrities in diplomatic, humanitarian, and development causes in a brief historical perspective. We argue that through Brand Aid, experts are becoming aid celebrities as their persona and aid work become inseparable. The chapter then analyzes the three celebrities who are the guarantors of the RED initiative: Bono, Jeffrey Sachs, and Paul Farmer. Afterward, we explore the relationship among aid celebrities, their claims to expertise, and their management of affect in international development.

Chapter 2, "The Rock Man's Burden: Fair Vanity and Virtual Salvation," studies the representational work of the Product RED campaign. Here we argue that Africa has long been the imagined place where well-meaning westerners could do good for distant others. Then we demonstrate how the RED campaign should be understood as an important player in representing African AIDS.

We describe the virtualism of AIDS treatment in which the privileged provision of drugs is disembedded from the social context or the experiences of Africans living with AIDS. Afterward, we look specifically at visual representations of African AIDS used in RED, and in the *Vanity Fair* Africa Issue. Finally, we explain how the virtualism of AIDS treatment in RED draws together nonsectarian versions of salvation and rebirth, and that these images must be understood within the context of selling images of AIDS in Africa, and using such suffering to sell products.

Chapter 3, "Saving Africa: AIDS and the Rebranding of Aid," places Brand Aid within the crisis of legitimacy that currently characterizes traditional forms of development aid, particularly that to Africa. We argue that RED and Brand Aid are driven by the need to continue mobilizing public support for "lost causes" and to combat the fatigue of individual philanthropists and institutional donors. We begin by briefly considering the current debates over the usefulness of aid (and of aid to Africa in particular) and the various forms of aid delivery. Then the chapter examines the aid given in response to the crisis of HIV/AIDS in Africa, and the particular emphasis given to AIDS treatment through the provision of ARV drugs. The Global Fund, the recipient of the RED funds, is analyzed. And finally, RED is examined as an "innovative mechanism" for providing funds to fight AIDS in Africa.

Chapter 4, "Hard Commerce: Corporate Social Responsibility for Distant Others," studies RED within the large umbrella of activities that constitute CSR. We demonstrate the economic logic behind Brand Aid of protecting capitalist accumulation from the threats posed by engaged activism that seeks to foster greater corporate social responsibility. We start by briefly examining the meanings of CSR, corporate philanthropy, and cause-related marketing. Then we conduct an analysis of the CSR activities of the companies that were RED's first cohort. We look at whether companies' activities appear to impact the "normal" functioning of their business or whether they are "disengaged" and work like charity or philanthropy. The chapter charts some of the rules and functioning of the "hard commerce" context in which the RED companies operate, then it compares their CSR profiles, and finally looks at each company's involvement with RED.

Chapter 5, "Doing Good by Shopping Well: The Rise of 'Causumer' Culture," looks explicitly at RED's promotion of a "causumer culture" (doing good through shopping) and a particular form of commodity fetishism. This chapter explores one of the book's key concepts— consumption—and how RED relates to other forms of ethical consumption. Specifically, we examine sustainability labels and certifications. Then we move on to analyze branding and how the ( )^{RED} embrace can be a good co-branding investment. Finally, the chapter articulates the relationship between RED and commodity fetishism in its promotion of causumer culture to save Africa. We argue that not only are the social relations of RED commodities obscured, but that these social relations stem from and enable continuing forms of dispossession. Brand Aid as a strategy protects companies' brands from ethical attack while producing value from the commodification of "lives saved."

The Conclusion, "Celebrities, Consumers, and Everyone Else," offers insights on the exemplary case of RED and what it might teach us about Brand Aid. Brand Aid is skillfully tapping into a growing constituency of Western consumers who want to be part of changing the world. Within the context of global capitalism, Brand Aid is a response for brands to do more good and for aid to be done better. Within Brand Aid, aid celebrities serve as the guarantors of the development interventions and as the totemic representations of consumers' desire to help. Brand Aid comes at a time when development aid, especially aid to Africa, suffers from poor public perception and is in need of rebranding, and when business is a popular solution for the problems ailing aid. Brand Aid is a gaunt form of CSR that focuses on distant and disengaged initiatives. Increasing consumption, of the appropriate kind, is at the core of Brand Aid. And when Brand Aid is given, it is to recipients who are worthy of the compassion of consumers, through simple but effective interventions that work at a sufficient distance not to risk intermingling the shoppers and the helpers.

Penélope Cruz's advertisement for Gap is the cover image for the Financial Times *"Business of Fashion" supplement for Spring 2007. Reproduced from the* Financial Times.

⟨1⟩ BAND AID TO BRAND AID
Celebrity Experts and Expert Celebrities

The popular magazine *Nature* described the image on the facing page as: "the actress Penelope Cruz is seen reclining across an advertisement sporting a cute red tee-shirt that proclaims the clothing chain Gap's commitment to fighting AIDS in Africa."[1] How an advertisement showing a beautiful, famous actress in a red shirt stamped with the word "DESI(RED)" has come to symbolize a company's effective engagement in an international development cause is fundamental to understanding the workings of Brand Aid. In Brand Aid, the link between product and cause, providing both legitimacy and exposure, comes from aid celebrities. Celebrities have a long history of involvement with international good causes, and they have perfected the form over time. Experts have taken up the celebrity modality as a response to the crisis in international development. Celebrities learn from the experts how to make arguments and influence policy, and experts learn from the celebrities how to create "buzz," cultivate popular audiences, and manage affect. In the aid celebrity modality, expertise becomes celebritized and circulated, while affective commitment is bestowed on emotional sovereigns for management.

The phenomenon of aid celebrities can be linked to the rise of celebrity politics in the United States (see Marks and Fischer 2002 among others) and to the rise of celebrity diplomacy internationally (Cooper 2008a). Celebrities share in an unprecedented management of the spectacle in promotion of international "good causes" and their own brand.

Celebrity has become a way of mediating between proximity and distance in the global as well as the specific context. As the paradigms of "people we know so well" that are simultaneously "just like us" and "exemplary," celebrities have become proxy philanthropists, statesmen, executives, and healers. As celebrities are endowed with expertise, experts are reconfigured as celebrities. As relations of international development are perceived as increasingly complex and "unmanageable," celebrities are the new totems of possibility.

Celebrities' engagement with social causes mainstreamed international development issues, like "fighting AIDS in Africa," into the mass media. Offering support for global charities through "confessions of caring" that take place on transnational terrain has become part of the celebrity job description and the hallmark of established stars (Littler 2008). This "celebrity do-gooding" through public displays of support for "the afflicted" raises the celebrities' profile from the material and commercial to the quasi-religious realm of altruism and charity (ibid.). Not surprisingly, celebrities insist on "playing the hero," and as de Waal writes, "their mental scripts have predetermined that they will be the saviors, or at least the instigators of salvation" (2008, 44).

International development experts, associated with celebrity activists in mutually beneficial ways, also became aid celebrities themselves. Celebrated development icons embody a new positive, win-win approach toward solving poverty and disease. "What is needed to sustain the status quo is the manufacturing of the public's consent. Absent the initiative of the public, this consent must be simulated, and media-driven celebrity activism now leads the way" (Marks and Fischer 2002, 393). "One of the things that happens when your organization signs up with celebrity is that personality can become policy."[2]

The celebrity is constitutive of what we are calling "Brand Aid" with Bono's RED initiative as the exemplary case. However, we are not arguing that celebrities are taking over aid, but instead show how the mechanism of celebrity has become increasingly important in international development as celebrities are called upon to play "expert" roles, while experts perform as celebrities. We argue, to borrow terms from Collier (2007), that "development buzz" is not simply "a headless heart" but in fact becomes legitimate "development biz." The aid celebrity modality dominates new forms of aid like RED and legitimates the ways that policies and institutions are shaped by individual aid celebrities. RED is full of global media celebrities in its advertisements and in those of its products as well, but it is also made possible as a legitimate development initiative by the work of aid celebrities known for their expertise on international development and AIDS treatment. As a popular Chicago newspaper article entitled "Bono, Oprah and Kanye Converge Downtown to Launch Campaign" reported, "the convergence of celebrity worship, American consumerism and the desire to make the world a better place makes the time ripe for a project like Red to take hold."[3]

In this chapter, we begin with an analysis of the meanings of "celebrity" and how the celebrity modality is becoming integral to international development. Then we outline a history of celebrity involvement in international do-gooding. Next, we highlight the aid celebrity trinity who made the RED initiative possible: Bono, who clearly sits in the center of the celebrity and expert modalities, and then Jeffrey Sachs and Paul Farmer who were both recognized experts before becoming famous aid celebrities. Finally, we analyze the link between the management of expertise and affect in the aid celebrity realm.

WHAT IS A CELEBRITY?

Legitimacy in the process of consumption of Brand Aid is guaranteed by aid celebrities. Boltanski and Thévenot (1991, 222–30) define "celebrity" as a state of superiority in a world where opinion is the defining instrument for measuring different orders of "greatness." In their approach, being a celebrity is characterized by having a widespread reputation, being recognized in public, being visible, having success, being distinguished, and having opinion leaders, journalists, and media as your testimonials. The test of celebrity is the judgment of the public (ibid.). According to Jamie Drummond, head of Bono's organization DATA/ONE, the best celebrities are "masters or very experienced people at managing their own brand."[4]

Celebrities are those select persons "who are given greater presence and a wider scope of activity and agency than are those who make up the rest of the population" (Marshall 1997, ix). While resembling in many ways other forms of charismatic leadership (see the classic discussion by Weber 1968), celebrity differs in its dependence on social distance and its mediation through the media. From "the movie star on the famine stage" (de Waal 2008, 44) to the "AIDS heroes" of China (Hood 2009), the past decade has seen a proliferation of celebrities appearing in development productions. An Internet site entitled "Look to the stars: inspiration for a better world" provides exclusive interviews and a database where fans can learn about their favorite stars' good deeds and boasts coverage of "1,580 charities and 2,254 celebrities and counting."[5]

Celebrities are constituted by components of both fantasy and purposive rationality. As such, they must be considered within both domains of irrationality (through metaphors of magic, charisma, pathology, or delusion) and of rationality—the media industries that work on publicity and promotion (G. Turner 2004) that produce the "celebritariat" (Rojek 2001). Scholarship within cultural studies has explored the political meaning of celebrity primarily through the examination of the performance of democratic and capitalist ideals through the media (G. Turner 2004; Rojek 2001; Marshall 1997). However, celebrities are now beginning to be taken seriously as actors in international politics (Cooper 2008a, 2008b), environmental conservation (Brockington 2009), and liberal democracies (Marks and Fischer 2002).

Yet even as celebrities are now being considered as social actors worthy of study in social science, they are often analyzed as a "symptom of a worrying cultural shift" (G. Turner 2004, 4). Some critics argue that celebrities are problematic because they symbolize a shift "towards a culture that privileges the momentary, the visual and the sensational over the enduring, the written and the rational" (ibid.). The vacuity of celebrity is taken to represent the center of false value—success that has come without the requisite association with work. In Marxist metaphor, the celebrity sign is pure exchange value cleaved from use value that articulates the individual as commodity (Marshall 1997, xi). Yet, today, it seems impossible to imagine that no "work" actually goes into making, performing, or being a celebrity.

Other critics have expressed that "celebrities lack a mandate to become active in global politics" (Dieter and Kumar 2008, 262). Because their legitimacy is derived from their personality, and this persona is a manufactured stage production, celebrities' actual dealings, their ethical actions, should be held to close scrutiny. Thus, Bono's business practices, tax evasion, personal charitable contributions, and staffing of his organizations with mostly white men from the "Anglo-sphere" simply add insult to injury as his celebrity ensemble trivializes development challenges (Dieter and Kumar 2008, 263). Celebrities, as shown by Littler (2008) and Gopal (2006), are able to use narratives of "justice" and social change without actually acknowledging inequalities in global social systems that make celebrity possible. Raising consciousness about social justice does not necessarily entail sharing responsibility for the cause of inequality or for its perpetuation.

The classic characterization of a celebrity is that of Boorstin who exclaimed "the celebrity is a person known for his well-knownness" (1971, 58). While the benefits that celebrities can bring to their chosen causes are easily imagined, the reception of their input by "traditional" aid actors has been less than celebratory. For example, some workers inside humanitarian NGOs see the "cult of celebrity" as a threat to their own organizational identity. According to an officer of the UN's agency UNICEF, "when most people think of the UN now they think of Angelina Jolie on a crusade, not the work that goes on in the field . . . celebrity is at the heart of every Unicef campaign these days and the association is being sold incredibly cheaply."[6] Magubane writes that these "celebrity-fueled spectacles" are particularly damaging to representations of Africa in which "their suffering bears a direct correlation to their utility in helping a celebrity build his or her brand."[7]

The link between spectacle, celebrity, and Africa has been critiqued by some as "celebrity colonialism" in which celebrities go to Africa to make themselves feel "special." In this scenario, Africa "has become a stage for moralistic poseurs," but it is not only the celebrities that reduce Africa to a simple morality tale; politicians follow suit.[8] The conflation between Africa and affect, as opposed to rationality, has historical roots but has seen a revival with the celebritization of campaigns like "Make Poverty History" (Gopal 2006). Furthermore, as Magubane points out, the cult of celebrity interest in Africa reinforces beliefs about the continent as a place that lacks its own systematized knowledge: "the Africa created by the American celebrity machine, while not populated by spear chucking savages, is also completely bereft of doctors, politicians, musicians, or actors."[9] As for the African celebrities, they have been conspicuously left out of large-scale "global" celebrations, including Live 8, a fact that has been remarked upon but only superficially debated. Magubane gives the example of when Femi Kuti, a Nigerian superstar, said of Bob Geldof and his cronies that "maybe they don't know black artists."[10] Geldof responded that African stars do not hold any "political traction." This was followed by an American television host's commentary that "[Geldof's] point is that the future of Africa is ours to shape. His, yours, and mine, whether we are famous or not." Thus, Magubane concludes, even ordinary Americans are portrayed as holding greater political traction than African superstars.

But why would celebrities then be interesting to "real world" experts and thus how could celebrities have become powerful actors in international development issues? In a classic text on celebrities as "the powerless elite," Alberoni (1972) examines the rise of cinema in the first half of the twentieth century and its accompanying film stars produced by the American film industry to star in audiovisual products. Alberoni concludes that celebrities are "a transitional phenomenon that identifies the need of the general community for an avenue through which to discuss issues of morality—family, neighbourhood, of production and consumption etc.—that are insufficiently or ineffectively handled in the rational sphere of evaluating political power elites" (cited in Marshall 1997, 16). Bestowing the power of intercession onto celebrities who act between the people and the system has been a common way of explaining why the mechanism of celebrity is powerful. Why individuals become so attractive for mass audiences has been attributed to their ability to tap into discourses of "authenticity" in which the balance is skillfully maintained between the person, the persona and the characters (Gledhill 1991), and their charisma—the extent to which the celebrity can act as a mirror for normative societal tensions (Dyer 1979).

While celebrities are well known for product promotion, advertising, and marketing efforts of various kinds, the emphasis on individuality as a product that can be consumed blurs the boundaries between celebrities and products. Celebrities themselves fall into commercial categories: they are objects of consumption. The existence of celebrities also legitimates a particular social order. Marshall explains how "the celebrity as public individual who participates openly as a marketable commodity serves as a powerful type of legitimation of the political economic model of exchange and value—the basis of capitalism— and extends that model to include the individual" (1997, x). Celebrities themselves are a sign, "an organizing structure for conventionalized meaning," and a representation of something other than itself (ibid., 56–57). Rojek (2001) develops Gamson's (1994) concept of "the celebrification process" that can inform our understanding of the mechanism of celebrity. Rojek uses "the celebrification process to describe the general tendency to frame social encounters in mediagenic filters that both reflect and reinforce the compulsion of abstract desire" (2001, 186–87).

In this chapter, we concentrate on the role of one type of celebrity— the aid celebrity—in producing a type of development intervention we call "Brand Aid." We are sidestepping discussions of what aid does for the celebrity, why celebrities choose to do one thing or another, and whether celebrity involvement in "good causes" is authentic. We draw support from G. Turner's seminal book on celebrity where he argues: "Celebrity has the potential to operate in ways that one might deplore or applaud, but neither potential is intrinsic" (2004, 137). As celebrities have become increasingly involved in international development aid, the mechanism of celebrity has become more acceptable, leading to the "aid celebrities" we will analyze later in this chapter.

CELEBRITIES IN ACTION: A BRIEF HISTORY

Prominent celebrity activism has been taking place since the 1960s. Before then, musicians and actors engaged in only the safest social causes. Two world wars, music and film's escapist entertainment of the 1930s, and the post–World War II anticommunist witch hunt in the United States worked against artists taking up prominent controversial social causes—with some notable exceptions like Paul Robeson and

Woody Guthrie (Huddart 2005, 21). Huddart describes celebrity activism from the 1960s onward as a succession of "waves." A first wave took place during the U.S. civil rights movement. It took inspiration from Martin Luther King Jr. and combined "heroic voices" (such as Joan Baez and Bob Dylan) with "convenors" (Harry Belafonte), who enrolled a group of celebrities (Marlon Brando, Burt Lancaster) to add moral weight to just causes, increase public interest, and reduce anxiety with familiar faces (ibid., 31–32). A second wave coalesced around the antiwar movement and opposition to the military draft in the United States from the mid-1960s. Celebrities functioned as well-known members of established, grassroots social movements. Unlike the role they would come to play later, celebrities were participants, not leaders, of these movements (Marks and Fischer 2002).

Grassroots organizations were engaged in activism, and celebrities were called in to join them, to contribute their resources and media attention to the existing movement. Todd Gitlin argues, however, that "as these media-savvy leaders became the focal point for the movement, the movement message became eclipsed by the star power of these charismatic leaders. This eventually undermined the very movements these organizers were supposed to serve" (1980, 176). In fact, once the celebritization began, it became possible for celebrities who had no experience in grassroots activism to emerge from it as political figures in their own right, eventually undermining the movements they were meant to work with (Marks and Fischer 2002, 385). During this time, the first "benefit concerts" took place.

A third wave followed from the 1970s, where activism aimed at responding to global concerns, from George Harrison's Concerts for Bangladesh in 1971, to the 1974 "Evening for Salvador Allende" and the No Nukes concerts of 1978–79 (Huddart 2005). But perhaps the most important events that marked the growth of celebrity activism were Bob Geldof's recording of "Do They Know It's Christmas" in 1984 and the related Live Aid concerts of 1985. An estimated two billion people watched the concerts, and the telethon raised almost $150 million, the largest ever at that time. Geldof's use of sponsorship at Live Aid made it possible to minimize costs and maximize the amount of donations to the cause. "Live Aid's use of highly emotional televised images to stimulate donations . . . subsequently changed the face of international fundraising" (Huddart 2005, 37). Now we are saturated with these images, so much that we do not need to refer to them; they are always out there in the collective subconscious. This allows Bono and RED to focus on cool, sexy branding rather than on poverty, inequality, and disease as we will discuss later in the book.

While the focus of celebrity activism broadened to solving "world problems," the increasing legitimacy of the celebrity as a form of political engagement was epitomized by the election of Ronald Reagan to the U.S. presidency in 1980. A B movie Hollywood star, Reagan ushered in an era of politics in which "celebrities in tuxedos and gowns (sporting the AIDS ribbon) supplanted the activist demonstrations of the previous political cycle" (Marks and Fischer 2002, 377).

Following Live Aid, celebrity activism and charity involvement became much more widespread. From the mid-1980s to the early 2000s, the focus shifted back and forth from addressing systemic problems to coalescing attention around "urgent issues." From the late 1990s onward, celebrity activism, reinvigorated by Bono, culminated in the Jubilee 2000 campaign, and the 2005 Live 8 concerts. The popularity of these initiatives permitted celebrity activists to become increasingly involved in political lobbying from the stage.

We contend that the RED initiative opens a fourth wave of celebrity activism that marks a fundamental break with the past, moving from "Band Aid" to "Brand Aid." Although sponsorship has become accepted practice after the success of Live Aid, the fundamental linkage of product, cause, and celebrity is unique to the fourth wave of activism that supports Brand Aid. For example, in RED the marriage of consumption and social causes has become one and indivisible.[11] Bono brought the work of Geldof and others to new heights and indeed, with RED, to a new form. The primary goal of RED is not to push governments to do their part, but to push consumers to do theirs through exercising their choices. This contemporary era of celebrity activism will be more eclectic, with different kinds of celebrities holding power in various realms and with shifting alliances between various kinds of celebrities holding sway over diverse constituencies. RED provides us just one example of the union of supermodels, macroeconomists, rockers, and doctors.

THE RED AID CELEBRITY TRINITY

Aid celebrities are participants in this fourth wave of celebrity activism as expert celebrities who do international development aid. As such, they are development "experts" and celebrities whose persona is inseparable from their aid work, but whose claims to expertise extend beyond formal qualifications. In a debate in *Global Governance,* Cooper (2008b) argues that Sachs has built his fame on achieved status while Bono's comes from ascribed status, and thus the two diverse aspects work synergistically to produce mutual celebrity. We argue that aid celebrities actually merge achieved and ascribed status, distinguishing them from other stars who simply engage in do-gooding. The Global Fund rests on the foundational work of the three aid celebrities—Bono, Jeffrey Sachs, and Paul Farmer. Interestingly, it is not written on either the history of the Fund or in Sachs's curriculum vitae that he was one of the aid celebrities who began the fund.[12] However, in Sachs's (2005) popular audience book *The End of Poverty,* he describes his role, and his vision, together with that of the other aid celebrities, Bono and Farmer.[13]

Sachs writes that Bono was an "enthusiastic supporter" of the World Health Organization (WHO) Commission on Macroeconomics and Health, chaired by Sachs for two years from 2000.[14] Sachs describes how "none but the incomparable Bono has opened the eyes of millions of fans and citizens to the shared struggle for global equality and justice" (2005, xii). It was in the context of the WHO commission that Sachs began to push the idea of a global fund to fight AIDS and malaria. However, as Sachs writes, "one more piece of the puzzle was needed" (ibid., 205): it was still believed that AIDS treatment was impossible to implement in poor countries. As told by Sachs, "my colleague Paul Farmer put those arguments to rest for me and, in some ways, for the world" (ibid.). Sachs, Farmer, and two other colleagues from Harvard prepared the "Consensus Statement by Members of the Harvard Faculty" to show that treatment was possible and scale-up could be practical in poor countries (ibid., 206). On the basis of Sachs's advice, the UN secretary-general announced his support for the creation of the Global Fund at the Abuja Summit on AIDS in April 2001. This was followed in the coming months by support from the then U.S. president Bush, the UN General Assembly, and the G8 leaders—and thus the Global Fund was born.

Aid celebrities become trusted advisors on issues of international development that extend beyond the actual scope of their research experience, and their presence is invoked to stand in for important beliefs and social values. Being an aid celebrity does not imply that one was not also a legitimate expert in some aspect of international development. In fact, it is on the basis of the high profile of their development work that aid celebrities came to be celebrated in the first place. As one of the seminal texts on contemporary celebrity explains, "We can map the precise moment a public figure becomes a celebrity. It occurs at the point at which media interest in their activities is transferred from reporting on their public role (such as their specific achievement in politics or sport) to investigating the details of their private lives. Paradoxically, it is most often the high profile achieved by their public activities that provides the alibi for this process of 'celebritisation'" (G. Turner 2004, 8). In addition to producing their own professional products (books, scholarly articles, and conference presentations for Sachs and Farmer, songs and concerts for Bono), aid celebrities are also active in the mass media. All three aid celebrities are well known in the popular print and television media and appear on a wide variety of fora supporting diverse initiatives.

Aid celebrities—Bono, Sachs, and Farmer—are called upon to speak truth to public health. Their field experiences are recounted as narrative devices in various and dissimilar publications. For example, a World Bank working paper authored by a team of macroeconomists outlines a monitoring model for the Millennium Development Goals (MDGs) (Agenor et al. 2005). As a text, it is characterized by decimals, Greek letter coefficients, and tables of regression results. Yet the introduction consists of a lengthy quotation from Bono's interview with a popular American news program, NBC's *Meet the Press*. The celebrity totem says the things that the economists cannot—"it is the most extraordinary thing to watch people dying three in a bed, two on top and one underneath, as I have seen in Lilongwe, Malawi" (cited in Agenor et al. 2005, 3). Sanitized sensationalism is intended to link the arduous work of constructing quantified targets for monitoring each goal of the MDGs with the "avoidable catastrophe" of human suffering. The same story is told in slightly different words in the first chapter of Jeffrey Sachs's *End of Poverty* (2005). What distinguishes this vignette is not its description of an African clinic mired in poverty, but the fact that it is repeated, nearly word for word, like a mantra by aid celebrities. And why is it more likely to be an American economist or an Irish rock star that credibly updates the world on the state of African health care instead of the thousands of African doctors or nurses or counselors who work in these clinics? The transformative magic of the celebrity totem brings the possibility of an improbable faith: that macroeconomic models of MDG monitoring will improve the plight of sufferers in this Malawian clinic.

More than simply exercising their networking capabilities, celebrities act as emotional sovereigns, in the classical republican sense where the sovereign manifests the true will of "the people." Bono recognizes his sovereignty and voices his relationships in terms of imagined representativeness:

> The reason why politicians let me in the door, and the reason why people will take my call is because I represent quite a large constituency of people. Now, I do not control that constituency, but I represent them in a certain sense, even without them asking me to, in the minds of the people whose doors I knock upon. That constituency is a very powerful one, because it is a constituency of people from eighteen to thirty, who are the floating vote.... They're the most open-minded, and that's why politicians pay attention to what's going on in contemporary culture and what a rock star might have to do with all of this: because of the people I represent. (Assayas 2005, 233)

Interestingly, Bono describes his role here as interceding both between the politicians and "the people" and elsewhere between "Africa" and the rest of the world. The celebrity as intermediary, as guarantor, in relationships of international development is central to Brand Aid. In the following discussion, we describe the aid celebrities—the bard, the teacher, and the healer—who guarantee the "cool quotient," the management, and the target of the Brand Aid modality as epitomized by RED.

The Bard

Only Bono, the quintessential celebrity ambassador, could have started RED. "Bono is a bit unique and in some ways he is American just as French people think he's French and Germans think he's German. That's how he manages his brand and gets away with it," according to DATA founder Jamie Drummond.[15] Bono is compelled to reconcile the "divides that separate Northern Ireland from the Irish republic, rich from poor, Catholic from Protestant, Democrat from Republican, aggressor from victim, Christian from Muslim" (Huddart 2005, 54). Now he has reconciled corporations and inequity, branding and disease. Rojek calls him a "rock shaman" who promotes a creed of living that "all you need is love," which is a "truism, but one that obviously glosses over many difficulties and inconsistencies" (2001, 70). Yet Bono, in his unique position of having moved from "celebrity" to "expert" to "aid celebrity," is taken quite seriously as an actor in the international arena. Cooper makes the analogy "As Henry Kissinger is to official diplomacy, Bono is to celebrity diplomacy" (2008a, 119).

Bono's appeal lies in his rock-star charisma and his "authenticity." U.S. senator Richard Durbin refers to this saying "Many of these stars are counseled by their agents to show a human side . . . Bono's different. He's clearly committed, and he knows what he's talking about."[16] Bono's social activism record, while much more visible in recent years, goes back at least to the mid-1980s. Bono and his band U2 supported Amnesty International, the Sandinistas, and a nonviolent solution to peace in Northern Ireland. During the decade of the 1990s, Bono's letters to newspapers, public challenge to Tony Blair, and meetings with world leaders are thought to have had a direct impact on debt cancellations that the G7 offered in 1999 and on the U.S. contribution to the Heavily Indebted Poor Countries (HIPC) initiative.

More recently, Bono joined the campaign against pharmaceutical companies to lower their prices for antiretroviral (ARV) treatment against AIDS. He was photographed with George W. Bush in Monterey in 2002, when the president announced that the United States was to increase its foreign aid budget to $5 billion between 2004 and 2006— in what was termed a Compact for Global Development. Later in 2002, Bono and then U.S. treasury secretary Paul O'Neill took a ten-day tour of Africa, also known as "The Odd Couple Tour of Africa 2002." They swept through foreign aid projects in Ghana, Uganda, South Africa, and Ethiopia. The itinerary included AIDS clinics, schools, clean-water schemes, and orphanages. O'Neill, Bono said, is "the man in charge of America's wallet and I am looking to open it."[17] Perhaps not surprisingly, Bono "the bard" prepared for his Africa tour with O'Neill by having a similar one with "the teacher" Jeffrey Sachs.

Bono's and Bob Geldof's initiatives have overlapped several times in the last few years, and the latter provides a more confrontational foil against which Bono can be the consensus-building diplomat (Cooper 2008a). Geldof was a member of the Commission for Africa, set up by then UK prime minister Tony Blair in early 2004. Its final report, "Our Common Interest," was published shortly before the G8 summit in 2005. Its goal was to propose measures for "a strong and prosperous Africa." Although it was Bob Geldof who organized the Live 8 series of concerts in 2005 to put pressure on G8 leaders meeting in Gleneagles, Bono played a key part as well. Geldof and Bono praised the G8 summit for pledging to double aid to Africa to $50 billion, saying that "the move will save the lives of hundreds of thousands of people who would have died of poverty, malaria or AIDS."[18] Later, Bono chastised the G8 countries in brash media-savvy headlines like "Harper [then Canadian prime minister] Risks Tainting Legacy by Ignoring Africa: Bono."[19] Subsequently, Bono was named *TIME* magazine person of the year in 2005.

According to Live 8 promoters, "the G8 leaders have it within their power to alter history. They will only have the will to do so if tens of thousands of people show them that enough is enough. By doubling aid, fully cancelling debt, and delivering trade justice for Africa, the G8 could change the future for millions of men, women and children. LIVE 8 is calling for people across the world to unite in one call—in

2005 it is your voice we are after, not your money."[20] Interestingly, Bono's RED turns this statement on its head, implicitly suggesting that "we are after your money, not your voice." RED is about individual consumption, not about public engagement in activism or advocacy. It is a private commitment showcased by wearing RED products in public, with Bono guaranteeing the cool quotient.[21]

Religious engagement plays a foundational role in Bono's creative ambiguity as a diplomatic actor. He has many different lineages at play in his presentation of a hybrid identity: Bono has a Roman Catholic father and a Protestant (Church of Ireland/Episcopalian) mother, and his lead guitarist and drummer were members of a Charismatic Christian group (Cooper 2008a). Bono has directed pivotal meetings with religious leaders in support of his causes and his own brand of celebrity. For example, he met with Pope John Paul II during his work with the Jubilee 2000 campaign and famously praised the pope as "a great showman as well as a great holy man" (ibid., 39). He has also emphasized his evangelical Christian connections and long-term commitment to shared missions to bring together diverse conservative allies such as former U.S. senator Jesse Helms, the global evangelist Billy Graham and his son Franklin, the famous U.S. televangelist Pat Robertson, and the former Nigerian president and devout Baptist Olusegun Obasanjo (ibid.). After meeting with Bono, Jesse Helms said, "I was deeply impressed with him. He has depth that I didn't expect. He is led by the Lord to do something about the starving people in Africa."[22]

Bono's celebrity brand is that of the "good looking Samaritan." In his book *Celebrity Diplomacy,* Cooper describes how Bono "has brought to the cause a candid emotionalism—with a strong religious sensibility— that shapes his sense of public purpose" (2008a, 37). In an episode for the television show *American Idol,* Bono interviews a little Tanzanian boy orphaned by AIDS. His "take home" message for the child and the global audience comes from a didactic exchange in which Bono asks the child, "Do you believe in God . . . Even after all that has happened to you?" The child nods his affirmation and Bono responds, "Well, Deloy, God believes in you, too."[23] Religion here is the appropriate form that emotion can fill in response to what would otherwise be problems solvable by rational science. Bono's identity as both "Christian" and "cool" is integral for RED's ethos of compassionate consumption. The profits from the RED initiative go directly to support the Global Fund. In the process, identities are performed indicating who is meant to save whom from what. Aid celebrities bring legitimacy to Brand Aid as a way to save Africans dying from AIDS.

The Teacher

Jeffrey Sachs guarantees that the mission of RED is achievable. As he proclaims in his public speeches, "Africa's problems are tougher, but solvable" and "Africa is a great puzzle for a development economist and a great challenge for all of us involved in policy to try to do something about it."[24] Sachs is the economist behind many of the initiatives to cancel debt and "eradicate poverty" that have emerged in the public realm in the last decade. The Harvard-trained economist, who in 1983 became full professor of economics at Harvard at age twenty-nine, has piled up an impressive number of high-pedigree positions in the development arena. He is director of the Earth Institute at Columbia University, professor of Sustainable Development, and professor of Health Policy and Management at the same university. He is director of the UN Millennium Project and special advisor to the UN secretary-general on the MDGs. In such capacity he has been influential in setting the MDGs to reduce extreme poverty, disease, and hunger by 2015. Sachs is a true celebrity, and not only in development circles. He was named in the list of "100 Most Influential People in the World" by *TIME* magazine in 2004 and 2005. He has been advisor to the International Monetary Fund (IMF), the World Bank, the Organization for Economic Cooperation and Development (OECD), the WHO, and the UN Development Programme (UNDP). He was deemed the "most important economist in the world" by the *New York Times Magazine* and "the world's best-known economist" by *TIME* magazine. Bono has characterized Sachs as the "Jimi Hendrix" of the "Woodstock of Global Health" (Bono's term for the *TIME* Global Health Summit held in New York, November 2005).

Sachs has developed the style and communication skills of celebrities but he uses them in his economic realm. At a public lecture attended by the authors, Sachs introduced his ideas in a speech as "my own perspective" noting that he was "familiar enough to have some credibility."[25] Developing trust and agreement from listeners based on their familiarity with your persona is one way that the celebrity modality is being embraced by aid celebrities like Sachs. Sachs also simplifies complex and contentious debates in international development into questions of "simple humanity" and "simple common sense" that focus in his words "not on what is new, but on what is right."[26] By conflating multifaceted technical and political debates with calls for simple moral efficacy, Sachs uses the voice of an evangelist, not that of an economist.

In 2006, a nonaffiliated political group in the United States organized a not-for-profit corporation called the "Sachs for President draft committee" to enlist Sachs to run for president. His qualifications for high public office included being "one of the world's most renowned economists" and that "his globe-trotting, high-profile work on Third World poverty-related issues has made him a sort of academic Bono."[27]

The status he has achieved as a "progressive" economist is even more striking, considering that in the late 1980s and early 1990s, Sachs spent most of his time advising Eastern European and former Soviet Republics on "shock therapy," a series of economic reforms that were meant to help former communist regimes to find the path of capitalism painfully, but quickly. Generally, Sachs in the 1980s was part of the wave of economists that crisscrossed the world to advise developing and transition country governments on structural adjustment and market liberalization. He was a key advisor to Solidarity and to the first postcommunist government in Poland. From 1991 to 1994, Sachs led a team of economic advisors for Russian president Boris Yeltsin on issues of stabilization, privatization, and market liberalization.

Then, in the mid- to late 1990s, Sachs went through a populist transformation, repackaging himself as a progressive economist. He became interested in the macroeconomics of public health and went back to his early career interest on debt reduction and restructuring, now modified into debt cancellation. He also became more interested in Africa. He collaborated with Ann Pettifor in raising the public profile of the Jubilee 2000 debt cancellation campaign, to which he was economic advisor. He became friends with Bono, accompanying him on many occasions—both of them embodying the image of relatively young, successful professionals that carry the torch of "soft capitalism" and Western values. Both men, in separate occasions, met with Pope John Paul II—Sachs did it twice. Bono, in the foreword of Sachs's book *The End of Poverty*, writes: "[Sachs] is an economist who can bring to life statistics that were, after all, lives in the first place. He can look up from the numbers and see faces through the spreadsheets" (2005, xv). Yet many of the poor and diseased Africans Sachs is now trying to save may have become so partly as a result of the reforms he advocated in the 1980s—public sector retrenchments, rollbacks from the provision of public goods and services, and the elimination of parastatal entities that controlled commodity trade and exports and that used to cushion farmers from commodity price shocks. His celebrity persona extends far beyond his professional accomplishments as exemplified by the lead-in to a feature on him in *Vanity Fair:* "Jeffrey Sachs—visionary economist, savior of Bolivia, Poland, and other struggling nations, adviser to the U.N. and movie stars—won't settle for less than the global eradication of extreme poverty."[28]

RED is not the only program of Brand Aid that Sachs is supporting. He has written a contribution to a book (Cole 2008) documenting an initiative undertaken by Kenneth Cole called "Awearness." The program includes a Web site, a clothing and accessories product line, and a holiday shopping appeal that supports selected charities. In his chapter in the *Awearness* book, Sachs plays on similar notions of cultural Christianity and even concludes with a reference to the wisdom of Bono.

> Religious traditions called on the religious community to tithe . . . for the poor. Now as a global society we are so rich that even less than one percent of our income . . . can be sufficient. . . . Invested properly, with expertise, and in the spirit of cooperation, ours will be the generation that ends extreme poverty on Earth. As Bono sings about our good fortune as human beings, "We get to carry each other." (Sachs 2008, 93)

Sachs as an aid celebrity asks for what he terms "enlightened globalization" (Sachs 2005, 358). He acknowledges that the antiglobalization movement has the "right moral fervor" (ibid., 356), but that private

"THE SQUEAKY WHEEL"
Sachs speaking at a school in the village of Ruhiira, Uganda, January 2007. Ruhiira is participating in Sachs's Millennium Villages Project.

Jeffrey Sachs's $200 Billion Dream

Jeffrey Sachs—visionary economist, savior of Bolivia, Poland, and other struggling nations, adviser to the U.N. and movie stars—won't settle for less than the global eradication of extreme poverty. And he hasn't got a second to waste

By Nina Munk

In the respected opinion of Jeffrey David Sachs—distinguished Quetelet Professor of Sustainable Development at Columbia University, director of the Earth Institute, and special adviser to the secretary-general of the United Nations—the problem of extreme poverty can be solved. In fact, the problem can be solved "easily." "We have enough on the planet to make sure, easily, that people aren't dying of their poverty. That's the basic truth," he tells me firmly, without a doubt.

It's November 2006, and Sachs has just addressed the General Assembly of the United Nations. His message is straightforward: "Millions of people die every year for the stupid reason they are too poor to

stay alive. . . . That is a plight we can end." Afterward, as the two of us have lunch in the crowded U.N. cafeteria, overlooking New York's East River, he continues: "The basic truth is that for less than a percent of the income of the rich world nobody has to die of poverty on the planet. That's really a powerful truth."

Sachs, 52, is devoting his life to this all-powerful truth. As one exhausted member of his staff explained to me, "It feels like we're running a campaign—all the time."

Day after day, without pausing for air, it seems, Sachs makes one speech after another (as many as three in one day). At the same time, he meets heads of state, holds press conferences, attends symposiums, lobbies government officials and legisla-

tors, participates in panel discussions, gives interviews, writes opinion pieces for newspapers and magazines, and connects with anyone, absolutely anyone, who might help him spread the word.

One week in early December, Sachs scheduled three overnight flights in five days. First, after a full day of teaching at Columbia, he flew from New York to Rio de Janeiro, São Paulo, and Brasília for two days of meetings with President Luiz Inacio Lula da Silva's Cabinet. From there he headed to Washington to attend the White House Summit on Malaria, hosted by President and Mrs. Bush. Afterward he left for San Francisco, where he made a presentation to the founders of Google. That same day, a Friday, he flew home to New York.

Jeffrey Sachs photographed in Ruhiira, Uganda, one of his "Millennium Villages." Reproduced from the Vanity Fair *Africa Issue, July 2007.*

companies are superior to public organizations, and thus, they should be the drivers of change in the global economy. Sachs writes, "They know, in short, how to get the job done when the incentives are in place for them to do the right thing" (ibid., 358).

The Healer

When Bono claimed at the Global Health Summit that "a world without malaria or TB is no longer unthinkable," the reference was to Paul Farmer. A physician and medical anthropologist, Farmer has shown by example that ARV treatment can resurrect patients suffering from the late stages of AIDS, even in the poorest circumstances.

> You might think it's too difficult to get these drugs to the people who most need them. A couple of years ago when DATA (Debt, AIDS, Trade, Africa) lobbied President Bush, Tony Blair and Jacques Chirac to do more on AIDS we went to experts about this. From Bill and Melinda Gates, to Dr Paul Farmer working in the poorest places on the earth, to Dr Coutinho in his AIDS clinic in Uganda. Is it easy? No. Is it impossible? No. Can we do it? Absolutely.[29]

In 1990, Paul Farmer received MD and PhD degrees from Harvard. He is an accomplished scholar, with over one hundred publications, and a clinical physician with dual practices in the United States and Haiti. And, according to at least one of his former patients, he's a god. Farmer began his lifework while still a medical student at Harvard when he set up a community-based healthcare delivery system in Cange on the central plateau of Haiti, the poorest country in the Western Hemisphere. To support the work, he founded a Boston-based charity called Partners In Health in 1987 together with Ophelia Dahl, daughter of the writer Roald Dahl, and with financing from Tom White, an Irish American developer who made his fortune in construction and then turned toward philanthropy. Partners In Health supported the work of the Haitian center Zammi Lasante. Its mission, according to Farmer, is both medical and moral, and it is based on solidarity rather than just charity. He began with a one-building clinic. "Today, the well-equipped facility, with its operating rooms, blood bank, satellite communications, laptops, and other components of modern medicine, is a global model for delivering public-health services."[30] Farmer's work in Haiti was a pivotal factor in the country's selection as the first in the world to receive money from the Global Fund.

Farmer's revolutionary tactic of "social medicine" includes providing lifesaving medicines and surgical care together with clean water, food, housing, education, and social services. Partners In Health tackles the most daunting challenges in infectious-disease control including multidrug-resistance tuberculosis, malaria, and HIV/AIDS affecting the poor in Boston's inner city, as well as in Haiti, Guatemala, Peru, Rwanda, Russia, and Mexico. In 2005, they received the world's largest humanitarian award, the $1.5 million Hilton Prize, for their multifaceted and unconventional approach to aid. Partners In Health is now a multimillion-dollar operation receiving funding from the Bill and Melinda Gates Foundation, the Clinton Health Access initiative, and the Global Fund, among others.

Farmer's books link his medical and moral missions with an important political message of "putting the poor first" (Farmer 1992, 1999, 2003). He has become the first "global doctor," known through the anecdotes and photographs of his Haitian community members, and substantiated with science, effectiveness, and efficiency. Thousands of people around the world have seen the photograph of Joseph Jeune, who was dying of AIDS and tuberculosis at age twenty-six, but after receiving access to ARV drugs through one of Farmer's Global Fund expansion sites, is shown as a healthy man with his niece propped on his hip.[31] Farmer's presentations then show Joseph when he was *really* a changed man, a year later as he gave a talk as an activist at a health and human rights conference.

Farmer also performed at the "Woodstock of Global Health" where he was asked to address "the case for optimism." He proclaimed that "doing the right thing for people living in poverty and facing disease will allow us to start a 'virtuous social cycle,' even if we began by attacking AIDS, tuberculosis, malaria or maternal mortality."[32] Farmer is regularly featured in the mass media and has been the subject of a Pulitzer Prize–winning biography entitled *Mountains beyond Mountains: The Quest of Dr. Paul Farmer, a Man Who Would Cure the World* (Kidder

2003). In an interview published in the *Huffington Post*, Farmer is the awe-inspiring doctor. "Farmer isn't some sort of far-out idealist touting universal health care for all. Instead, he proved that not only is adequate care possible in impoverished communities, denying that treatment is unjustifiable."[33] Farmer's version of "proven morality" on his famous "AMCs" (Areas of Moral Clarity) leaves little room for dissent. However, much of the writing on Farmer, including his biography, demonstrates how his persona, his character as the global doctor, and his charisma are never contradictory. His personal authenticity, perhaps even beyond that of the other aid celebrities, is his greatest asset.

Farmer has stated that there are no inaccuracies in his biography, but he also acknowledged that the power of his story exceeds the professional achievements of his work. In other words, he has celebrity power. Farmer explains in an interview:

> Tracy Kidder [Farmer's biographer] was writing his book at the same time I was writing *Pathologies of Power*. So a lot of issues he wrote about are covered somewhat differently in my writing. But his is a bestseller; mine is not.[34]

Farmer himself, the aid celebrity, has more mass-market appeal than his complicated international health work around the globe. Like Bono and Sachs, Farmer uses his celebrity to speak for others, most frequently poor Haitians, who otherwise would have no input in global debates. However, when Farmer tells interviewers that "I've been trained by the Haitians,"[35] it comes with the backing of two prestigious Ivy League degrees.

While Paul Farmer has not been directly involved in the RED campaign media thus far, his work as an aid celebrity has made the initiative possible. His effective advocacy for the right to treatment is taken out of the context of his actual work that includes intensive community support structures that expand far beyond the purely medical realm. While Farmer's moral tone and ascetic lifestyle do not at first glance seem compatible with the flashy, bling image of RED, such an approach would have been impossible without his revolution in the potential of AIDS treatment, embodied in his own totemic role as the healer. Doing global health differently, in ways that work, under the logic of pragmatism not ideology, can be taken up by very different kinds of approaches toward international development.

EXPERTISE AND AFFECT

Aid celebrities are not circumventing "the system" in international development: they are forming the system. Celebrities are not perceived as fundamentally inauthentic, and thus a detriment to overcome, but are actually the faces of doing good, credibility, and believability in international development. While sharing some of the overall qualities of celebrity in general, aid celebrities must be distinguished from other kinds of celebrities who might participate in international development or humanitarian causes. Many different kinds of celebrities engage in promoting global "good causes" in a wide variety of ways, most of which fall outside the scope of Brand Aid. However, it may be the case that the credibility of the aid celebrities transfers also to other nonexpert celebrities who ally with the same causes. One interesting aspect of aid celebrities is not that the celebrities must follow the rules, but that the institutions, the system, must function like a celebrity to be considered credible by the general population.

Because of aid celebrities, consumers can have faith in international development. However, the development they actually connect with is not the messy, on-the-ground interaction between different people, challenges, and values. Brockington (2009) highlights the ways that celebrities have enabled people to vicariously reconnect with their natural world through conservation spectacles. Celebrities and the "highly staged and carefully framed encounters" with nature are linked through mutually constitutive symbolic processes. However, by restricting their possibility to "mediagenic" conservation, celebrities empower those forms of conservation most, even when their social impacts are highly questionable (ibid., 14). Brockington's book rests on the intertwining of celebrity and conservation: "Celebrity conservation produces images which are commodities in themselves and sold, [or] else used to elicit donors' support, and which are consumed with little awareness of these images' origins or conditions of production" (ibid., vi). By intertwining development with consumption and celebrities, RED produces a virtualism of AIDS treatment that we describe in chapter 2.

RED is based on celebrity validation, which is based on personal capacity. The RED Web site contains links to "learn" about RED, HIV/AIDS in Africa, the crisis and the solution, how RED works, partners, and results.[36] The "crisis" is summarized in bold statistics. But the hard science representation of numbers and facts does not hold the power to make consumers believe in the RED campaign.

The aid celebrities that guarantee RED operate in ways that appear fundamentally different from the current spate of certifications, labels, and codes of conduct that characterize "ethical and sustainable" trade and corporate social responsibility. Celebrity at first sight seems contradictory to the "audit culture" that underpins these processes (Power 1997; Strathern 2000) and that aims at "impersonal" and systemic solutions to problems of quality, food safety, environmental impact, and social conditions of production (see chapter 4). Labels and certifications for "fair trade" or "organic" products, for example, are systemic, based on auditing and certification. However, from the consumer point of view, both labels and celebrities provide a similar simplification of very complex socioeconomic environmental processes. The label is a "sign" that performs a simplified complexity, and celebrity does the same work. But, instead of an aura of science, the celebrity is vested in the performance of persona.

The reason that celebrities are becoming more acceptable guarantors at this particular historical moment may be related to larger trends in the "democratization of expertise" linking new media technologies (the blogosphere) and the basic contradictions of liberal democracy. S. P. Turner (2003) argues that the traditional models of expertise are giving way to new, more pluralistic and "democratic" models. In these new spaces, the boundaries between experts and lay people are increasingly porous.

In traditional models of expertise, experts speak "as experts" within the limits of accepted knowledge within their own group and produce a science that is "neutral." Within this framework, the role of the journalist is to translate expert statements for public consumption. In the process of this translation, the media creates celebrity experts by using expert statements to back trivial arguments, which then assume an aura of authority. However, this traditional model has been undermined by the blogosphere where the distinction between the expert and the nonexpert becomes blurred, multiple views and controversies abound, and in the process the celebrity experts are exposed, sometimes to ridicule. This potential for greater democracy in the creation of knowledge also exposes the contradictions in liberalism between the need for control, moderating the blogosphere, and the calls for openness (S. P. Turner 2003).

RED emphasizes a community created in the blogosphere that could, in theory, produce a multiplicity of views that differs from the traditional aid models based on a "consensus" among the "community of experts." This increased complexity through "open" expertise creates a need for greater simplification. This may be one reason why experts become aid celebrities—to spread messages through their own charismatic translation. Yet, paradoxically, the content thus far on the RED blog suggests homogeneity, unquestionable support for the initiative and its products, and predictable, if rare, discussions of Africa as we elaborate in chapter 2. As Banet-Weiser and Lapsansky argue, in "the RED campaign . . . the space available for consumers to participate in the process of meaning-making is relatively limited. . . . RED is a case where the producers [meaning the RED companies], not the consumers, are in control" (2008, 1254).

Aid celebrities, like other celebrities more generally, must forgo nuance and argumentation and promote a set of easy-to-grasp policy prescriptions to "save" Africa as a question of faith, not rationality. And as in organized faith, the room for questioning is tightly delimited. Ironically, the RED blogsite posted a reflection by a regular contributor on the difference between celebrity and saint, the latter constituting a distance too great to sustain the relationship between RED consumers and aid celebrities like Farmer and Bono:

> tonight at the university of washington, author Tracy Kidder [Paul Farmer's biographer] in referring to Paul Farmer stated how making him out to be a saint would separate and detach

him from the potential let alone responsibility we all have to do what we can and should, and so it can be said of Bono. but with both men their inspiration and influence cannot be measured.

i'm proud to be a fan of his and coworker in making poverty history. someone, if you would, thank him for me, please? or, if possible, thanx Bono. you deserve this and so much more.
stay close,
sammi f(red)enburg
seattle.[37]

Collectively, the three celebrities totemically embody the "good" and have their lives' stories to guarantee for that. After more than three decades of development pessimism burdening the conscience of left-leaning development enthusiasts, and increasing suspicion of the vacuity of consumerism, totemic aid celebrities merge disparate longings into a new modality for resolving the disparity between rich and poor, well and diseased.

The virtualism of RED rests on AIDS treatment in Africa, and these images must be reproduced to suit the needs of the RED interests. Celebrities are critical for drawing attention to the spectacle, legitimating the virtualism of RED that is meant to "solve" it. De Waal uses the example of the indigenous leader and Nigerian martyr Ken Saro-Wiwa, who fatally overestimated the power of Western publicity in preventing the failure of the Ogoni people's struggle and his own hanging, to draw lessons for other humanitarian struggles like the one in Darfur (2008, 55). He concludes: "the moral hyperventilation of celebrities hasn't helped and probably has hindered. But who needs empirics when there is a good story to tell?" (ibid.).

Celebrity status sanctions power on emotive and irrational claims. Celebrities are leaders in emotion. Marshall constructs an analysis of celebrity that is based on existing studies of leadership, arguing that the representations of public figures from politicians to film stars hold much in common as a unified system of celebrity status is created (1997, 19). "The celebrity system is a way in which the sphere of the irrational, emotional, personal, and affective is contained and negotiated in contemporary culture" (ibid., 72–73). Central to the power of celebrity is the concept of "affect." The term is used by psychology to refer to "the middle ground between cognition and behavior: the affective realm is connected to this chain of causality between something experienced and the formulation of a reaction to that experience" (ibid., 73). According to theorists of celebrity such as Marshall, Alberoni, and Grossberg, our contemporary culture is characterized by the following scenario:

> a crisis in our ability to locate any meaning as a possible and appropriate source for an impassioned commitment. It is a crisis, not of faith, but of the relationship between faith and commonsense, a dissolution of what we might call the "anchoring effect" that articulates meaning and affect. It is not that nothing matters—for something has to matter—but that we can find no way of choosing, or of finding something to warrant our investment. . . . Meaning and affect—historically so closely intertwined—have broken apart, each going off in its own direction. (Grossberg 1992, 222; cited in Marshall 1997, 74)

Celebrities are able to provide an expression of and an anchoring for affect in contemporary society, and they can do this in ways that ordinary individuals cannot.[38] Rojek summarizes: "post-God celebrity is now one of the mainstays of organizing recognition and belonging in secular society" (2001, 58). Marks and Fischer take this further into the political realm where rationality should have replaced myth with the loss of charismatic authority, yet citizens manufacture celebrities out of "bits and pieces of existent political ideology. The authority of celebrities thus derives from their ability, *through the force of their personality,* to translate political ideology *into the person* of themselves as legitimate rulers" (2002, 383; emphasis in original).

It is through their management of affect, the emotional in political culture, that celebrities are able to unify disparate constituencies and to "stitch together a functional unity" in a context where disunities are obvious, acting as a legitimating apparatus for the symbolic representation of the people (Marshall 1997, 240). As people become increasingly delinked from their closest social relations, and as "parasocial" relations[39] (interactions across a significant social distance with people we do not know) become more important, the celebrity figure serves as a new dimension of creating community through the media (G. Turner 2004; Rojek 2001). Celebrities are there to provide meaning, to promote order, and to achieve social integration (Rojek 2001).

AID CELEBRITIES AND BRAND AID

Aid celebrities are created to brand affect in international development. The rise of an aid celebritariat (to borrow and qualify Rojek's term) is linked to the institutional failures of international development and African aid as we describe in chapter 3. The "sleepy backwater that development had become"[40] created a need for grounding the international impulse to do good. As development aid became increasingly subjected to criticism, consumers, citizens, or "the masses" were exposed to an increasing proliferation of development "news" or data. The growing complexity and confusion for rational decision-making created a demand for aid celebrities.

The felt need for affective grounding may also explain why readers find it legitimate to consider both Bono and Sachs as aid celebrities, but dispute the inclusion of Farmer, who is "really good," as an important aid celebrity. As we state in the introduction, this book is not making light of the impulse to "do good" globally, for Africa or elsewhere. However, we bring attention to the power of Brand Aid that exists beyond the material realm of stylish clothes and smart gadgetry: it exists through the mobilization of affect to produce certain kinds of donors who care. As Harding and Pribram argue, "people care if they are invested. If people care, certain effects are produced: they feel and act in certain ways . . . subjects are 'affected,' that they are constituted into specifically contoured kinds of feeling beings" (2004, 879).

Aid celebrities can appeal to the international aid community. They communicate to an increasingly discerning crowd of consumer-citizens, and unlike celebrities from other arenas like films or sports, aid celebrities combine expertise and appeal. However, debates that are taking place over the role of celebrities in international humanitarian causes have only recently begun to consider the role of the aid celebrities like Bono, Sachs, and Farmer. Some of the contentious issues are that aid celebrities close debate by embodying consensus on issues where there is none; they cannot represent complexity; they are celebrated because of a link to expertise in a "local" realm that can only partially be translated to make sense in "global" terms. Because they are celebrities on the basis of a local rootedness, their celebrity status reinforces a provincial appeal and the prejudices of those who have "chosen" them. Celebrities cannot provide global solutions, but they can represent, embody, the possibility that such answers can be achieved. Bono is hip, Sachs is serious, and Farmer is good.

(2) THE ROCK MAN'S BURDEN
Fair Vanity and Virtual Salvation

RED's celebrities and its images draw on religious metaphor to create unlikely allies in a cause-related marketing campaign to benefit Africa. In this chapter, we demonstrate how RED weds existing colonial imaginaries with technological faith to produce a depiction of AIDS that can be solved by proper shopping. In the process, the RED brand rebrands Africa as "cool" in a neomissionary option for consumers who can now take up the "rock man's burden." RED, like philanthropy in general, has its genesis in early Christian charities' questioning of the ability of market mechanisms to ameliorate human misery caused by unchecked capitalist growth. With RED, a new social contract is created to generate a sustainable flow of money to support the Global Fund to Fight AIDS, Tuberculosis and Malaria. And, like the classical social contracts of Locke and Rousseau, this one is also premised on Christian foundations. This chapter will demonstrate that RED also recycles eighteenth- and nineteenth-century representations of the holy trinity of Christianity, Civilization, and Commerce (Magubane 2008; McClintock 1994). The representational work of the RED campaign works to help a negotiated and distant "Africa," while selling products through the marketing of the difference between "us" and "them."

Here, the RED campaign is examined as a meaningful player in representations of African AIDS that draw on deeply embedded cultural logics that condition what seems real.[1] We have selected a sample of such representations from the RED campaign in various popular media. This chapter analyzes text and photographs from the *Vanity Fair* RED Africa Issue, blogs published on the RED Web site and MySpace, a RED video titled *The Lazarus Effect*, the cover image from *The (RED) Independent*, and a print advertisement for the RED American Express card. True to RED's vision of harnessing the strengths of marketing and advertising from business, the RED campaign includes striking photography of what we argue are iconic images. While most of these pictures are high-gloss fashion advertisements, some are also showing the African beneficiaries of shopping RED. In these photos, we argue, consumers are given an opportunity to regard suffering at a distance through the medium of photography (see Sontag 2003).

One of the claims made by RED is that it raises awareness, so we consider what it is that Western consumers are being made aware of. Focusing on the treatment of African AIDS medicalizes and normalizes the disease as heterosexual, thus distancing the RED consumers from previous generations of gay AIDS activism and representations of unsafe sex (see Watney 1987). RED's explicit emphasis on women and children aligns it clearly with the camp that tackles the "good AIDS" ascribed to the heterosexual population, as opposed to the "queer AIDS" acquired by those "who got what they deserved" (Gurevich et al. 2007, 14; see also Patton 1996). The UN pointed to the importance of gender as part of how we understand and grapple with AIDS in which it is "the unequal relationships between men and women, as well as gender stereotypes" that "fuel the spread of HIV" (2008, 25). Gendered power relationships and sexual stereotypes also affect the possibilities available to women who live with the virus, limiting both women's physical enactment of sexuality and their identities as sexual beings (Gurevich et al. 2007). These stereotypes are of course not simply a gender problem for societies that receive international development assistance and philanthropic donations, but are also part of the constitution and representations of aid and giving.[2]

In *Globalizing AIDS*, Cindy Patton argues that "the legacies of colonialism and modernization allow for the spectacular and insidious recycling of racist, sexist, xenophobic, and homophobic ideas as though they were 'scientific'" (2002, xxvi). RED weds a Western faith in science as it focuses on treatment technologies with a religious understanding of the burden of caring for deserving others. RED relies on a nonsectarian, cultural Christianity, which is fundamental for much of the engagement of international development by non-Africans to fight AIDS in Africa. Drawing on Treichler's (1999) work that the representations of AIDS are critical to shaping the possibilities for understanding, intervening, and living with the disease, this chapter suggests that explicitly Christian referencing throughout the campaign is used as a foil, and perhaps a distraction, for the promotion of material values and perpetuation of stereotypes of African AIDS. By pulling together the understandings of Western consumers that draw on cultural Christianity and the faith that Africans need their help, the RED virtualism of treatment (see later in this chapter) allows the possibility of believing that conscious consumption and antiretroviral (ARV) pills will save Africa.

RED's representations are deeply problematic, not simply in the ways that Africa is "reimagined" and thus can be assumed by Western consumers to be suffering from some imaginative lack, but more fundamentally in the ways that AIDS in Africa is made into something that you can know from a distance. RED's pictures of AIDS provide answers and preempt questions in ways that are easily accessed, morally upstanding, and stylistically cool. However, all of the important questions of how power conditions the entry of RED, its pictures, and its products into the global marketplace of ideas and objects are brushed aside. A rock man's burden—imagined along familiar constructions of sex, gender, race, and place—frames African beneficiaries' receiving process. When relationships of donation are created, the fundamental imbalance between the givers and the recipients, in this case the Western consumers and the women and children with AIDS in Africa, is not part of the problem to be solved. In the words of Kleinman and Kleinman, "the authorization of action through an appeal for foreign aid, even foreign intervention, begins with an evocation of indigenous absence, an erasure of local voices and acts" (1996, 7). Brand Aid in general and the RED initiative in particular thus resemble old forms of international aid and charity in their reliance on a scripted suffering other. RED depicts images of African AIDS and the Western savior so beautifully as to distract the viewer from their stereotypes. As global relations of exchange appear increasingly complex, these stereotypes become reified and rigid as part of the industry of image making, and consumers may become "tempted to cling desperately to clichés which seem to bring some order into the otherwise ununderstandable" (Adorno 1991, 147). Representations in RED draw on powerful cultural logics to allow the campaign to naturalize global inequalities of race, class, and gender while approving consumer engagement to mediate their worst effects—producing what we call "the rock man's burden." RED's images construct feminine, partial, neoliberal subjects (African women and children) who are consumers of advanced biomedicine who are then twinned with masculinized (ironically, since consumers of "soft" goods are typically women), whole, neoliberal subjects (Western consumers) who are consumers of "cool Africa."

AFRICA IN THE HIERARCHY OF DEVELOPMENT IMAGINARIES

A secularized belief in Christian charity can be traced at least as far back as eighteenth-century Europe, when a "new humanitarianism" embraced the notion of human misery as a preventable evil (Curtin 1964, 260). Notions of progress, based on the moral value of spreading Western civilization, were linked to economic motivations for spreading commerce. Like RED, these early manifestations were not limited to "saints" but were taken up by "secular reformers" and even "enlightened unbelievers" who could share some aspects of the missionary zeal to carry the light of "civilization" to the "dark places" (ibid.).

Furthermore, there is over a century of history that suggests that appeals to some form of "The White Man's Burden" has been marketed to sell consumer products.

> Take up the White Man's burden—
> Have done with childish day—
> The lightly-proffered laurel,
> The easy ungrudged praise:
> Comes now, to search your manhood

Through all the thankless years,
Cold, edged with dear-bought wisdom,
The judgment of your peers.[3]

Rudyard Kipling's famous poem, credited by some as promoting or by others as satirizing the imperialist impulse, was published in *McClure's,* an illustrated monthly magazine popular in America around the turn of the century. This is the same magazine that, just four years later, published Ida Tarbell's series on the abuses committed by John D. Rockefeller's Standard Oil Company. These early examples of "investigative journalism" or "muckraking" focused popular attention on the negative externalities of capitalism and resulted in state intervention to impose limits on corporate power, while setting the foundations for a reactive prototype of corporate social responsibility as we will discuss later in this book. The final line in the last stanza of Kipling's poem concludes with a clear demarcation of boundaries of race, gender, and class—defining "who counts" and outlining the parameters of privileged masculinity and "difference." The poem is foundational for displacing the "half-devil and half-child" sullen peoples from those who will judge "your manhood"—your peers.[4]

Soon after its publication, the popular notion of "The White Man's Burden" was used in a cause-related marketing campaign of the 1890s for Pears soap. The advertisement claims that its product "is a potent factor in brightening the dark corners of the earth as civilization advances." Pears soap, a "technology of purification" has been central to understanding the historical links between commodity racism[5] and gendered empire (McClintock 1994, 131).[6] Anne McClintock explains:

> Both the cult of domesticity and the new imperialism found in soap an exemplary mediating form. The emergent middle-class values—monogamy ("clean" sex, which has value), industrial capital ("clean" money, which has value), Christianity ("being washed in the blood of the lamb"), class control ("cleansing the great unwashed") and the imperial civilizing mission ("washing and clothing the savage")—could all be marvelously embodied in a single household commodity (1994, 134).

The first step towards lightening

The White Man's Burden

is through teaching the virtues of cleanliness.

Pears' Soap

is a potent factor in brightening the dark corners of the earth as civilization advances, while amongst the cultured of all nations it holds the highest place—it is the ideal toilet soap.

Admiral George Dewey washes his hands with Pears soap. Courtesy of Library of Congress.

In the Pears advertising campaign, the aesthetic space around the domestic commodity, in this case soap, was invested with the commercial cult of empire (ibid., 511). We argue that the RED campaign draws on these nineteenth-century "discoveries" of advertising to promote products for domestic consumption while drawing on imaginaries of saving Africa. The RED theme of saving the "others" to raise your own status among your peers is thus not without precedent. In postcolonial society, explicit referencing to "The White Man's Burden" would be unlikely to sell products; however, RED reenacts such an ideology in which products are used to promote virtue and save savages, what we call the "Rock Man's Burden."

RED grants are made through the Fund's best-performing programs for AIDS in Africa; funds have gone to Ghana, Lesotho, Rwanda, and Swaziland, and more recently also to South Africa and Zambia. As we will discuss in chapter 3, this is the first time that a contributor has been able to "hand pick" successes from the Global Fund's repertoire of programs. RED chooses receivers that are both "successful" and "African." That RED's beneficiaries are African is not coincidental, as reimagining Africa is part of the RED vision. Mbembe (2001) has argued that the real and the imaginary are interwoven in the category of "Africa." J. Ferguson (2006) takes this further by suggesting that "Africa" has a particular place in "globalization"—a "place" understood as both a location in space and a rank in a system of social categories. The "forcefully imposed position in the contemporary world—is easily visible if we notice how fantasies of a categorical 'Africa' (normally, 'Sub-Saharan' or 'black' Africa) and 'real' political-economic processes on the continent are interrelated" (ibid., 7). Mbembe describes, "More than any other region, Africa thus stands out as the supreme receptacle of the West's obsession with, and circular discourse about, the facts of 'absence,' 'lack,' and 'non-being,' of identity and difference" (2001, 4). Indian feminist Uma Narayan (1997) argues that representation of "other" cultures in the mainstream Western media is not a problem of omission, but instead that Western representations have been deeply involved in perpetuating negative stereotypes and imputations of cultural inferiority. It is in the "reductive repetition" that African underdevelopment becomes popularized (Andreasson 2005).

Yet imaginations of African AIDS go even beyond Said's Orientalism of "Otherness" (see Mbembe and Nuttal 2004). In Bayart's classic critique of Afropessimism, he describes "the AIDS pandemic, a sinister companion of conflict, which decimates those populations which war has spared" (2000, 217). In post-9/11 geopolitical terms, Africa remains relevant for its oil and minerals, as the proving ground for Western generosity and virtue, and perhaps for sport and adventure. Jean Comaroff articulates:

> [D]isease-ridden Africa epitomizes another otherness, a product less of an axis of evil than an axis of irrelevance. . . . The continent disappears once more behind colonial images of nature red in tooth and claw. Once more it becomes a site for European philanthropy and adventurism. (2007, 201)

That the continent finds little space in the popular imaginary beyond suffering and safaris poses no problem for selling RED. Bono articulates the RED rationale for "Africa as adventure": "We needed help in describing the continent of Africa as an opportunity, as an adventure, not a burden. Our habit—and we have to kick it—is to reduce this mesmerizing, entrepreneurial, dynamic continent of fifty-three diverse countries to a hopeless deathbed of war, disease, and corruption."[7]

Bono's call to kick our habit of Afropessimism, including a reference to the fifty-three countries that comprise the continent, might have been able to communicate a meaningful message to a popular audience, perhaps even beginning to destabilize what we believe we already know about "Africa" and our relationship to "Africans." However, like all texts, this one must be placed within its context as part of its meaning. Bono's statement is in the magazine *Vanity Fair*, which we discuss in more detail later in this chapter. It is located on the facing page of an advertisement for Dolce & Gabbana, "a producer of men's and women's fashion wear for a 'modern hedonist'" (Hintzen 2008, 78). Percy Hintzen analyzes Bono's quotation alongside this imagery in detail.[8] Hintzen concludes: "I was struck, but certainly not surprised, by the seamlessness with which all the tropes and figurative representations of white supremacy, (cross)racial desire, sexism, developmental historicism, and materialism combined in the juxtaposition of the two sentence Bono quotation and the advertisement.... Africa... appeases profligate consumption while offering up to the modern sophisticate the unlimited sexual pleasures of the jungle in its naked freedom, bereft of the staid heteronormativity of Victorian-like sensibilities" (ibid., 78–79).

In its predictable portrayal of saving African women and children, RED markets the difference between "us" and "them."[9] The category of the "African woman" is constructed through RED as in many other interventions as being, on the one hand, the remarkable and resilient hero of the pandemic, caring for orphans and holding together fragile families, and on the other hand, a passive victim of both individual men and patriarchal African "culture" (O'Manique 2004). Africa seems the obvious "place" where RED money could buy pills to save women and children with AIDS, and where the constructions of donor and recipient would not be challenged, as Africa's "place" in the hierarchy of development is well established.

TREATMENT TOURISM FROM THE BLOGOSPHERE

The possibility of saving Africans with AIDS through your choice of sunglasses is constituted by the virtualism of ARV treatment in RED. In RED, ARV treatment must be distanced from any of the other important social, economic, psychological, or even medical factors in the lives of the Africans to be "saved." This disembedding of AIDS treatment activities from their context creates a different reality of treatment. Polanyi describes this disembedding in relation to economics as that in which economic activities are removed from the social and other relationships in which they had occurred and are carried out in a context in which the only important relationships are those defined by the economic activity itself (cited in Carrier 1998, 2). The reembedding of these activities in their own self-referential context creates a virtualism. The result is based on the belief that the abstracted and reinscribed description of the world is not just a parsimonious description of what is really happening, but a prescriptive of what the world ought to be (ibid.; see also Miller 1998). The representations of ARV treatment in RED's campaign abstract the economic accessibility of ARVs (if there was simply more money for more pills, the people who need those pills would get them and their lives would be saved) from their social, psychological, and political relationships and then reinscribe this distilled "reality" into imagined relationships. The virtualism created relies on what westerners "know" about Africans with AIDS (that they need treatment and are too poor to afford it) and as such perpetuates narrow imaginaries of the "Other" (Spivak 1985). Boltanski (1993) and others (for example, Butt 2002; Kleinman and Kleinman 1996; Littler 2008) have theorized the importance of understanding the meaning of bringing suffering at a distance close up through mediated images. RED produces a virtualism of AIDS treatment that relies on the proximity and distance of Western consumers and African sufferers.

As part of the RED Web site, there is a blog spot that usually includes updates from the field on RED activities around the United States and Europe. It also provides short travelogue-style briefs on what RED money is actually doing in Africa, through the Global Fund. This travel blog constitutes a form of AIDS treatment tourism in the virtual realm. Readers are encouraged to read and "follow" the daily travails of Dr. Ryan Phelps, a physician from Texas who is now working in a clinic in Swaziland as part of the Baylor International Pediatric AIDS Initiative. Early in the Phelps blog of life as an AIDS pediatrician, he writes: "Every reader of this blog knows what an anonymous dying child looks like."[10] Certainly, the proliferation of highly visible and believable images of African AIDS in the media has convinced Western consumers that we have seen these things before (see Johnson 2002). On the contrary, we would argue that the fact that most readers of the RED blog, *Vanity Fair,* or even this book probably do not know what a dying child looks like marks the vast geopolitical distance that separates the helpers from the sufferers in RED. Yet the representation in "Stories of Sipho" posted on the RED blog Web site shows us a "prescriptive not descriptive" version of a "reality" that becomes a virtualism of AIDS in Africa. Sipho's story is a well-written narrative of a child whose life has been, so far, transformed by his access to ARVs. Dr. Phelps has his own blog site[11] separate from RED that gives a somewhat wider variety of stories, including some that describe insufficiency, uncertainty, and doubt; these stories are not incorporated into the virtualism of RED's AIDS treatment tourism.

RED uses virtual communities to create a sense of social space in cyberspace, a place where race, gender, HIV status, or geopolitical disadvantage may in theory be overcome by the democratization of the Internet. However, the comments by RED members on the popular social networking site MySpace suggest that transgressing boundaries and creating global community is given little attention, while shopping and cheering are most common. An analysis of RED on MySpace showed that 593,266 "friends"[12] had posted over four thousand comments on RED during 2006 and 2007 (Anderson 2008, 44). In 2007, the comments were categorized and subjected to a content analysis that demonstrated that most commonly remarked was simply "people's love of RED," the second most common theme was the love of and desire for RED products, and the third category consisted of remarks on the cause or the "good work" of RED (ibid., 44–45). The comments in the latter category were generally more concerned with "solving a problem" than with anything specific about the problem that RED is designed to engage. Of all the comments analyzed, "a mere eight people wrote about Africa specifically, and only thirty-five wrote specifically about AIDS," and when they did write about Africa, they did so using "stock scripts," such as "Very cool. i think what you have done is awesome. Some people out there are still ignorant of these diseases. Ignorant because of the lack of knowing. Like in Africa. I think red is a great Cause."[13] The representation of Africans as people who are "out there" and "ignorant" not only reiterates tired stereotypes, but it legitimizes the concern of everyday consumers who can take up the "great cause." In the interactive RED fora on social networking sites and within the RED Web site itself, the primacy of consumption, of product and prestige, overshadows the cause itself in anything but the most superficial generalizations. It is in these examples that we see the images of connectedness that are portrayed between RED consumers and their products, bereft of any of the complexity or potential benefit of real social relations (see also Sarna-Wojcicki 2008).

VISUAL REPRESENTATION AND AFRICAN AIDS

Representations matter, and in order to begin an understanding of what is at stake in RED's representations of Africans with AIDS, we must first diverge into a discussion of pictures. A picture "refers to the entire situation in which an image has made its appearance—as when we ask someone if they 'get the picture'" (Mitchell 2005, xiv). Sontag brings us closer to understanding the power that pictures have over language: "In contrast to a written account—which, depending on its complexity of thought, reference, and vocabulary, is pitched at a larger or smaller readership—a photograph has only one language and is destined potentially for all" (2003, 20). Pictures have long been used in international development campaigns and advertising, and in representing images of all sorts. This world of images, according to the painter David Hockney, claims a relationship to visual reality.[14] This relationship and its claim are powerful and often left out of mainstream debates over power and social control. Mitchell argues that the world has seen "the pictorial turn" as understood by Heidegger as "the modern age in which the world has become a picture—that is, has become a systematized, representable object of technoscientific rationality: 'World picture . . . does not mean a picture of the world but the world conceived and grasped as picture'" (Heidegger 1977, 130; as in Mitchell 2005, xiv). Yet Mitchell differs from his philosophical predecessors in that he does not argue that we can move beyond these pictures to grasp something more authentic, or real. The pictures themselves, according to Mitchell, provide our ways of making the world (ibid.). So what kind of world is made and remade through the RED pictures? And how might these pictures be seen after other pictures of African AIDS have already been and continue to be shown?

Today, war photography that shows grievously injured bodies in intimate depictions of suffering is still most likely to come from Africa or Asia where it is assumed that these are the bodies of someone to be seen, not someone (like us) who also sees (Sontag 2003, 72–73). For centuries, African bodies have been shown in published photographs meant to exhibit their "exotic" suffering. Magubane links nineteenth-

century Christian missionaries' success with their ability to strategi-
cally package and disseminate images of African suffering—"African
primitives who could only be lifted out of their misery by the charitable actions of benevolent Europeans."[15] It was in the pictures, the
"ethnographic showcases" that the truth of civilization was created.
"Publication was essential to the missions. Unlike the government or
the traders, they lived on voluntary contributions. If the missions in
the field were to continue their day to day operations, the missionary
societies at home had to maintain a regular flow of contributions. . . .
The link between publicity and fund raising was established early in the
century."[16] Missionary fundraising, like RED, promised that you could
save Africa through your consumer choices, although the missionaries
actually sold Africans to save them.[17]

Global HIV/AIDS has been described as an "epidemic of signification" (Treichler 1999) in which the representations of the disease are intrinsically related to the ways in which the disease is perceived and managed at all levels. Within global AIDS, Africa remains
a "dark zone"—"a dark, untamed continent from which devastating
viruses emerge to threaten the West" (Kitzinger and Miller 1992,
cited in Bancroft 2001, 96). It has become a common understanding
that "African AIDS" has relied upon and perpetuated stereotypes
of Africa as "Other," particularly in sexually exotic and exceptional
ways (Stillwaggon 2003). This understanding and differentiation of
African AIDS is reflected in our images depicting Africans with AIDS.
Photographic images play a particular and significant role in representations of AIDS in Africa, serving as "visual quotations." In their classic
work on suffering "in public," Kleinman and Kleinman describe how
"the photograph is a professional transformation of social life, a politically relevant rhetoric, a constructed form that ironically naturalizes
experience" (1996, 9). In a recent analysis of photographic representations of African AIDS specifically, Bleiker and Kay argue that "at a
time when we are saturated with information stemming from multiple
media sources, images are well suited to capture issues in succinct and
mesmerizing ways" (2007, 140). As elaborated by Sontag, "the photograph provides a quick way of apprehending something and a compact
form for memorizing it. The photograph is like a quotation, or a maxim

or proverb. Each of us mentally stocks hundreds of photographs, subject to instant recall" (2003, 22).

Using images of suffering in raising attention and funds for humanitarian causes has been widely contested (Burman 1994; Campbell 2004; Cohen 2001; Moeller 1999; Van der Gaag and Nash 1987; all cited in Manzo 2008, 637). Still, from Live Aid onward, the dominant images of African AIDS are those of suffering, more likely to generate pity than compassion, portraying Africans as victims with no agency set in circumstances that are far removed from the Western lifestyle. Yet RED's Africa is not full of suffering; in fact, the only images that call forth concern are clearly staged as "before" pictures in a before-and-after scenario.

African AIDS provides the quintessential cause as the outlet for Brand Aid's hard-commerce approach to doing good, because, as we stated in the introduction, like fashion, rock music, or celebrity, AIDS is about money, power, and sex. AIDS appears as a dichotomy: HIV-positive/negative. As argued by Browning, "this seems to be a division which allows all the other divisive oppositions to proliferate" (1998, 137). Furthermore, the distance between RED and its recipients obscures the contradictions between an initiative embedded in privileged, heterosexist frameworks and the actual gendered struggles of preventing and living with AIDS in Africa. Western consumers are encouraged to express their sexuality, their attractiveness, and their desire through consumer choices. It is good to be sexy and it is good to buy prestigious commodities. Women's bodies become the repository for sexuality and consumption, selling the self with the stuff. RED never connects this to the exchange of sexual services for consumer goods within its recipient societies most affected by AIDS.[18] The use of stereotypical imagery of sexy, scantily clad women to sell products to consumers is perhaps too commonplace to merit mention; however using these images to raise funding for international development efforts to respond to AIDS in Africa is distinctive. Beginning over a decade ago, research has shown that AIDS is "a different disease" for poor women (Ward 1993), yet it is the poor woman in Africa who has become the epitome of the suffering stranger (Butt 2002) with AIDS.

FAIR VANITY? WE ARE ALL AFRICAN

In July 2007, Bono guest-edited a special issue of the magazine *Vanity Fair*—the purpose of which was to "rebrand Africa."[19] Given the legacy of slavery and colonialism and the history of extraction of resources and supply of armaments to the continent, it is difficult to imagine a time when the rich have not been interested in Africa. Assuming that Africa is far from the minds, lives, and income-sources of the rich readers of *Vanity Fair* contributes to the myth that there is no real linkage between the rich and the poor, between the entrepreneurs and Africa, or between capitalism and disease.

Vanity Fair[20] is a monthly, middlebrow entertainment magazine. It features reviews, celebrity interviews, trend stories, and usually one highbrow feature with literary ambitions (Iraq War, women's prisons, AIDS, etc.) per issue. *Vanity Fair* has a controversial history in representations of African AIDS having brought the search for an origin of HIV to a popular audience with its publication of Alex Shoumatoff's "In Search of the Source of AIDS," which claims that "to the Western man in the street, however, the question of the African origin of AIDS is important" (cited in Browning 1998, 29). In this depiction, Africa is a figure representing the very origin of death (ibid.). Simultaneously, much of what *Vanity Fair* depicts is the chasing of "cool." Bono encapsulates the appeal of this intervention in his promotional video for the issue: "That's what this issue of *Vanity Fair* is all about. To bring some sex appeal to the idea of wanting to change the world."[21]

With no indications that this was intentional irony, the UK version of the Africa Issue came bundled with a seventy-eight-page insert advertising, of all things, diamonds.[22] While the topic of focus is explicitly "Africa" there are recurrent reminders that this is Africa from a neoliberal, American perspective. The inability to think beyond the world as constituted by American foreign policy is illustrated first by the issue's "Editor's Letter" justifying the choice of "Africa" as a topic. The editor sets the time frame as "sometime after 9/11."[23] The editor of *Vanity Fair* is reminding readers that after the fall of the twin towers in New York, Africa's strategic importance dropped considerably (see Comaroff 2007), thus a justification is necessary for a focus on Africa.[24]

One of the twenty-two "historic" covers photographed by Annie Leibowitz from the Vanity Fair *Africa Issue, July 2007.*

After dividing the world into geopolitical time units, the editorial then makes reference to the place "in what is now Ghana" and describes that "there was once a mini-empire called Bono, ruled by kings called Bonohene." There is a marked and skillful shift in time perspective from the contemporary and urgent reference to New York to the timeless and ahistorical reference to "Africa." The less-than-oblique imagined history of Bono as the miniemperor of Africa stands in for the complex history of the independent country that has been called "Ghana" for half a century, but places well into a virtualism of a continent plagued with suffering where Western celebrities and consumers have a responsibility to intervene.

RED relies on coexisting notions of familiarity and distance between the shoppers it tries to engage and the beneficiaries it tries to help. Let us present a few examples from the magazine. The masthead of *Vanity Fair*'s contributors to this issue are annotated with the staff member's "haplogroup." A text box explains: "Thanks to minor genetic mutations that have occurred over tens of thousands of years of human history and are shared by large groups of people, scientists can trace the migrations of early human beings from Africa to the far corners of the world."[25] Spatial imagery is interesting here, representing Africa as a place from which everyone has moved. From this we learn that Bono's matrilineal ancestry is linked to the same African mother as that of the magazine's London editor, and his patriline pairs with that of *Vanity Fair* U.S. editor Graydon Carter. Such a genetic map tracing its contributors back to their "African roots" reinforces a notion of primordial, genetic identity while also fundamentally destabilizing notions of who is the African. There is no action or sentiment required, no claims to be made or fulfilled, but a community is imagined and everyone simply is part of it in a truly cosmopolitan sense. This creates a relation described by Fadlalla as "familial globality" (2008, 210). With no claim to culture or place, genetic Africans are everywhere. We are all so close to Africa that we are actually African. Thus, a cosmopolitan call for compassion to help suffering others in faraway places re-creates our own agency and limits the possibility for activism by those slotted as "helpless." Magubane describes how "people living on the Continent today, must simply sit and wait, with the hope that someone will take pity on them and write them into history. This is Sontag's 'applied Hegelianism' taken to the extreme. The Other completely ceases to exist except insofar as a tiny remnant of her survives in us. The Other is not even a memory, she is only the vaguest genetic trace" (2008, 102.22). As "we" move back to Africa, the "Africans" in fact must cease to exist. Africa in RED is only possible at a distance. As Western consumers increase our proximity to Africa, we consume it and reproduce a virtualism of "Africa" in our image. Africa is lacking while we are abundant; Africa is receptive while we are forthcoming; Africa is suffering while we are curative. Yet, simultaneously, Africa is exciting while we are anodyne; Africa is wild while we are tame and we can consume, at a safe distance, some of the exoticism and sexiness of the African adventure without risking our souls: causumerism (see chapter 5) allows us to buy into the nineteenth-century myths of Africa wedded with twenty-first-century notions of good global helping.

Between rather stereotypical notions of bourgeois beauty and wild adventure (an article profiling the first "woman of color" to be named as "The Face of Estée Lauder" and one titled "Congo from the Cockpit"), this issue of *Vanity Fair* published a story called "The Lazarus Effect."[26] Two African women and two men, all aged between twenty-four and thirty-four, were shown in paired "before" and "after" photographs "showing how ARV treatment has allowed them to resume their lives."[27] This "Lazarus Effect" was chronicled, perhaps with yet another biblical analogy, in two images taken forty days apart in Lusaka. The article begins with the heading "A Population on the Mend," but the text refers not to urban Zambia, as one might expect from photographs taken in Lusaka, but to a health center in Kigali, Rwanda. It is one of our contentions in this chapter that the slippage between countries that border Congo is not merely a lack of professional attention to detail by one of the world's most successful magazines, but a rudimentary marker of the effacement of Africans with AIDS into one smooth, global subjectivity in which there is no great difference between being a Rwandan or a Zambian.

The faces of AIDS are shown in dramatic black-and-white photography; three of the subjects are partially unclothed so that the viewer cannot fail to identify the contours of their collar and rib bones. The "before" photograph of Silvia Ng'andwe shows her staring wide-eyed into the camera lens with only her face and upper shoulders visible. Her shirt has a western-style collar with studded embellishment, and her hair is tightly braided to her scalp. Behind her, but mostly obscured from the lens, we see the small head of a child whose face is covered by her hand. The background of the photo is blurry, but we can make out what appears to be a bed, small table, child's toy, and metal walking aid. The setting produced is that of intimate domestic space of caregiving, a room in which a mother is with her child. The rocking horse toy with its associations of (western) play and lightness is preempted by the metal walker that supports crippled movement, associated with debilitation and degeneration of age or illness. The bed of course can mark the conjugal and heterosexual nature of African AIDS, rest and repose, and succumbing to sickness. Nancy Malaku sits in profile, staring up at a man whose only presence in the photograph is that of his right arm, which rests on Nancy's left shoulder. Her naked right shoulder is revealed by an unbuttoned shirt, which is left to slip from her body, as she touches at her sternum with her left hand. The gesture and position of the gaze appear vaguely like expressions of contrition. None of the objects in the background of this photograph are easily identifiable. These photographs, intimate and pleading (Bleiker and Kay 2007) to illicit pity from the readers, are quite unusual in the RED campaign. In fact, in the entire *Vanity Fair* Africa Issue, it is only these four Zambians with AIDS before they began taking ARVs whose images indicate any obvious allusion to suffering.[28]

The "after" photographs show color images of a young mother, Silvia, with her toddler, of Nancy holding a head of cabbage in front of a cement house with a small plot in the background, and of one young man, Elimas, sitting with his wife while the other young father, Nigel, poses with a wife and three small children. Silvia is radiant and beautiful with loose, shiny hair as she cradles the head of a little girl dressed up in a fancy pink western-style dress. In the background, we see a shelving unit displaying a domestic collectable and a colorful poster hanging on the wall. Nancy, shown from a slightly more distant perspective, appears more reserved, yet smiling as her right hand cradles a large green cabbage. She is dressed in a western-style blouse paired with a "traditional" African cloth wrapper as a skirt. Behind the stone-block house with its glass windows, potted plants, and wooden trimming we see a dirt road flanked by bushes with no other houses in view. A blue plastic tub sits inside a red one close to the house, suggesting the continuity of domestic labor. All the "after" photographs are smiling representations of a return to domestic productive and reproductive life. We do not know if Nancy will find a market for her produce or even if she has access to land, nor do we know which ones, if any, of Nigel's three small girls have the virus or how many other siblings they have. Yet in this depiction, we are led to believe that conjugal marriages involving caring spouses and healthy children are part and parcel of the Lazarus Effect of ARVs.[29]

From these images, it is difficult to understand anything about the relationships, or even the disease vectors, between the people in the photographs. It would be difficult to speculate on whether or not the partners and children of these families had been tested for HIV, and whether they also were on treatment, or needed it. However, the supposedly transformative focus of treatment is on the domestic self, the husband, mother or father, or home-gardener. The African family has been central to constructions of African AIDS as a distinct and distant manifestation of the disease.[30]

We are also left somehow with visual finality, a sense of completion and closure that the domestic transformation is finished. Of course all of these Zambians live in a culture that values childbearing and fertility, and they would be likely to want to have more children when they are returned to health, but that would open up a difficult and complicated story about the possibility of reproducing while on AIDS treatment (Richey 2008; Richey 2011; Smith and Mbakwem 2007). Finally, we do not know how these four individuals were persuaded to be photographed when they were ill in the first place.

Also, it is quite difficult, even for a trained Africanist scholar, to identify with much specificity the background of the photographs. What is the likely social or economic situation of these people: a stone-brick house with windows and plants in pots appears decidedly middle-class, while a straw mat over a stone floor seems less prosperous, but these are only guesses at best. And how do we know if the large, wooden-framed mirror into which Elimas gazes forlornly at himself in his "before" shot is actually part of his home's interior design or is a prop brought along by the photographer? These may appear as petty or irrelevant questions, but these images illustrate the point that the representations of AIDS treatment, like the representations of AIDS suffering before it, are bound up with the identities and expectations of the producers and consumers of these images and have little to teach us about the lived experiences of Africans who are managing treatment.

VIRTUOUS OR VIRTUAL?

Sontag reminds us that even though ordinary language makes the distinction that an artist "makes" drawings while a photographer "takes" pictures, such an image "cannot be simply a transparency of something that happened—it is always the image that someone chose; to photograph is to frame, and to frame is to exclude" (2003, 46). Innovative photographer Alison Jackson creates "mockumentary" films and stills that use celebrity look-alikes posed in discomforting situations to force viewers to confront their own expectations, voyeurism, and reluctance to question the truth of the visual.[31]

Jackson's work confronts our literalist expectations that a photograph is meant to show, not to evoke. "If you get the right composition, you can tell a whole other fantasy story that exists in the public imagination which is totally different from the truth—and that's what photography does."[32] Jackson's "fake" images satisfy the viewer's expectations, play effortlessly into their tight attention span, and show exactly what one imagines would be real.[33]

The same photographs of Silvia, Nigel, and Elimas from *Vanity Fair* also provide the only video imagery for a video posted on YouTube from RED titled *The Lazarus Effect*.[34] This video's message in thirty seconds is as follows: Written text fills the screen with "4,400 people die every day of AIDS in sub-Saharan Africa." This slide is followed by the words "Treatment exists." Then Silvia's "before" photograph fills the screen as an American female voice explains: "In about sixty days, an HIV patient in Africa can go from here [Silvia before] to here [Silvia after]. We call this transformation 'the Lazarus Effect.'" The voice continues as

Nigel's and then Elimas's before and after photos fill the screen: "It's the result of two pills a day taken by an HIV/AIDS patient for about sixty days. Learn more about how you can help give people this chance at life at joinred.com." The message of the thirty-second film is powerful and compelling because the images, like the art of Alison Jackson, tell Western consumer viewers more than simply the objects that are shown. While no products are actually shown, these images use visual tropes of nineteenth-century advertising and its Christian themes that visually perform the rock man's burden. For example, Elimas, seated, gazes at his self "before" ARVs in an oversize mirror. The mirror freezes time and creates spectacle: we are permitted to gaze at Elimas because he is reflected as a commodity. In her classic analysis of nineteenth-century soap advertisements, McClintock elaborates on the situated meaning of the mirror:

> Mirrors glint and gleam in soap advertising as they do in the culture of imperial kitsch at large. In Victorian middle-class households, servants scoured and polished every metal and wooden surface until it shone like a mirror. . . . The mirror became the epitome of commodity fetishism: erasing both the signs of domestic labor and the industrial origins of domestic commodities. (1994, 135)

The mirror in the RED visual creates a spectacle in which the commodity fetish pills are linked to unseen RED products themselves. The framing of this photograph, and the others, is iconic: Western consumers now have a visual snapshot to help them understand the problem of African AIDS and how they hold the power to help solve it. The promise is not dissimilar to that of nineteenth-century advertisements showing a white boy "bending benevolently over his 'lesser' brother," who has a white-washed face and black body: "the magical fetish of soap promises that the commodity can regenerate the Family of Man by washing from the skin the very stigma of racial and class degeneration" (ibid., 137).

Why would the promotional videos for RED rely on the same six photographs that had already been disseminated to a popular audience in the *Vanity Fair* magazine months before? Surely of the 1.4 million people as of September 2007 who, according to the RED Web site, had received treatment for HIV/AIDS provided by the Global Fund, there were other subjects who could represent the Lazarus Effect—perhaps even those living in the countries where RED's support is channeled (as opposed to Zambia, which at that time was not receiving RED funds). The power of these images, like the art of Alison Jackson, comes from their framing and sense to their viewers that they feel real and meaningful. In fact, many of the most iconic photographs providing intimate glimpses of love or death over time have been staged photographs (including the best-remembered pictures from the Second World War, thus predating contemporary photoshop technologies), yet with time, these turn into historical evidence (Sontag 2003). The RED Lazarus Effect images provide a powerful snapshot of the resurrection of Africans with AIDS through the power of ARVs. Yet the Lazarus Effect as representation is a virtualism: it is a prescriptive demonstration of reality that relies on the replication of iconic images. These icons draw on nonsectarian Christian scripts of salvation and rebirth.

When the Lazarus Effect images are compared to other RED pictures, their claims to authenticity are even more marked. One could argue that the image that most closely resembles the bodily emaciation, the shadowlike framing, and the claims of urgency of the "before" photos of AIDS victims is in fact the cover of the RED edition of *The Independent,* which shows not an African living with AIDS, but super-model Kate Moss in blackface titled "Not a Fashion Statement."[35]

In this "blackface" cover of *The (RED) Independent,* "skin is used as a means of invoking the experience of an African woman by performing a surface-level transformation of an iconic British supermodel" (Sarna-Wojcicki 2008, 19). African women's experiences with AIDS become phenomena to be invoked, not shown, and not subject to scrutiny, interrogation, or understanding. Certainly, women's bodies have historically been conduits and not subjects in the representations of AIDS in which "women's bodies were situated between infected man and infectable baby, or they were the shuttle between infected and uninfected men" (Patton 2002, 68). In a competing British newspaper, *The Guardian,* Hannah Pool writes of the Moss cover:

The blackface cover photograph of Kate Moss from The (RED) Independent.

I suppose it is meant to be subversive, but what does it say about race today when a quality newspaper decides that its readers will only relate to Africa through a blacked-up white model rather than a real-life black woman? What does it say about the fight against HIV/Aids if that is the only way to make us care?[36]

RED is about redeeming sex and stylizing gender relations. Percy Hintzen's detailed critique of the text in the *Vanity Fair* Africa Issue from both its features and its product advertisements draws out the appeal of racialized sexuality of "Africa." He argues "that the targeted 'modern sophisticated consumer' is to be enticed by sexual desire produced by 'stunning photography' to create 'demand.' This is to be accomplished through 'popular dialogue' and 'social commentary.' It is the very (stunning but unsurprising) template evident in the juxtaposition of Bono's plea for Africa with the 'stunning photography' of sexual desire" (2008, 79). Of course, the racialization of sexuality long predates contemporary initiatives like RED, but RED puts a new spin to allow the West to reclaim sex as healthy. The sexy blacked-up body of a supermodel is able to stand in for the body of an African woman dying from sex. We as viewers do not need to actually confront literal images or experiences of suffering; we can have the virtual mediation of a familiar translator. As other critical scholars have also noted, RED has not taken onboard any of the central messages of feminist scholars of development, and "a Hollywood standard of heterosexual sexiness prevails, which may be good marketing but fails to provoke deeper analysis of broadly viable models of sexuality" (Cameron and Haanstra 2008, 1485). We push this argument further because the RED images constitute a "familial globality" as described earlier that actively reinforces, rather than destabilizes, notions of sexualized distant others.

Our argument is not that the RED pictures are purposefully misleading, distorted, or lying; whether or not this is the case is in fact beside the point. We argue that there are always implications of relying on representations as "truth" and that RED must be understood within the existing history of selling images of AIDS in Africa. We must also consider the meaning of using images of suffering to sell products. The easy response to our critique is to suggest that it is instead "Africans with AIDS" who should be responsible for the production and circulation of "legitimate" pictures.[37] Africans should create their own media. Predictably, however, this answer is insufficient. In perhaps the most famous attempt to circulate self-produced images of African AIDS, the Long Life project, a social outreach project blending techniques of art therapy and narrative, sent its own self-portraits known as "body maps" into exhibition across South Africa, the UK, and the United States. At first glance, these "body maps," made by poor women with AIDS to exemplify how they navigate the complexities of living with the disease, may appear quite remote from RED images of the virtualism of AIDS treatment. Yet we argue that they are plagued by similar constrictions of possibility, as they are both also "cast as spectacle, reproductions of which have become fetishised commodities that can be bought or sold" (Thomas 2008, 217). As concluded by one of the "body map" project's founders and most reflective critics, "representations of the bodies of black HIV-positive women in South Africa cannot be read as transparent. To take such representations as points of access to the truth of the subjects they represent is to disavow the relations of power that continue to determine how such images appear and how they can be read" (ibid., 223).[38] The "body maps" become valuable commodities, worth something, because of their assumed connection to something "real," accessible, and culturally specific. Yet the portraits "represent rather than reflect the 'real,' so too these images are constructed and produce what they purport to reveal" (ibid., 219). RED's AIDS treatment virtualism also uses constructed images that are depicting and producing reality, not simply revealing it.

As we move into a period of AIDS treatment in Africa where we no longer have to defend the possibility of treatment, its relevance to the people who receive it, or whether international funding will be amassed to support it, we can begin to acknowledge, document, and analyze the fundamental social conflicts that arise in the processes of treatment. The surplus value of images of AIDS and treatment cannot be ignored when viewing an image like the print advertisement for the RED American Express depicting a supermodel embracing a

This photograph of Gisele Bündchen and Keseme Ole Parsapaet was used in the RED American Express campaign "my card" (referring to the supermodel), "my life" (refering to the Maasai warrior), a spin from the company's previous campaign "my life, my card." The image appeared in outdoor landmark sites around London and in high-end glossy magazines in September and October 2006.

Masaai moran. In some versions of the print ad, the model was tagged with a caption reading "my card" while the "African" was captioned "my life."

The "life" of Keseme Ole Parsapaet, the Masaai model, was described in the media: "Parsapaet's world in the acacia-strewn bush of southern Kenya is very different from the glitz and fabulous wealth of the fashion industry. His nomadic lifestyle is one he does not want to leave."[39] Drawing on obvious tropes of "traditional nomadic life" (huts, malaria, livestock, flies, slender elegance), the article notes that the experienced goat and cattle herder with no formal education was blessed by his father's pouring of milk over him before boarding the airplane to London for the photography session with "one of Britain's leading fashion photographers." Nowhere does the article mention the nearly 8 percent national HIV prevalence rates in his country, nor does it address the sexual relationships Parsapaet does have; it only speculates on what his apparently nonexistent relationship to model Gisele Bündchen means to him. He "admits" to never having heard of the model who earned a Guinness World Record for her wages of $17 million in a single year, while he was paid $5000 for his famous photography shoot for RED.[40] Barbara Browning's analysis of the Benetton AIDS advertising campaign argues that "to make difference visible, you need contrast, and for contrast, you need contact—skin on skin if possible" (1998, 151). The American Express ad markets the difference between "my card" and "my life" as the caption suggests, and does so in ways that make this difference safe, manageable, and not politically challenging.

The virtualism of AIDS treatment tourism that supports RED is crafted with greater style and bling than most of the justifications for international development assistance. When one considers a popular RED promotional video in which a troop of supermodels is shown touring southern African AIDS clinics to the musical accompaniment of the archetypical "native" choir, which is meant to provide the link between consumers and Africans with AIDS, it is easy to levy criticism of their representations of distant others.[41] The distance between the supermodels and the "suffering strangers" is obvious and indeed vast. Yet this distance allows the consumers, as "real people," to step in and help. In fact, Brand Aid representations may share more than a vague family resemblance to the other international development representations of the need to intervene and save the lives of the worthy but ineffective citizens of "Africa."[42]

LOW-COST HEROISM

Mitchell describes images such as the RED visuals: "As objects of surplus value, of simultaneous over- and underestimation, these stand at the interface of the most fundamental social conflicts" (2005, 105). This statement is integral to the focus of this chapter on representations of AIDS, gender, and domesticity by a co-branding, cause-related marketing initiative.

RED, with its glam and "hard commerce" approach to combating moral wrongs, promotes a consumer-based salvation relation in which westerners are actors and Africans are acted upon. RED is not so much a deviant as a derivative of aid itself. At the same time, in RED, Bono is the totem of "compassionate consumption," steering attention away from the causes of poverty, such as the inequities of systems of production and trade, by focusing on one of the outcomes, HIV and AIDS. The beauty of this celebrity simplification is that it provides the possibility that everyday people can engage in low-cost heroism. As an American Express RED promotional states, it provides "the union of consumerism and conscience, demonstrating how something as simple as everyday shopping can now help to eliminate AIDS in Africa."[43] The reduction of a complex disease of biology and economy into "fragmented knowledge . . . packaged in the oversimplified moral categories" (Fadlalla 2008, 209) resembles most closely perhaps the contemporary "Save Darfur" campaign in its creation of the helpless African and the compassionate Western helper (Flint and de Waal 2005). Mobilizing an army of shoppers is even easier when the fight is against a disease, something that no one could actually be "for."

The rock man's burden justifies why the aid agenda for Africa is being pushed by aid celebrities like Bono, and how wealthy Western consumers should shop to the aid of their less-fortunate global citizens. Bono states, "I represent a lot of [African] people who have no voice at all. . . . They haven't asked me to represent them. It's cheeky but I hope they're glad I do."[44]

But it is important to remember that the "suffering strangers" (Butt 2002) or "'iconic figures' of misfortune" (Fassin 2007, 22) abound in social science as well as popular media. Through these representations, we argue, Africans living with AIDS are defined, isolated, and stripped of their own public voice: they are neither producers nor consumers of images or products, but are simply "the face of AIDS." As Patton succinctly condemns: "If we as a society continue to desire a 'face of AIDS,' it will not be to show that we are all basically the same but, rather, to show that those who are already projected as deviants do not live here" (2002, 121). It is now "Africa" as the embodiment of developing countries that is the new face of AIDS (ibid., 130). This is why the images used in RED must be taken seriously. Sontag reminds us of the complicity involved in such representations: "The imaginary proximity to the suffering inflicted on others that is granted by images suggests a link between the far-away sufferers—seen close-up on the television screen—and the privileged viewer that is simply untrue, that is yet one more mystification of our real relations to power" (2003, 102).

The common understanding of an icon is that it is an image, representation, or likeness that stands in for something else, something meaningful. The signage to Christianity throughout brand Bono and RED allows a slippage between the material and the spiritual. The Lazarus Effect of ARV treatment for African AIDS, as represented in the iconic photographs of four Zambians, illustrates the work that cultural Christianity does for RED as it shuffles religious metaphor and neoliberal values, salvation and resuscitation.

RED creates a virtualism of AIDS treatment in Africa in which access to ARV drugs (and only first-line treatment at that, for only 40 cents per day) is the modality for achieving the Lazarus Effect—the mystical coming back to life that can happen with AIDS treatment. The essayist Annette Schouten Woudstra describes this miracle:

> I'm sure that those who saw the first Lazarus-effect never forgot it. Jesus, full of emotion and love for this dead man and his sisters in John chapter 11, weeps when he sees the grave-site, when his sister Mary who has not come out to meet Jesus in her despair (in anger, exhaustion, confusion?) finally comes and falls at his feet. She knows. Mary knows that if Jesus had been there, Lazarus would not have died and she says so, out-loud. Jesus, convicted, raises the dead, weeping as he does.[45]

The RED virtualism, in its iconic images, locates the meaning of salvation in ARV technology that can restore African bodies, as it has been doing for over two decades with Western bodies. However, the complexity of the Lazarus reference is never taken up: Mary knows that if Jesus had been there, Lazarus would not have died. This marked absence, perhaps the complex social (and economic and political) conflicts that brought AIDS to the bodies of Silvia, Nancy, Elimas, and Nigel, falls outside of the virtualism. Only by placing faith in the representation of these iconic images can it really become plausible that buying a RED product "over here" will save African women and children "over there," and that there can be fair vanity or virtual salvation.

(3) SAVING AFRICA
AIDS and the Rebranding of Aid

In the conclusion of his most recent popular book, the aid celebrity Jeffrey Sachs likens the provision of life-saving AIDS treatment for poor Africans with the American quest to "conquer" the moon. Sachs writes:

> John Kennedy said the following about the challenge of going to the moon: "We choose to go to the moon in this decade and do the other things, not because they are easy, but because they are hard, because that goal will serve to organize and measure the best of our energies and skills, because that challenge is one that we are willing to accept, one we are unwilling to postpone, and one which we intend to win, and the others, too." (2008, 316)

Saving Africans with AIDS is the "complex problem par excellence" as described by Sachs: "A pandemic disease is ravaging Africa, a technical solution exists to transform the disease from a killer to a manageable condition, yet that solution is utterly beyond reach of those who need it" (ibid., 317). Just as "we" have lifted a man to the moon, we can extend the reach of antiretroviral (ARV) medicines all the way to Africa. The challenge is formidable, and just as the moon exists to measure the best of our energies and skills, so too follows the story of Africans with AIDS whose lives are saved, and thus counted to measure the best of our international development efforts.

The level of hyperbolic discourse on the mission of international development—its worthiness, immediacy, and practicality—is indicative of the current crisis of legitimacy of international aid. Into exactly this moment of uncertainty, Brand Aid provides a convenient win-win solution based on a probusiness platform. In this book, we define Brand Aid as the combined meaning of "aid to brands" and "brands that provide aid." Brand Aid emerges in a context of increasingly popular and emotional debates about international development aid. While aid has always been controversial, and the distinction between aid for humanitarian reasons of helping others and aid for strategic reasons of helping the donors themselves has never been completely separate, the debates have intensified over the past decade.

Aid debates proliferate in the popular media. In a spate of recent books by international development experts, the public is given two broad themes—aid is bad, and/or aid to Africa is bad. What these books share in common is their criticism of public or government-provided aid and their positive disposition toward the idea that business methods and business itself should be used to solve the problems of third world poverty. As a response to the crisis of legitimacy in international aid, Brand Aid helps to rebrand aid itself (and aid to Africa in particular) and to justify using commerce and consumption as vectors for aiding distant others.

In the first half of this chapter, we place our case study of RED and the emerging form of Brand Aid within the broader trends and debates over international aid to Africa. We take an expansive definition of aid that includes the evolutions and overlaps between public and private giving. We also go beyond aid to briefly examine other financial flows to Africa. We provide a picture of the relative importance of public vis-à-vis private aid, of aid in general vis-à-vis other flows to Africa (such as foreign direct investment and remittances), and the interpretations of these trends by interested parties. We show that RED disrupts traditional dichotomies between public and private in meaningful ways. It is a form of "giving" but it is also good business because it helps companies sell products and manage brand image. It is a private source of funds that are then channelled through a public-private partnership (the Global Fund) that is still largely funded by public sources. Specific projects in beneficiary countries of RED funds can be implemented both by governments and by NGOs. This analysis is essential in order to understand why and how the supporters of private aid portray public aid as being in a crisis, and therefore why Africa needs something like Brand Aid or indeed RED.

Then in the second half of this chapter, we focus on aid in response to AIDS in Africa, on treatment (the provision of ARVs) and the Global Fund, one of the "vertical mechanisms" of channelling aid. We argue that RED comes at a time when interest in aid to African AIDS was already high and growing. But the aid, like RED, is mostly concentrated on the provision of pharmaceutical inputs, much less on strengthening health systems. In the penultimate section, we describe and critique RED's beneficiary, the Global Fund, which is the exemplary model of public-private partnerships in popular aid debates. In this section, we demonstrate how RED makes financial contributions to the Global Fund, but it also makes unprecedented demands in the governance of the Fund itself. Nonetheless, the fact that the Global Fund takes the RED initiative seriously and expresses interest in having more, not fewer, initiatives like it suggests that Brand Aid may come to characterize other relationships with the Global Fund, as well as with other aid initiatives.

Both academic and popular criticisms of aid claim that the international aid system has serious shortcomings, stemming from too much aid or too little. Radical critics argue that international aid is beyond repair and should simply be eliminated. Other critics suggest that perhaps the system could be salvaged if it were sufficiently reformed to become more flexible, efficient, businesslike, and based on partnerships. The reformist position states that aid needs more funds and/or new funding mechanisms and that those funds need to be spent wisely through better aid delivery mechanisms. Whether the problem is understood as inhering in "aid" or in "Africa," business is consistently promoted as the creative solution in the face of decreasing confidence in governments. We show how RED is one important response to the increasing criticism of aid: it raises funds through consumption; it is a business solution to aid financing; and it uses one of the existing "innovative" vertical funds for delivery. In sum, we argue that RED and Brand Aid are driven by the need to continue mobilizing support for tough but noble causes, as traditional public and institutional aid is systematically discredited.

DEVELOPMENT AID AND AFRICA: RECENT PUBLIC DEBATES OVER "THE WEST" AND "THE REST"

Foreign aid to the world's poorest countries, most of which are in sub-Saharan Africa, has been mired in controversy since its inception. Former U.S. senator Jesse Helms notoriously disparaged aid to poor regions such as Africa as throwing money "down a rathole" (Goldstein and Moss 2005, 1289).[1] In spite of such perceptions, when Bono took then U.S. treasury secretary Paul O'Neill on a tour of Africa in 2002, O'Neill declared that more money would be given to poor countries, but that this money must be used with more efficiency than in the past. At the same time, local activism, selected leadership, and international celebrities pushed Africa into the center of aid debates. For example, the "Make Poverty History" campaign, coupled with the UK Commission for Africa, the Live 8 concerts, and the focus on aid and poverty at the Gleneagles G8 meeting led some observers to label 2005 as "the year of Africa" (Harrison 2006). Yet as African aid has come back to the forefront of public debate over the last few years, the debates on whether aid is needed at all, efficient, or effective have been particularly virulent. An assortment of books advocating extreme positions for and against international aid have become best sellers, while numerous other contributions have attempted to navigate this ground on the basis of more technical issues.[2] In this section, we examine selected exemplary texts from the first set of books dedicated to a more popular audience. Serious consideration of these is important for understanding the context of Brand Aid that plays simultaneously to constituencies of traditional aid interventions and to new "players" in international development aid—consumers. In the popular debate, the broad issues of aid legitimacy, including what aid should do, who should do it, and who should benefit, are played out. Other debates, not covered here, examine the forms, mechanisms, and coordination of aid delivery and the evaluation of its impact.[3] In the same way that aid celebrities were described in chapter

1 as merging both the celebrity and the expert roles, Brand Aid should be understood as emerging from debates within both the popular and the technical fields of aid to AIDS and Africa.

The polarization in the more popular debate has played along two main parallel axes. The first is that aid is bad because there is not enough of it. From this perspective, a grand plan, or a big push, is needed to get the poorest countries out of their predicament (especially in Africa) and more aid is proposed. The second is that aid is bad because there is too much of it going to the wrong places. This perspective argues that aid is wasted due to bad governance in recipient countries (especially in Africa) and proposes solutions ranging from less or even no aid to promoting more targeted and efficient aid. In practice, supporters of the big push theory (notably, Jeffrey Sachs) tend to undermine the effect of corruption on aid delivery and growth; supporters of smaller, more targeted aid (notably, William Easterly, Robert Calderisi, and Dambisa Moyo) tend to place more importance on corruption and argue that less aid, not more, is needed, because more money will inevitably lead to more corruption. While from a scholarly perspective, these debates appear fatally simplistic, engaging in a chicken-and-egg–type debate over whether increasing aid or decreasing corruption in fact comes first, these are important for understanding the power of Brand Aid. The celebritized form of these debates and the target audience of "nonexperts" is significant, but perhaps more significant is the skillful management of affect in these texts. Thus, statements that are both simplified and generalized to the point of being indisputable form the engagement between a caring public and their international development possibilities. One cannot dispute with evidence arguments that are not based on evidential claims. Yet what really counts in these debates is the appropriate ideology to support the management of compassionately taking on the rock man's burden.

The big push approach to aid (and especially to aid to Africa) is most clearly spelled out by Jeffrey Sachs in his book *The End of Poverty* (2005) and is embedded in the UN Millennium Project.[4] According to Sachs and his colleagues, Africa is locked into a "poverty trap" resulting from a complex web of structural and sociopolitical factors. One major factor is that "Africa carries a disease burden unique in the world"

(McCord, Sachs, and Woo 2005, 28). In order to lift people out of the poverty trap, a massive increase in aid is needed, coupled with the use of technology that already exists. Thus, the appeal of Sachs's message is that poverty is a problem that can be solved with the resources we have available in the North; resources simply must be allocated toward more aid and bigger scale-up to provide a "big push." This big push, according to Sachs (2005), can achieve massive results at a relatively low cost and in just a few years. This optimism about the potential for using science and technology to lift millions of people out of poverty leans on the assumption that "Africa's governance, on average, is no worse than elsewhere after controlling for income levels" (McCord, Sachs, and Woo 2005, 24). According to Sachs and his many supporters, the rich world has the ability and the moral obligation to save all Africans from poverty.

At the opposite end of the debate, we find one of the most famous aid books of the last decade, William Easterly's *White Man's Burden* (2006). According to Easterly, most aid is useless[5] and success stories (both in aid and in business) happen through trial and error, sometimes by pure chance. Easterly accuses well-meaning "planners" (these are named explicitly: Jeffrey Sachs, Tony Blair, Gordon Brown, James Wolfensohn) of harming the poor. According to Easterly, ending poverty will not be achieved by planners, but by "searchers" (such as Muhammad Yunus, the Nobel Prize winner and founder of the Grameen Bank), who explore solutions "by trial and error experimentation . . . accept responsibility for their actions . . . [and] adapt to local conditions," all of this in an unplanned, spontaneous way (2006, 6). Bluntly put in Easterly's characterization, "Planners determine what to supply; Searchers find out what is in demand" (ibid., 6; capitalization in the original). This dichotomous view of the downfall of aid is analogous to comparisons drawn between old-fashioned development assistance done by governments and new forms of aid done by philanthropists, corporations, and consumers.

> In foreign aid, Planners announce good intentions but don't motivate anyone to carry them out; Searchers find things that work and get some reward. Planners raise expectations but

take no responsibility for meeting them; Searchers accept responsibility for their actions. Planners determine what to supply; Searchers find out what is in demand. Planners apply global blueprints; Searchers adapt to local conditions. Planners at the top lack knowledge of the bottom; Searchers find out what the reality is at the bottom. Planners never hear whether the planned got what it needed; Searchers find out whether the customer is satisfied. (Ibid., 5–6)

This theme that aid is failing because it cannot think and act like business is explicit in Easterly's work and in many of the recent contributions to the aid debate. Easterly argues that economic success is uneven and unpredictable, and many large companies are successful because they were able to scale up accidental discoveries (2008b, 18–21). This sort of flexibility for seizing opportunities is notably lacking in the old structures of aid. One contributor to Easterly's edited book, *Reinventing Foreign Aid* (2008a), explicitly argues that aid agencies should act more like business (Hoffman 2008). Easterly (2006) himself has even proposed the idea of "aid vouchers," which would be issued to poor people in developing countries who could then use them to buy social services from providers competing in the marketplace; those supplying aid could be any combination of traditional aid agencies, NGOs, business, or other local providers. In this model, the kinds of "goods" that aid should deliver are directly translated as commodities that can be bought and sold, ideally with as little market regulation as possible.

Both the "aid is bad because it is too little" and the "aid is bad because it is too much" camps agree that government interventions and "traditional" aid are not likely to hold the solution to either problem. Business, however, is viewed favorably by all sides. The most extreme of the "business can solve development problems" arguments comes (perhaps not surprisingly) from the business school literature. The clearest and most popular version of this perspective is spelled out by C. K. Prahalad in his best-selling book *The Fortune at the Bottom of the Pyramid* (2005). The key to helping the poor to help themselves is to convince CEOs of multinational corporations (MNCs) that "Bottom of the Pyramid" (BOP) markets are important. Prahalad argues that BOP markets should be the key objective of strategies of MNCs. The private sector is seen as the key solution in addressing poverty. It can "create opportunities for the poor by offering them choices and encouraging self-esteem" (ibid., 5). For Prahalad, providing products or services for free is the traditional approach used to create the capacity for poor people to become consumers. Yet this perspective does not address the conditions of inequality and/or poverty that are responsible for their inability to consume in the first place. Prahalad wants to encourage consumption in BOP markets by making unit packages small and more affordable (due to the poor's unpredictable income flows) and by using new purchase schemes (such as providing credit to consumers in new ways—he provides the examples of Casas Bahia in Brazil and microcredit schemes such as the Grameen Bank) (ibid., 16–17). Not only is there money at the BOP, and profit-making potential, but these markets are also brand conscious. What is needed, according to Prahalad, is a "market-oriented ecosystem" that allows the private sector and social actors to act together to create wealth. Such an ecosystem includes MNCs, small and medium enterprises, micro-enterprises, NGOs, cooperatives, and other civic groups (ibid., 65). A key component in the working of such an ecosystem is "transaction governance capacity" (ibid., 79), that is, transparency and contract enforcement. Prahalad takes the big solutions of Hernando de Soto (2000) and makes them even bigger, arguing that there are trapped assets in BOP markets. This is because assets cannot become capital due to poor contract law and lack of legal titles. The poor are not really poor; they just do not know that their assets can be used to get capital.[6] Business, not aid, is the solution to the problems of international development.

So far, we have seen that "aid does not work" arguments led their proponents to place more emphasis on trial-and-error and business-based solutions. Yet in the popular literature, whether the problem of aid is that there is not enough of it (the Sachs "big push" camp) or whether the problem is that the aid model is faulty (agreed by both the Easterly "over-planned" and the Prahalad "business first" camps), the area of the biggest challenge is consistently Africa. Now we move from general debates over "aid is the problem" to debates over "Africa is the problem for aid." This discussion is particularly relevant to our case study of RED as it pertains to the particular problems that Africa has with development and produces for development. The problems have been magnified and broadcast into the aid debates through the megaphone of two books by Dambisa Moyo (2009) and Robert Calderisi (2006).

Moyo, an Ivy League–educated Zambian economist formerly with Goldman Sachs, is the woman that can provide an "African voice" (see the foreword to the book by Niall Ferguson 2009) for the arguments brought forward by Easterly and other white men critical of aid. Her book titled *Dead Aid* (Moyo 2009) is dedicated to a famous critic of foreign aid, Peter Bauer, and argues that aid, rather than the solution, has been the main cause of Africa's economic problems. She advocates a "shock therapy" of eliminating aid to all African countries within a period of five to ten years. She suggests that alternative financing mechanisms can be found through the issuing of sovereign bonds in African countries, the boosting of foreign investment, more trade (and less protectionism in industrialized economies), and microfinance.

Calderisi, in his book *The Trouble with Africa* (2006), selected by the *Economist* as one of the best books of 2006, also agrees that "aid does not work" in Africa, but his explanation is linked to the fact that Africa is populated by Africans. While for Easterly the "Planners" are the bad guys, and for Moyo aid itself is the source of the African "problem," for Calderisi it is Africans themselves who hide behind a raft of "excuses" (debt, colonialism, the global economy, and others) instead of realizing that it is their own corrupt leaders and "African culture" that keeps them where they are. The West is only responsible because it is not "politically correct" to say such things (anymore). Not surprisingly, Calderisi's main conclusion is that aid to Africa should be reduced, not increased. Aid can be permitted to continue in the five countries that have done well (Uganda, Tanzania, Mozambique, Ghana, and Mali), while all other African countries should see their aid cut in half.

Calderisi argues that aid money and African corruption and culture are the problems, and that less aid is better. Furthermore, while

Easterly's approach is somewhat anarchic and reliant on happenstance in its recommendations, Calderisi comes close to explicitly stating that Africa needs a new sort of colonization. Among his "ten ways of changing Africa," we find that the West should supervise all elections and run the educational systems, and take over the HIV/AIDS programs in Africa. He even goes as far as to recommend that 100–150 international supervisors per country should be deployed to "prevent the siphoning off of funds and abuses at the local school level" (Calderisi 2006, 213).

Calderisi's "Africans" are depicted in stereotypically racialized sexual terms, as being out of control of their sexuality and thus contributing to public health crises like HIV/AIDS and overpopulation. He writes that "Africa has the youngest and most sexually active population on earth. . . . African women have been open to practicing birth control, but their governments and husbands have failed them. Public services have been slow to provide condoms and counseling services, while fathers insist on having larger families" (ibid., 169–70). These depictions of "out of control" Africans are unfortunately not new or limited to a single book, but derive from global overpopulation debates that have persevered since the end of World War II (Richey 2008) and have played out in some debates on global AIDS as well (Stillwaggon 2005). The call for Westerners, particularly white men, to come and save African women from their own men resonates with the rock man's burden we analyzed in the previous chapter.

Of specific relevance to RED, Calderisi's book concludes that it is particularly in the fight against HIV/AIDS that Africans are failing and need help from the West. Calderisi writes:

> The fight against HIV/AIDS is too important to leave to the whims of African governments. The scale of organization needed to provide information to vulnerable grounds, and the logistical network required for storing and distributing pharmaceutical products, is without precedent for most countries. Reductions in the price of HIV/AIDS drugs have created opportunities yet to be exploited in Africa, partly for practical reasons, but also because of inadequate political commitment.

Countries that have put themselves on a war footing, for flimsier reasons, in the past need to be accompanied by the international community on this new battleground rather than left to react as local resources, fatalism, and prejudice allow. (2006, 214)

Calderisi's call to the West to "save Africa" has been received with acclaim from both popular and policy audiences (and mirrors RED's own take). He has appeared in numerous interviews in print and television in North America and Europe. In 2008, he was asked to serve on the Commission on Effective Development Cooperation of Denmark, an important donor in several African countries. Calderisi perpetuates the idea that Africa is a lost cause and that "culture" hinders its development (one of the chapters of his book is titled "A Clash of Values"). By arguing against "political correctness," he places himself as the ambassador of many silent others. He brings the argument of African exceptionalism extremely close to colonial arguments of racial inferiority, this time justified by African "culture and values [that] ... have been perverted to condone oppression on the continent" (ibid., 8). Calderisi claims that "if character keeps Africans fatalistic and corruption binds their elites together, political correctness in the West adds a final touch to Africa's misery" (ibid., 91).

Whether the popular debates are that aid is the problem or that Africa is the problem, the RED initiative cuts across them and indeed contributes, we argue, to rebranding aid to Africa. RED is based on the understanding that technical solutions and science can solve Africa's problems, if only enough money is spent. RED channels its funds through the Global Fund, a public-private partnership. RED is based on the premise that business and commerce are appropriate bases upon which resources for aid are drawn. Yet at the same time, RED's glitzy, cool, positive take on Africa comes as a breath of fresh air—given the abysmal portrayals of Africa in much of the aid literature. Finally, the perceptions of AIDS as an exceptional situation, even to RED's sexy rebranding of Africa, make it possible to continue mobilizing public support for the West's responsibility and capacity to save Africa.

PUBLIC AID, PRIVATE AID, AND OTHER FINANCIAL FLOWS TO AFRICA

Brand Aid initiatives are situated as a new modality in contrast to traditional aid from public donors. However, the flows of finance to Africa go well beyond public aid and encompass private aid, foreign direct investment (FDI), remittances, and other non-FDI flows. Table 1 summarizes the picture of these flows. As we can see, in real terms, official flows increased significantly from 1995 to 2005–7, but less so if only grants and not loans are taken into account. Private flows increased much more dramatically, both proportionally and in absolute terms. Growth has been especially marked in relation to equity (FDI and portfolio investment), long-term bank lending, and remittances—although much FDI growth is linked to the extraction of natural resources. Clear limitations on data availability and reliability suggest caution in making strong claims. The data on private aid (labeled "private grants (net)") included in Table 1 is particularly problematic as OECD data suffers from severe underreporting. However, triangulation with other sources provides some indications of the sources of money to Africa.

The Index of Global Philanthropy (Hudson Institute 2008) provides some data on U.S. sources of what they call "private giving." These are summarized in Table 2. It is not our intention here to discuss the strengths and limitations of the analysis (private giving even includes volunteer time and support to foreign students, which seems to be overstretching the boundaries of the concept to us). But if one accepts the estimate of $39.3 billion of private giving to developing countries from the United States (in constant 2000 prices), then it becomes clear that private aid is an important source of financing, even surpassing overseas development assistance (ODA) from the United States in 2006.

The United States has a much longer and deeper tradition of private giving than other OECD countries, especially countries in which welfare states are most developed and where a high proportion of GDP is allocated to development aid (such as the Nordic countries and

TABLE 1. Net official and private flows to sub-Saharan Africa (US$ billion, constant 2000 prices)

	1995	2000	2005	2006	2007
Official flows	18.1	10.9	24.9	30.7	26.8
Grants (nondebt)	13.5	9.3	18.0	19.6	22.4
Debt relief (net)	0.7	0.8	7.9	13.3	3.0
Credits (including IMF)	3.9	0.7	−1.0	−2.3	1.3
Private flows	14.0	14.6	39.7	47.1	63.9
Net equity flows	5.0	9.1	20.5	26.6	31.1
Direct investment	1.8	5.0	13.8	13.2	22.3
Portfolio equity	3.2	4.2	6.7	13.4	8.8
Net debt flows	3.7	−0.8	7.1	7.7	18.7
Bonds	0.9	1.0	1.2	0.1	5.0
Banks (long-term)	−0.5	−0.7	3.4	−1.4	10.5
Short-term and other	3.3	−1.1	2.5	8.9	3.1
Remittances	3.5	4.6	8.4	9.2	9.4
Private grants (net)	1.8	1.7	3.6	3.7	4.7
Total (excluding debt relief)	31.4	24.7	56.7	64.4	87.7

Source: Jones (2009)
Note: Sums may not exactly match the addition of individual entries due to rounding.

Holland). So, if one expands the analysis above to all traditional donors (see Table 3), the picture is quite different. In this case, ODA represents a large majority of all giving. It should be noted, however, that private giving figures for many donor countries are of poor quality and therefore the total is likely to be underestimated.

On the basis of the data in Tables 2 and 3, private giving is documented as an important form of help to developing countries. In Table 1, while underestimating the total, the data suggest that private giving is increasing in absolute terms for Africa, without the purchase of branded consumer goods. However, we do not know for sure if private aid is becoming proportionally more or less important than public aid in Africa. Beyond what the "real" picture of private aid (and RED's contribution) may be, what is relevant here is that the supporters of

TABLE 2. Private giving to developing countries from the United States (2006)

Source of giving	Estimated amount (US$ billion, constant 2000 prices)	
Foundations	4.5	
Corporations	6.2	
Private and voluntary organizations	12.0	
Value of volunteer time	2.5	
Private support to students from developing countries	4.2	
Religious organizations	9.9	
Total private giving	39.3	(62%)
Total overseas development assistance (ODA)	23.9	(38%)
Grand total of giving to developing countries	63.2	(100%)

Sources: Private giving is calculated from nominal values included in Hudson Institute (2008). Total ODA includes total U.S. ODA to developing countries (grants, concessional loans, and debt relief); http://stats.oecd.org/.

private giving, such as the Hudson Institute, want to promote the idea that "traditional" public aid is in crisis and that private forms of engagement, especially from business, provide the way out of the impasse. The Hudson Institute writes: "Whatever it is called—social entrepreneurship, philanthrocapitalism, venture philanthropy, or the latest label by Bill Gates, creative capitalism—the lines between business and philanthropy continue to blur. This trend in philanthropy has been dubbed the 'double bottom line,' or making money and helping a charitable cause at the same time" (2008, 6). According to the same report, cause-related marketing is becoming increasingly important and accounts for $1.5 billion (although it is not clear whether that includes all campaigns or only those targeted at developing-country beneficiaries) (ibid., 6).

The excitement over "new aid" is predicated on an underlying mistrust of "old aid." New aid is portrayed as being about choice and linking up in new communities, unlike government aid, which is outdated. The Hudson Institute claims: "The new global philanthropy is coming at a time of increased scrutiny and criticism of traditional government

TABLE 3. Forms of giving from Development Assistance Committee (DAC) countries to developing countries (2006)

Source of giving	Value (US$ billion, constant 2000 prices)	Percentage of total
Private giving	48.7	29.2
ODA	117.8	70.8
Grand total	166.5	100.0

Sources: Private giving is calculated from nominal values included in Figure 1 in Hudson Institute (2008). ODA includes total net disbursements of bilateral and multilateral ODA (grants, concessional loans, and debt relief); http://stats.oecd.org/.

foreign aid programs. There is *widespread agreement* that the government foreign aid mode—top-down, central planning—has failed" (ibid., 9; emphasis added).

The Hudson Institute (along with RED) appears to be leading to its own solution for the aid debates: the turn to business. "In order to help people in sustainable ways, foreign aid needs a completely new business model. This new paradigm should be grounded in what William Easterly calls an 'opportunistic innovation' model that looks for targets of opportunity, not long-range rigid goals set by donor agencies" (ibid., 10). The Hudson Institute's figures on private giving, coupled with a dubious "widespread agreement" that aid as we know it does not work, leads to a justification for using less public aid and more private innovation. In such we find a call for proportionally less taxpayer money going to foreign aid and more "direct" involvement by corporations and consumer-citizens. As written in *The Index of Global Philanthropy*:

> This model has already been proven in countless public-private partnerships where government aid, now the minority partner in the development world in terms of financial flows, links its funds with ongoing private ventures. In this way, government aid can be involved with private endeavors that have passed a critical market test: they have raised outside dollars and volunteer time. (Ibid., 10–11)

In this model of business aid, government aid is portrayed as being "minority" (in contrast to the evidence shown in Table 3 above) and governments need to raise "private dollars and volunteer time" to "pass the test." Issues of evaluation of private aid and accountability do not feature prominently in such discourse, and although we are told that private entities are "beginning to take efficiency and impact more seriously," we are not told how they will achieve this (ibid., 11). What the Hudson Institute and others want to portray is that "traditional public aid" is in need of "rebranding" to stave off a portrayed crisis of legitimacy. This opens up an enabling environment for Brand Aid within debates over aid legitimacy and modalities.

The criticisms of public aid and the attacks to its legitimacy have indeed stimulated some changes in how aid is financed and delivered. RED is one example of financing, but new mechanisms of aid *delivery* have also been multiplying in the past decade.

Many of these have taken place through the organization of new institutions or setups, rather than the reform of existing structures. This, on the one hand, has allowed the easier implementation of innovative forms of delivery; on the other hand, it has added to the proliferation of agencies and institutions, and of their reporting and supervision requirements from recipients. Among the most important new initiatives emerging in the 2000s, we find the U.S. Millennium Challenge Account (MCA),[7] the Global Alliance for Vaccines and Immunisation (GAVI), and the Global Fund to Fight AIDS, Tuberculosis and Malaria (see Radelet and Levine 2008 for a brief review of the three). Many of the new initiatives are focused on a narrow set of issues and on vertical systems of aid delivery. Health and HIV/AIDS have been particularly popular realms of intervention.

AID IN RESPONSE TO AIDS IN AFRICA

Aid to Africa, and specifically aid to AIDS, has become a popular way to disburse public monies in recent times. In spite of the comparably low proportion of its money given to development assistance,[8] the United States embraced aid to Africa under former President George W. Bush, with a $30 billion African AIDS initiative as its flagship.[9] "At that time, the United States' ODA to fight HIV/AIDS increased by 26.1 percent to USD 3.4 billion" in 2007.[10] As the actual amount of money given in foreign aid grew by 5.9 percent per annum between 1993 and 2003, the share of funds devoted to health, AIDS, and population increased from 5.5 percent to 6.7 percent of total development assistance (MacKellar 2005). The most dominant and continuing trend among donors has been the shift toward funding that targets sexually transmitted infections and HIV and AIDS. But if money given for HIV and AIDS is taken out of the calculation of funding, then health actually declined as a share of ODA, from 5.4 percent in 1993 to 5.0 percent in 2003 (Sachs 2005, 308). The importance of responding to HIV and AIDS from a gender perspective reminds us that the umbrella of reproductive health might have been an opportunity for broadening a population-control agenda to include many aspects of health, including prevention of HIV and treatment of AIDS. Yet international commitments have been notoriously lacking (Chesler 2005). Donor initiatives make up 68 percent of all funds, public and private, spent on AIDS in developing countries for 2005—far higher than the 8 percent share that was agreed upon as the appropriate input from donors at the world population conference in Cairo in 1994 (van Dalen and Reuser 2005, 36). And within health, HIV/AIDS is unique in experiencing rising shares of international development assistance: "basic health care and infrastructure, health education and personnel development, reproductive health and family planning, and basic nutrition, all pro-poor interventions, have experienced declining shares" (MacKellar 2005, 308). A later analysis of trend data demonstrated again that funding for HIV/AIDS and sexually transmitted infections contributed most to health sector growth and received 21 percent of all aid to health by 2004, up from 8 percent in 2000 (Kates, Morrison, and Lief 2006, 188). HIV and AIDS account for almost all development assistance for control of sexually transmitted infections (MacKellar 2005).

AIDS receives far more dollars per DALY (disability-adjusted life years) than any other cause (ibid.). AIDS is being allocated a much higher share of official development assistance than can be explained by its share in the burden of disease (ibid., 301).[11] Activists and the many affected by HIV and AIDS would argue that this is a reasonable response to the disease burden of AIDS. Why? Effective advocacy, the fear factor that if not controlled in developing countries, AIDS could have a greater impact in rich countries, and a well-publicized "efficiency" argument (slowing the spread of HIV was the highest-priority cost-effective development intervention as rated by the Copenhagen Consensus of Economists)[12] provide some of the answers. Analysis of the arguments for and against "AIDS exceptionalism" are beyond the scope of this book,[13] but the debates over whether AIDS is, in fact, overfunded date back at least to 2001, a "turning point in the global response to AIDS" with a special UN session on the disease, and the formation of the Global Fund. The debate was taken up again in the *British Medical Journal* when one critic called for the closure of UNAIDS on the basis that "HIV exceptionalism is dead" (England 2008, 1072). England argued that the imbalance between spending on HIV and other diseases is damaging health systems, stifling necessary reforms, and undermining basket funding, ultimately increasing aid dependency (ibid.). The blame for bias in donor financing is placed squarely on the global AIDS industry. According to England: "We have created a monster with too many vested interests and reputations at stake, too many single issue NGOs, too many relatively well paid HIV staff in affected countries, and too many rock stars with AIDS support as a fashion accessory" (ibid.).

Overall, there have been two major changes in global health over the past decade: the vast increase in international aid for health, and the declining influence of formerly dominant donors (bilaterals and the UN organizations) (Hanefeld et al. 2007). The most well-known initiatives in public health development assistance are public-private partnerships, also known as global health initiatives,[14] such as the Global Fund, the International AIDS Vaccine Initiative, PEPFAR, GAVI, Stop TB, and Roll Back Malaria. In spite of the publicity given to these new modalities, they are financed mostly by the traditional sources of public aid: donor-country governments as represented in the Development Assistance Committee of the OECD and, to a lesser extent, multilateral institutions like the World Bank (MacKellar 2005, 294). Not only have HIV and AIDS been increasingly favored by donors, they have also gained mass appeal as popular global causes.

This unusual level of popularity is epitomized by the November 2005 *TIME* Global Health Summit, flagged by Bono as "The Woodstock of Global Health."[15]

AID FOR ANTIRETROVIRAL AIDS TREATMENT

There is a global consensus that AIDS in Africa is a serious problem worthy of international attention. Sub-Saharan Africans made up 67 percent of the total of people living with HIV across the globe and 72 percent of AIDS deaths in 2007 (UNAIDS 2008).

In rich countries, AIDS transformed from a fatal to a chronic disease through widespread treatment with combination ARV therapy in the late 1990s. While ARVs do not cure AIDS, when taken regularly they can significantly slow the replication of the virus and suppress symptoms of illness. Yet, as Biehl's work reminds us, "healing, after all, is a multifaceted concept, and 'healing' is no more synonymous with 'treatment' than 'treatment' is with 'drugs'" (2007, 1104). Nonetheless, increasing access to ARV treatment has been an important part of all recent health initiatives on a global scale, including the WHO's 3 by 5 initiative (aimed at getting three million people on treatment by 2005), the G8's goal of universal access to AIDS treatment by 2010, and the MDG target 7 ("the spread of HIV/AIDS should be halted and reversed by 2015"). In developing countries, fewer than 5 percent of the people with HIV who needed treatment were actually receiving ARVs in 2001, while as of December 2007, an estimated 31 percent were receiving ARVs (UNAIDS 2008).

Still, it is worth remembering that most people who need AIDS treatment in Africa are not receiving it. Furthermore, the number of new HIV infections is still overtaking the number of people accessing treatment by a scale of 2.5 to 1 (UNAIDS 2008, 131). The vast debates over achieving an appropriate balance between international aid for treatment versus aid for HIV prevention extend far beyond the scope of this book; however, it is worth noting that treatment continues to receive the lion's share of funding compared to any other single input for healthcare.[16] The U.S. PEPFAR II requires that "at least half" of all funds be spent on treatment and care, regardless of recipient countries' potentially different priorities. A comparative analysis of PEPFAR, the World Bank's Multi-country HIV/AIDS Program (MAP), and the Global Fund activities in three African countries found that resources from all these donors appear disproportionately focused on treatment and care at the expense of prevention (Oomman, Bernstein, and Rosenzweig 2007, xii).

In spite of such high priority given to treatment in the global governance of AIDS, there are many challenges to bringing ARV provision to the scale necessary to provide care for those who need it in developing countries. Some challenges can be understood as barriers to implementing treatment occurring in most if not all resource-poor settings, while other problems may be found in one context but not another. Overall, drugs needed for lifelong treatment and diagnostic and monitoring equipment are costly, and most must be imported. Some second-line treatments require refrigeration, a difficult feat in areas without a functioning cold-chain. Drugs are also required to treat opportunistic infections that occur in people living with AIDS.

The influx of vast amounts of funding for ARV treatment in Africa has been accused of causing "collateral damage" in other parts of countries' health systems (Therkildsen 2005). Health systems in African countries have had their capacities strengthened to provide ARVs, building more laboratories and clinics and hiring more doctors, nurses, pharmacists, and health supporters. However, in most countries, scarcity of sufficient personnel has led to shifting from low- to high-profile activities. Furthermore, the pressure to achieve measurable targets in a short period of time, and effective leadership to meet these goals, has magnified the collateral damage to programs aiming to provide other services that are not contributing to the AIDS treatment statistics, even in relatively well-resourced areas (Richey 2008). We are not arguing that treatment should not be provided for Africans living with HIV and AIDS, but that other non-AIDS-specific health-care services should also be strengthened by the kinds of inputs provided for treatment.

The RED campaign emphasizes that its funds go toward the provision of ARV drugs, which is one, but not the only, critical component of AIDS treatment and care. It is of course easier to quantify and count the number of pills provided and then to virtually transform these numbers into "lives saved" as discussed in the previous chapter. Drugs are a key input of any treatment program, as Shadlen argues, because they are irreplaceable (2007, 563). He argues that alternative, if not optimal, solutions might be crafted to solve infrastructural problems or staffing inadequacies, but "no amount of managerial and political creativity can create functional substitutes for ARVs: if drugs are not available, treatment is impossible, full stop" (ibid.). Yet because AIDS treatment is lifelong, and patients develop immunity and regimens need adjustment to continue suppressing the virus, there is a never-ending need for the supply of new drugs. "The drugs that work today will be ineffective tomorrow, meaning that the political, economic, and legal conditions that facilitate the availability of today's drugs must be continuously reproduced" (ibid., 565). Thus, we can expect the demand for ARVs to increase, as long as there is international funding, people remain alive to continue taking the drugs, and there is no cure. Yet, as Shadlen warns, the production-side challenges for continual supply of high-quality, low-priced generic drugs are complicated and often underconsidered. Furthermore, the transnational activists and their coalitions that have supported the production of generic drugs thus far are unlikely to provide sufficient incentives for continued production over the long term.

Thus, the supply of drugs to save African women and children with AIDS is a far more complicated affair than RED's version of "the solution" in which "just two pills a day that cost about 40 cents, can keep someone with HIV and AIDS alive."[17]

THE GLOBAL FUND

Product RED's beneficiary, the Global Fund to Fight Aids, Tuberculosis and Malaria, is an independent, private foundation governed by an international board that works in partnership with governments, NGOs, civil society organizations, and the private sector. It is an international mechanism to channel aid financing and not an implementing agency. Of course, money travels with power and the Global Fund controls the second largest pool of donor funds in the world (after the UN itself).[18]

In its annual report, the Global Fund includes praise from the aid celebrity Paul Farmer.

> The Global Fund has rekindled life and hope for countless patients and the communities in which they live. To Partners In Health and our sister organizations in Haiti, Rwanda, Russia and Peru, The Global Fund has brought the resources needed to scale up treatment rapidly and to see hundreds of people literally transformed before our eyes from dying patients to healthy community members and proud partners in combating pandemic HIV/AIDS, TB, malaria and poverty.[19]

Paul Farmer's quotation above points to the critical relationship between international NGOs, like his Partners In Health, and the monies from the Global Fund. The Fund's well-known motto is "raise it, spend it, prove it." RED has positioned itself uniquely by raising funds through product sales, spending them only in the best-performing programs, and proving RED's success by aid celebrity verification.

As we described in chapter 1, the Global Fund came about as a response to the then UN secretary-general Kofi Annan's meeting with African leaders in Nigeria in 2001. Under consultation of Sachs, guarantee of Farmer, and promotion of Bono, Annan's call led to an unusually quick response by the UN General Assembly, which called a special session on AIDS and committed to creating the Global Fund, while the G8 committed to funding it. By January 2002, a permanent secretariat was established in Geneva and the first grants were released to recipients in thirty-six countries. By 2010, the Fund had benefited over 120 countries. It maintains no in-country presence or technical assistance expertise, but relies heavily on partner organizations, particularly others within the UN system.

The Global Fund differs from bilateral initiatives in its governance structure and more balanced decision-making process that aims to include representatives from a broad range of donor and recipient constituencies, including developing country governments, NGOs, people living with HIV and AIDS, etc. Supporters have pointed out that the Global Fund was groundbreaking in its inclusion of civil society groups in decision making. The Global Fund is governed by a board of directors with support from four subcommittees. The board includes representatives from key global health organizations such as UNAIDS, the WHO, and the World Bank. To receive a grant from the Global Fund, a country must establish a country-coordinating mechanism (CCM). CCMs are multistakeholder bodies in each country that are responsible for receiving grant applications, for nominating worthy recipients to the technical review panel, and for oversight in implementation of awarded grants.[20] While the board of directors formally approves grants, the technical review panel decides which applications meet the criteria for funding. The Global Fund aims to support all countries with viable action plans, unlike the more politicized U.S. PEPFAR initiatives that channel funds bilaterally through U.S. embassies in selected countries.[21]

Financing comes to the Global Fund primarily from nation-states, but also from individuals and foundations, such as the Bill and Melinda Gates Foundation, on a completely voluntary basis, and thus commitments are not legally binding under any international law. One of the largest contributors to the Global Fund, the U.S. government, is not permitted by law to contribute more than 33 percent of the total paid-in funding, as an attempt to minimize disproportionate contribution and control over the institution. Table 4 summarizes the source of pledges and actually disbursed funds to the Global Fund as of November 2008. A total of $18.9 billion were pledged by donors, of which $11.8 billion was actually disbursed. Ninety-five percent of disbursed funds came from "traditional" bilateral donors. The remaining 5 percent came from private sources. Within private sources, "traditional" philanthropy provided the bulk (the Gates Foundation provided 72 percent of all private funding alone). RED was actually the second source of private funding, with $115 million disbursed as of November 2008—or 1 percent of total disbursements (public and private).[22] Note that there is no RED entry into "pledges" because RED contributions depend on the volume of RED product sales. The Global Fund cannot bank on RED, even though all RED corporate partners have made multiyear commitments to supporting the Global Fund. Given the high level of transparency in reporting in the Global Fund, it is quite remarkable that no breakdown is provided by RED company, nor the disbursements by year (only a grand total to date is provided; see Table 4). This means that consumers have no basis on which to choose between RED products in order to maximize their "help" for Africa.

With RED, it is the first time that the Global Fund has publicly permitted donations to be channeled to support particular types of grants (the best-performing AIDS programs benefiting women and children in Africa) rather than the Fund's overall activities. This may have more fundamental repercussions on the Global Fund as donors like RED set the priorities of the Fund on the basis of the areas where donor contributions be channeled. Also, the Fund writes that the in-house management of the RED campaign is almost the exclusive focus of the Global Fund's budget for private-sector support (Global Fund 2007a, 20).

Nonetheless, RED contributions have been singled out as "innovative" by the Global Fund, and in an interesting contrast to the genesis story promoted by the RED campaign (as resulting from Bono's creative musings on saving the world), the Fund reports that RED was the result of institutional collaboration over the year before the launch of RED.

> While private contributions comprise a relatively small portion of the Global Fund's income to date, fundraising efforts gained a considerable boost through Product RED, an innovative initiative designed by the musician Bono and Bobby Shriver, Chairman of Debt, AIDS, Trade, Africa (DATA). This initiative, the result of hard work by the Global Fund's Private Sector Board Delegation and Secretariat throughout 2005, is to be launched at the World Economic Forum in January 2006 and has the potential to raise substantial new funds for and significantly raise the profile of the Global Fund around the world. (Global Fund 2005, 20)

RED is here seen as part of a collaborative strategy to increase private funding and improve the brand value by linking aid celebrities with the Global Fund.

In addition to collaboration with RED to promote business links, the Global Fund announced in January 2008 the launch of the Global Fund "Corporate Champions" program. Chevron Corporation was the program's inaugural Corporate Champion, making a commitment to invest $30 million over three years in Global Fund–supported programs in parts of Asia and Africa. "The Global Fund Corporate Champions program has been designed as an integrated platform for public/private partnership, giving companies the opportunity to make a substantial commitment to global health. Each Corporate Champion will make a financial contribution to Global Fund–supported programs in countries where it operates.... Chevron was selected as the inaugural partner as a result of its highly-successful community engagement programs tackling AIDS and malaria and its award-winning HIV/AIDS workplace programs."[23] We will compare forms of corporate social responsibility (CSR) with the RED initiative in the next chapter.

Other ways for corporations to be involved with Global Fund–related activities are through national level collaborations, including "participating in and supporting the national Country Coordinating Mechanisms (CCMs) which oversee Global Fund grants; providing technical and/or management assistance to implementers of grants; leveraging business infrastructure through co-investments which expand the reach of grants; and acting as a direct grant recipient and implementer."[24]

The Fund had at the time of writing approved grants in eight funding rounds. In awarding grants, it "gives priority to effective proposals from countries and regions with the greatest need, based on the highest burden of disease and the fewest financial resources available to fight these epidemics."[25] Table 5 illustrates the amounts and distribution of grants allocated by the Global Fund (as of November 2008). It has approved proposals worth $14.9 billion, concluded grant agreements with recipients worth $10 billion and actually disbursed $6.6 billion so far. Africa accounts for 61 percent of the value of approved proposals and over 50 percent of disbursements so far. After seven rounds, 61 percent of the value of grants was allocated to projects for HIV/AIDS, 25 percent for malaria, and 14 percent for tuberculosis.[26]

The four countries that had received RED funding through the Global Fund at that time have approved grants targeting HIV/AIDS totalling almost $880 million. RED, with its $115 million raised at that time, represented 13 percent of this total.[27]

TABLE 4. The Global Fund to Fight AIDS, Tuberculosis and Malaria: Pledges (nominal prices)

Donors	Pledges (US$ thousands)	Year	Total paid to date (US$ thousands)
Countries			
Australia	158,127	2004–10	95,669
Belgium	111,992	2001–10	78,542
Brazil	200	2003–4, 2006–7	200
Brunei Darussalam	50	2007	
Cameroon	125	2003, 2007	
Canada	100,000	2002–4	100,006
	709,419	2005–10	373,887
China	16,000	2003–10	12,000
Denmark	208,781	2002–10	148,091
European Commission	1,178,009	2001–10	789,911
Finland	15,419	2006–9	10,892
France	2,399,470	2002–10	1,396,882
Germany	1,232,784	2002–10	715,319
Greece	788	2005–7	788
Hungary	45	2004–6, 2008	45
Iceland	421	2004–5	421
	700	2006–8	700
India	11,000	2006–10	3,000
Ireland	219,176	2002–10	135,088
Italy	200,000	2002–3	215,160
	1,130,453	2004–10	793,101
Japan	1,406,120	2002–8, 2009	846,520
Korea (Republic of)	11,000	2004–9	4,000
Kuwait	2,000	2003, 2008	2,000
Latvia	10	2008	
Liechtenstein	425	2002, 2005–8	425
	117	2004, 2006	117
Luxembourg	24,015	2002–10	17,546
Mexico	200	2003, 2005	200
Netherlands	619,098	2002–10	321,556
New Zealand	2,169	2003–5	2,169
Nigeria	20,000	2002–3, 2006	9,081
Norway	340,369	2002–10	170,480
Poland	50	2003–6	50
Portugal	15,500	2003–10	7,500
Romania	436	2007	436
Russia	254,500	2002–10	154,854
Saudi Arabia	28,000	2003–6, 2008–10	16,000
Singapore	1,000	2004–8	1,000

Donors	Pledges (US$ thousands)	Year	Total paid to date (US$ thousands)
Slovenia	28	2004–6	28
	44	2007	44
South Africa	10,000	2003–8	8,000
	231	2006, 2008	131
Spain	751,547	2003–5, 2007–10	304,307
	63,900	2006	63,900
Gen.Catalunya/ Spain	7,579	2005–8	5,639
Sweden	539,232	2002–10	378,297
Switzerland	10,000	2002–3	10,000
	35,341	2004–10	16,920
Thailand	10,000	2003–12	6,000
Uganda	2,000	2004–7	1,500
United Kingdom	2,313,811	2001–15	674,644
United States	4,028,356	2001–8	3,328,837
Other countries	2,750	2001–4	1,675
Total	18,192,787		11,223,558
Other			
Bill and Melinda Gates Foundation	650,000	2002–4, 2006–10	450,000
Communitas Foundation	3,000	2007–9	2,000
Debt2Health—Germany; realized as restricted contributions from:			
Indonesia	33,879	2008–12	8,006
UNITAID	52,500	2007	38,692
CPEF (Idol Gives Back)	6,000	2007–8	5,500
(PRODUCT) RED™ and Partners			115,292
United Nations Foundation and its donors:			
Hottokenai Campaign (G-CAP Coalition Japan)	250	2006	250
Other UNF Donors	4,022	Various	6,510
Other donors		Various	12
Total	749,651		628,512
Grand Total	18,942,438		11,849,808

Source: Elaboration from Global Fund data, http://www.globalfund.org (Progress Summary 083; as of November 2008).

TABLE 5. The Global Fund: Proposals, agreements, and disbursements by round and region (US$ thousands, nominal prices)

	Approved proposals	Grant agreements	Disbursements
By All Round: All Regions			
Round 1	1,736,417	1,458,217	1,190,800
Round 2	2,589,821	1,822,704	1,501,040
Round 3	1,404,467	1,402,455	1,076,058
Round 4	2,818,358	2,647,281	1,589,705
Round 5	1,316,140	991,814	683,415
Round 6	868,832	868,832	444,733
Round 7	1,086,350	827,197	153,944
Round 8	3,059,157	0	0
All rounds	14,879,542	10,018,500	6,639,695
Regions as a percentage of the total			
East Asia & the Pacific	13	13	14
Eastern Europe & Central Asia	7	9	10
Latin America & the Caribbean	8	8	9
North Africa & the Middle East	6	6	6
South Asia	7	8	7
Sub-Saharan Africa: East Africa	28	26	25
Sub-Saharan Africa: Southern Africa	17	18	15
Sub-Saharan Africa: West & Central Africa	16	13	13

Source: Global Fund, http://www.globalfund.org (Progress Summary 083; as of November 2008)

Approved proposals include all proposal amounts approved by the Board Grant. Agreements include all amounts related to signed grants (re: grants signed by both the PR and GFATM Secretariat). Disbursements include all disbursements made (where instructions to disburse have been sent to the Trustee).

BALANCING RISK: CRITIQUES OF THE GLOBAL FUND

The Global Fund has been criticized for its activities in relation to the multiplication of aid initiatives to health, for governance from a distance, and for its limited focus on the megadiseases.[28] Officially, there are attempts to "harmonize international efforts" in response to HIV and AIDS between all donors with what is called "the three ones" initiative.[29] The Global Fund and other donor initiatives should be harmonized with the U.S. PEPFAR to prevent "overlapping efforts and conflicting priorities."[30] PEPFAR is also a major financer of the Global Fund, having provided $200 million in 2005 (van Dalen and Reuser 2005, 16). Official reports state that PEPFAR as of 2010 contributed more than $3.5 billion to the Fund since its founding contribution in 2001.[31] However, lack of sufficiently harmonized efforts in aid to AIDS on the ground has contributed to difficulties in managing the magnitude of funds that have come into certain countries over the last decade. The Fund has been faulted for the situation documented in some countries in which "governments and their partners were partially engaging with many (old and new) financing initiatives, in place of systematic and effective engagement with fewer initiatives and funding agencies, which was the perverse effect of too many poorly coordinated parallel financing mechanisms" (Brugha 2005, 8). Disbursement delays that have plagued the Global Fund's work in many African countries have been blamed on factors ranging from a "crisis of expectation" that a rapid financing mechanism would result in speedy implementation, to changing information requests from the Global Fund (ibid., 14–15). An analysis of the Global Fund as compared to the World Bank's MAP and PEPFAR found that "the flow of Global Fund monies has been impeded by bottlenecks that were primarily caused by challenges faced by ROs [recipient organizations] in managing resources" (Oomman, Bernstein, and Rosenzweig 2007, 42).

A lack of management and oversight capacity in Uganda resulted in one of the most publicized cases of aid corruption in the history of African aid. In Uganda, the Global Fund became synonymous with corruption, as tens of millions of U.S. dollars of the country's Global Fund grants "disappeared" into the accounts of high-ranking government officials. Similar mismanagement of Global Fund monies has been reported, but not yet substantiated, in Kenya and Nigeria.[32]

The Global Fund as an organization with global reach but minimal local presence has been criticized for its governance from a distance. One criticism is over the Fund's dual governance structure. When the Fund was established, there was insufficient time to recruit and train the secretariat, so an administrative service agreement was reached with the WHO.[33] Thus, the WHO formally employs those who serve in the central administration of the Global Fund. Referencing the WHO's lack of any whistleblowing policy to fight corruption, a Global Compact report noted problems of dual governance: "By virtue of being responsible for the final pay cheque every month, it may model behaviour that conflicts with the strategic intentions of the board."[34] Furthermore, the *Lancet* wrote that "the two organisations are tied through a series of bureaucratic tangles that deprive the Global Fund of the flexibility it needs."[35] Another criticism relates to the lack of on-the-ground coordination and in-country support personnel to facilitate grant applications or implementation (Rivers 2008). Finally, the biggest criticism over governance from a distance relates to the complicated and shifting processes for applying for funds and for reporting after monies are disbursed. In the words of Nathan Geffen, the then Policy Coordinator for South Africa's Treatment Action Campaign (TAC):

> [The Global Fund] is so complex that it has spawned an industry of expensive consultants with far too much power over the recipient organizations, even though their role is merely to manage the Fund's highly specific technical details. This cannot be right. TAC has far more technical expertise available to it than the vast majority of African NGOs, yet we are struggling to make sense of the GF mechanisms. (Quoted in Rivers 2008, 17)

If, as indicated above, the Global Fund's procedures are so complicated for what is probably the best-resourced NGO working on AIDS in Africa, then certainly the image of a smooth operation, accessible to those who need it, is misplaced.

The Global Fund has been limited by its disease-specific focus. In April 2007 the Fund agreed for the first time to consider proposals for comprehensive health program financing, but canceled the practice in subsequent rounds.[36] Still, the Global Fund's disease focus necessarily verticalizes its input, and as noted earlier, verticalization can weaken more generic health service components and draw attention away from the nonfocal diseases (Hanefeld et al. 2007, 26). The Fund continues to struggle with the paradox that while it depends tremendously on local capacity, it is unable to expand local capacity in health (Ooms 2008, 20). Seckinelgin's (2005, 2008) work on global governance in African AIDS demonstrates the complex relationships between languages and policies of the global AIDS funders and the depoliticization of people infected and affected by AIDS as recipients of aid. The long-term vision, leadership, and social change required for a sustained intervention for dealing with HIV and AIDS requires agency and coordinated response, not depoliticized and disparate "emergency" interventions that rely on NGOs.

Finally, the Global Fund has been criticized for its insufficient attention to gender issues. One review noted the lack of gender disaggregated data that the Fund uses for monitoring and reporting and an absence of programs addressing women's vulnerability to HIV infection and gender inequality or targeting gender violence (ICRW 2004). Also, the innovative CCMs could potentially provide spaces for women's political empowerment and recognition in the political process of AIDS governance. Yet so far, participation in the CCMs has been gender-biased in all regions, and only 32 percent or fewer of the CCM members in sub-Saharan Africa are women (Hanefeld et al. 2007, 25). Furthermore, the lack of integration between the Global Fund's projects and sexual and reproductive health services has been documented as draining staff and worsening a human resource crisis in some African contexts (ibid., 26).

RED's consumers are led to believe that if they want to spend their way to saving women and children with AIDS in Africa, the Global Fund is in fact the organization to make this possible. While the brief review of the critiques of the Fund above is not meant to suggest that the Fund's work is not valuable, it is important to recognize what is completely missing in the RED campaign: The Global Fund is a politicized and controversial organization. It has a noteworthy commitment toward working through local counterparts and participation, yet the governance from a distance limits the kinds of local organizations that might hope to navigate the Fund's processes. In spite of its "efficient" representations in the RED media, it has been accused of contributing to gross problems of coordination in recipient countries. Its focus on vertical programs fits well into the RED virtualism that two pills a day will save the lives of women and children with AIDS in Africa, but the

Fund itself is at odds with its limitations as a disease-focused entity and attempted expansion to accept comprehensive health program financing as a result. Finally, if RED is in fact so concerned with women and children, it should advocate better gender monitoring, representation, and integration of programs within the Global Fund.

AID, BUSINESS, AND AIDS

In this chapter, we have highlighted how "traditional aid" (intended as public aid coming from bilateral and multilateral donors) is being increasingly portrayed as in need of reform or even discontinuation altogether. Traditional aid is under incessant attack for being wasteful, irrelevant, and inefficient. Private aid is portrayed as flexible, innovative, and growing. Hybrid forms of both aid financing and delivery are emerging. We have also seen that private and public aid are only two of the sources of finances to Africa, and that other sources (such as remittances, FDI, and other capital flows) are very important to the continent. We highlight this aspect because the efficiency argument in aid has been closely linked with the assumption that African countries are the paradigms of "bad governance." Corruption, nepotism, the "big man" theory of leadership, and a dearth of accountability have become synonymous with notions of aid in Africa. But the trends we highlighted in this chapter suggest that Africa is not the bottomless pit of rich countries' taxpayer money. It is not the lost continent that needs recolonization.

RED has emerged at a time when aid suffers from a crisis of legitimacy. It is helping to "rebrand" some forms of aid. It is a new financing modality, and it uses a new channelling mechanism (the Global Fund) to deliver such aid. It is also based on business mechanisms to raise funds. This helps RED avoid efficiency criticisms that are often levied on aid interventions. To those who pointed out that RED companies spent well above the sum raised for the Global Fund in their marketing and advertising campaign,[37] Bobby Shriver (the cofounder of RED) replied that those expenditures would have been carried out anyway by those companies, on something else instead of RED.[38]

RED gives the impression that the work that it funds to respond to HIV and AIDS is innovative, outside of the usual bureaucratic mire of development aid, and reliant on individuals.[39] The 2008 UNAIDS report mentions RED specifically in its summary of the need for "innovative mechanisms" to sustain financing for the long term: "The quest for long-term financing for HIV response has led to a number of imaginative initiatives. For example Product RED, the brainchild of Bono and Bobby Shriver, chair of DATA" (UNAIDS 2008, 196). The Global Fund's Report to its fifteenth board meeting included a graph of RED revenue growth and argued that "Product (RED) has steadily demonstrated the power of corporate marketing and consumer spending as a means of private sector fundraising."[40] In an official announcement, Richard Feachem, then executive director of the Global Fund, encouraged the corporate expansion of aid financing: "The RED campaign, launched this week in London, enrols major corporations and their customers into our collective fight, and must be expanded to include more corporate partners in more markets."[41] However, Michel Kazatchkine was more circumscribed in his first interview after being named as the subsequent executive director of the Global Fund:

> I think this [the business sector] is an open space; we are still on very preliminary ground. I hope and believe we can increase the Product (RED) initiative; I hope it will spread more into Europe. I hope we can also have other business sector initiatives. But I hope also that businesses can get more into co-investment [in which businesses in developing countries contribute their clinics, doctors, etc. to projects that are financed by the Fund]. I don't think that the private sector has a culture yet of working with multilateral entities like the Fund.[42]

A Global Fund Task Force on Resource Mobilization noted that consumer-focused campaigns like RED have additive potential and do not compete with the Global Fund's other funders; however "consumer-focused campaigns, such as (PRODUCT) RED, do appear to hold the greatest potential as a significant, albeit somewhat unpredictable, supplementary revenue stream."[43] Thus, RED's relationship with the Global Fund could be seen as merging aid's "rule-abiding and rule-enforcing multilaterals and unruly yet very generous private funders" (Steiner-Khamsi 2008, 14). But, like the other major suppliers of development funding in response to HIV and AIDS in general, the Global Fund receives most of its revenue from donor governments, not from young fashionistas.

Therefore, it is questionable whether reiterative consumption by Western buyers is likely to carry the burden of generating a sustainable flow of money to support the Global Fund, especially under the current financial and economic crisis. Yet the power of RED in providing a "solution" to many of the current popular debates on international aid preempts possible criticism of the initiative and opens the doors for more successful initiatives of Brand Aid.

(4) HARD COMMERCE
Corporate Social Responsibility for Distant Others

The Web site for Converse includes an interactive platform for designing your own RED shoes or choosing a series of existing designs, including one called "Maphute Manamela 1HUND(RED) #83." This white shoe features a drawing of the traditional red AIDS ribbon with feet dribbling a soccer ball and the words "kick AIDS." The description reads: "Inspired by purposeful play ... 10% of the net wholesale price of these CONVERSE (PRODUCT) RED shoes will be paid to The Global Fund to Fight AIDS, Tuberculosis and Malaria (Geneva, Switzerland). No part of the purchase price is deductible under US law."[1] This RED shoe is interesting, not simply because of its clear signing of "Africa," but also in the ways it embodies the conflation of commerce and donation; hence the need for a disclaimer that while the product will guarantee a contribution to a good cause, this is not charity, which might be tax deductible under U.S. law.

Brand Aid is both a business practice and a development intervention. RED has been built upon the principle that business methods and "hard commerce" can be an appropriate vector for raising funds for good causes. In this chapter, we place the RED case study against the background of the "normal functioning" of the industries in which the RED companies operate, and in relation to the many aspects of corporate social responsibility (CSR). We examine how the corporations that are part of this initiative use RED to build up their brand profiles, sell products, and/or portray themselves as both "caring" and "cool."

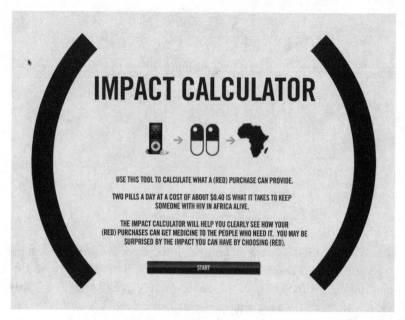

The impact calculator used on the RED Web site, http://www.joinred.com/Learn/Impact/Calculator.aspx.

Because managing a positive CSR profile is part of a company's effort to maximize brand value, it is important to see how RED contributes to such a process.

To understand the interface between business and aid in emerging Brand Aid initiatives, this chapter situates the RED case with a thriving literature that takes a reflective and critical look at CSR and development.[2] We concur with this literature that not enough is known on the actual impact of CSR activities in developing countries (Blowfield 2007; Newell and Frynas 2007) and that CSR can distract attention from the root causes of poverty and environmental destruction (Newell 2008). RED offers an unusual comparison in that the impact of the CSR intervention is easy to measure—consumers can click onto the RED Web site and use the online "impact calculator" to determine how many antiretroviral (ARV) pills are bought through the contribution generated by the purchase of a RED t-shirt. The RED "impact calculator" is a tool for calculating what a (RED) purchase can provide "to keep someone with HIV in Africa alive."[3] When the customer clicks on "start," a screen of RED products appears—an iPod, a t-shirt, sunglasses, a greeting card, a watch, a coffee cup—each with a button to add (+) or subtract (-) the product in the arithmetic of saving African lives. As you move the cursor over any product, you are informed of the amount of lifetime you will buy for an African with AIDS. For example, moving over the Armani watch calls forth the text "Can provide more than 30 days of lifesaving ARV treatment." The lifetime varies according to product price, as it would take four Hallmark cards with sound to buy one day of African life. But when consumers click on the "calculate" button, they are given their answer, and the reminder, "And remember that all of your (RED) purchases help save the lives of people with HIV in Africa." After finalizing your product-life equation, you are given two buttons of choice, "recalculate" or "Shop Product (RED)."

Of course, impact is meaningless outside of the context of possible impacts and other opportunities. We argue that Brand Aid shifts the kinds of activities that are represented as constituting "legitimate CSR," which has direct relevance for important questions of "development." First, this happens in terms of what groups are represented as constituting appropriate beneficiaries for CSR initiatives; second, it happens in terms of what kinds of benefits they receive. RED beneficiaries are explicitly "women and children affected by HIV/AIDS in Africa." The kinds of benefits they receive from RED are primarily limited to ARV treatment.

The chapter proceeds as follows. We first briefly explain the genesis of key concepts such as CSR, corporate philanthropy, and cause-related marketing. We then present the key analytical dimensions we use to sift through the company data to provide a comparative CSR profile of RED companies. We also summarize the "hard commerce" challenges that these companies face in their day-to-day operations, which are important in order to understand both their CSR activities more generally and the possible range of motivations for joining RED. In a section on the involvement with RED, we show what items or services these companies actually sell through RED and what portion of sales or profits they donate. In the conclusion to the chapter, we argue that RED engages corporations in profitable "helping" while simultaneously pushing the agenda of CSR toward solving the problems of "distant others"—as opposed to, say, the problems of workers producing RED products or minimizing the deleterious impact of production on the environment. In doing so, RED promotes a form of CSR based on hard commerce, one that, instead of addressing the three Ps (people, planet, profits) on an equal basis, puts the core objective of profit maximization ahead. RED improves a company's brand without challenging any of its actual operations and practices, and increases its value and reputation.

CORPORATE SOCIAL RESPONSIBILITY, CORPORATE PHILANTHROPY, AND CAUSE-RELATED MARKETING

Corporate social responsibility has operated under a number of names and definitions through its rapid development (Wartick and Cochran 1985). Although the issue of the social responsibility of business can be found in writings that go back centuries, examination of business as a social actor has expanded considerably in the last half century or so (Carroll 1999). The European Commission defines CSR as "a concept whereby companies integrate social and environmental concerns in their business operations and in their interaction with their stakeholders on a voluntary basis."[4] But other definitions of CSR expand responsibility to cover society as a whole, not just the immediate stakeholders.[5] More recently, the concept of "corporate citizenship" has also arisen, which on the one hand seems to suggest a more holistic view of responsibility, while on the other hand has been often used to mean the same thing as CSR.[6]

The term *corporate philanthropy* has also been used for activities that companies do to benefit the communities where they are located, for example donating funds to local schools and hospitals. But as companies have expanded the geographical reach of their operations and sourcing, they have become increasingly accountable for the direct and indirect consequences of their actions in disparate spheres and locations.[7] Philanthropy in general has its roots in nineteenth-century Christian organizations, which questioned classical liberalism's reliance on market mechanisms to ameliorate human misery caused by unchecked capitalist growth (di Leonardo 2008).[8] Two of the first proponents of *corporate* philanthropy were Andrew Carnegie and John D. Rockefeller. Carnegie believed that large, wealthy entities such as corporations had a responsibility to improve conditions for vulnerable groups—the disabled, the poor, and the elderly (Freeman and Liedtka 1991). Carnegie's was a charity-focused appeal, a call for companies to undertake the responsibility of lifting the poor as an extracurricular activity. But wages, working hours, or what would come to be known as "pro-poor" business practices were not an explicit part of his call to action. Rockefeller, like Carnegie, "espoused philanthropy that removed barriers to self-improvement and that empowered the poor" (Frumkin 2006, 8).

This kind of perspective inspired a backlash among business leaders and economists. Friedman stated unequivocally that "the social responsibility of business is to increase its profits."[9] Levitt (1958), another critic of corporate responsibility, advocated that companies' undertaking of ambitious social roles would usurp the responsibilities of government. (For a recent rehash of the debate on the social role of corporations, see Kinsley 2008.) Both Friedman and Levitt only dealt with a form of CSR that advocated shareholder-funded philanthropy. But beginning in the 1960s, issues such as labor practices, product safety, and bribery wriggled into the popular press, activist literature, and political speeches (Lantos 2001). Multinational corporations, not governments, were cast as the agents of such violations. Accounts of environmental damage and Third World poverty added to the growing public acceptance that company operations no longer affected only one area or one group of employees (Jenkins 2005). Corporations began to engage in "social responsibility" as a way of demonstrating their societal worth beyond the operations of their core business.

Deregulation, increased capital mobility, and industry consolidation saw the rise of outsourcing of production to developing countries in the 1980s and 1990s. Corporations became increasingly able to "shop" for developing countries to provide their labor, threatening to pull capital if factories were not given tax breaks and minimum wage waivers. It was in the background of these changes that the management literature started to examine whether "engaged CSR" and long-term profitability could be mutually reinforcing. The most prominent promoter of this discussion, framed as the "business case" for CSR, was R. Edward Freeman, through his "stakeholder theory" (1984).[10]

In the 1980s, philanthropic and social-responsibility activities started to be placed within companies' overall strategic plans. CSR activities became more focused, aligned to the companies' business goals and brand characteristics, and supportive of beneficiaries that could become customers (King 2006). This, together with the increased importance and visibility of branding (and thus, the vulnerability of brand image to negative campaigns) (Conroy 2007), led in the 1990s to an unprecedented level of scrutiny on company operations in developing countries, and reports of poor labor and environmental practices proliferated. The term "sweatshop," coined during the assembly-line era of the Industrial Revolution, made a comeback in profiles of Nike, Gap, and Kathie Lee Gifford. Industry leaders such as McDonald's and Nike were repeatedly attacked, and violations three or four stages of supply-chain separation from the companies themselves were reported with the language of direct complicity.

The 1990s also witnessed the development of corporate codes of conduct. Driven as they were by NGO campaigns and public "busts" of companies operating in poor countries, such codes emphasized negative, "thou shalt not"-style obligations for companies. Policies of monitoring and auditing set a baseline of human rights, labor standards, and environmental protection below which companies could not fall. High-profile issues such as child labor were a fixture of these efforts, both in the codes of conduct and in the public relation rollouts that followed (Blowfield and Frynas 2005, 512).[11]

Over the last two decades, CSR has also seen the mushrooming of *cause-related marketing* as "an established and prevalent form of corporate philanthropy" (Berglind and Nakata 2005, 443). In cause-related marketing, the marketing of a brand, company, product, or service is tied directly to a social cause, most often with a portion of the sales going to support the cause.[12] Otherwise known as "transactional programs," these are classic exchange-based donations, where a corporation agrees to give a specified share of the proceeds for every unit sold (Berglind and Nakata 2005). Cause-related marketing can also involve message promotion in which a donation may or may not be given, and licensing programs in which a nonprofit (such as the World Wildlife Fund) licenses the use of its name and logo to a company that uses it on their product in exchange for a contribution. Such a mechanism for fund-raising lends itself to meeting overarching business goals (including the drive for profits), and strengthens brand reputation and employee loyalty, aiding recruitment and retention (King 2006, 9). For the nonprofits, it increases funding, heightens their media exposure and even credibility through associations with well-known businesses, and provides marketing talent and business acumen that is often in greater supply in corporations than in nonprofits (Berglind and Nakata 2005, 448). This kind of CSR does more than just allow companies to differentiate their products from the competition. It shifts consumer attitudes, as they are represented as "yearning to connect to people and things that will give meaning to their lives" (King 2006, 11).

ANALYTICAL FRAMEWORK FOR CSR

The concept "CSR" is an extremely diverse receptacle of corporate activities, with the common goal of achieving the "triple bottom line"— based on financial, social, and environmental objectives. In more comprehensive definitions, CSR can also include activities that go beyond the reach of a company's operations, for example addressing social and/or environmental issues more broadly, participating in global fora such as the UN Global Compact, or donating through more traditional corporate philanthropy. In our analysis, we take "CSR" as a broad, comprehensive, umbrella term to include aspects such as corporate philanthropy and cause-related marketing. Recognizing that this is a contentious approach (some observers have argued against the catch-all use of the term; see Jenkins 2005), we bring together the diverse aspects of corporate "doing good" as a way to understand how RED is a manifestation of some aspects of CSR, but not of others. Thus, CSR as a concept is being shaped by the kinds of Brand Aid activities that operate as part of any business's engagement as socially responsible.

The analysis carried out in this chapter relies on the public availability of information. CSR activities are diverse, and companies clearly have strong incentives toward selective reporting of their CSR portfolio.

Many companies are reporting activities explicitly labeled as "CSR" as a way to get credit for things that they may have been doing for some time, which raise the morale of their employees but for which they do not receive credit from other stakeholders—particularly consumers. Interestingly, however, while the incentives not to report failures are obvious, there may also be perverse incentives not to report certain kinds of successes that could raise objections from Wall Street. One reason of course is that bragging may inspire others to attack your failures. All of the data under analysis here are from publicly available sources including reports written by advocacy NGOs, company CSR reports, press releases, and trade magazines. Attempts to obtain primary data on RED products through phone interviews with the seven companies and the RED initiative headquarters were, with a few exceptions, unsuccessful. Questions about which companies release what information, to whom, how, and when are beyond the scope of this book; however, it would be naïve to disregard the limitations of the public data.

The CSR activity matrix is a heuristic device to guide our discussion. It is not meant to be "filled in" in mutually exclusive ways, but is designed to help the reader distinguish between different forms (and combinations) of corporate concern related to labor issues, the environment, and/or the lives of distant others. By "engaged CSR activities" we mean activities that have a direct impact on company operations (this is what is known in much of the literature as "proper CSR"). In other words, this relates to how much a CSR activity appears to impact the "normal functioning" of doing business—such as supply relations (with immediate suppliers and beyond), treatment of the labor force, and environmental impact of the company's own operations or of its suppliers. At the other end of this continuum is "disengaged CSR," which is akin to traditional corporate philanthropy or charity. These are activities that are weakly linked (or not linked at all) to the operations of a firm. While these "disengaged" activities may have a positive impact on some people and/or environments (and thus, provide an ethical aura), they do not challenge any of the tenets of normal business conduct—on the contrary, the more successful a company is, the more money it can donate—no matter how and where that profit was obtained.

Type of CSR Activity

		Engaged	Disengaged
Location of CSR Activity Beneficiaries	**Proximate**	– Workplace conditions and policies at head-quarters or own plants – Addressing environmental impact and carbon footprint at head-quarters or own plants	– Cause-related marketing with beneficiaries in local communities of operation – Corporate philanthropy with beneficiaries in local communities of operation
	Distant	– Codes of conduct of suppliers – Addressing environmental impact and carbon footprint of suppliers and from trade/transport	– Brand Aid – Cause-related marketing with distant beneficiaries – Corporate philanthropy with distant beneficiaries

CSR activity matrix by location and type.

Extremely competitive practices and/or exploitative relations of production and trade can be justified ex-post by "doing good." On a larger scale, this is usually done through the establishment of charitable foundations. Engaged CSR, on the other hand, includes changes that may even undermine competitiveness and result in lower profitability (at least in the short term); yet it can have a positive impact on thousands of workers or primary agricultural producers in the South. In other words, it can go against the grain of the normal functioning of business. This is not necessarily the case, however, when profitability increases from lower waste and energy savings, for example, or a more palatable corporate image is built for a brand, and so forth.

Whether CSR activities are engaged or disengaged, their intended beneficiaries live in different places vis-à-vis the location of normal business operations. "Proximate CSR" takes place within the corporation itself, in relation to its own labor force or the impact on the environment in the location of its operations, and on the "working environment" as a whole (pay, benefits, equal opportunities, unionization, treatment in relation to gender and sexual orientation of workers). Proximate CSR can also include activities that are not related to the business in which the company is involved, but that take place within communities and environments adjacent to the sites of operation (support for local public schools, sponsoring the local symphony, employee volunteer projects in local communities, etc.). "Distant CSR," on the contrary, includes activities that address problems of communities where the company, its suppliers, or its stakeholders are not present. It is most common for companies to act locally to increase the sense of corporate belonging within their community; however, global causes with wide emotional appeal have also become popular. We may see even more global do-gooding as Brand Aid expands. The benefits of helping "distant others" include increased opportunity to build awareness or to educate on your issue, without extensive participation or back-talking, and thus potential critique, from your beneficiaries. There is also less local accountability for the corporation if they fail to succeed, as viewed by their target beneficiaries.

RED COMPANIES AND "HARD COMMERCE"

In this section, we provide a brief picture of the "normal conditions" under which the seven RED companies operate—that is, we spell out some of the rules and functioning of "hard commerce." This provides a background against which their CSR activities (including RED) will be analyzed—in relation to the continua of engagement-disengagement and proximity-distance highlighted above. The dynamics of each of these industries are distinct. However, general trends in the constitution of "normal conditions" for companies can still be highlighted. All RED companies are operating within the overarching context of global capitalism. Gibbon and Ponte (2005) describe the historical period starting approximately in the early 1980s and continuing at least until the onset of the financial crisis in 2007–8 as the "age of global capitalism." This period is characterized by the following:

1. *Intensified "economic globalization"*—at least in some respects; "globalization skeptics" (see, inter alia, Hirst and Thompson 1999) may be correct in pointing out that contemporary foreign direct investment (FDI) and global trade, far from being comprehensively "globalized," still take the form of flows mostly within and between the so-called triad (North America, Western Europe, and Japan). But it is also notable that—since the early 1970s—the tendency for the triad to dominate world exports has been halted or even reversed. Also, exports of merchandise trade from a developing country region *outside* the triad ("Asia other than Japan") has increased substantially—not only for basic manufactures like clothing, but also in more technologically sophisticated products.

2. *Increased internationalization of retail activities in Northern countries*—mainly as a result of mergers and acquisitions. As recently as the mid-1980s, almost all retailers, even leading ones, served only their domestic markets. World retail sales are today dominated by groups operating not merely across countries, but also across regions— including those regions typically characterized as "emerging markets."

3. *The emergence of corporate "financialization,"* or broadening popular participation in corporate shareholding, that has led to a partial reorientation of corporations quoted on the stock exchange from (mainly) increasing their market share to (also) increasing "shareholder value." Although these phenomena are more relevant to Anglo-Saxon countries, there are signs that similar prescriptions are spreading to other "business cultures" in Europe.

4. *Changes in industrial organization,* with the passage from a focus on internal scale economies (related to vertical integration) to one on external economies (via outsourcing), and a resulting tendency for large corporations to retain

control over product definition and marketing, and to outsource manufacturing, supply-chain management, and sometimes also inventory management.

5. *The rise of "global contract manufacturing"*—as lead firms have increasingly redefined themselves as specialists in branding and marketing, certain of their suppliers have chosen to specialize in the manufacture and/or provision of related production services. This allows (some) suppliers to reap the benefits of large economies of scale, to diversify their customer base, and to break away from a "captive" supply relationship (Gibbon and Ponte 2005).

6. Price increases and market expansion have been superseded by *supplier-related cost-cutting as the main source of profit making* in the last decade or so (Milberg 2008). In other words, "squeezing value out of suppliers" has become one of (if not the) main instrument of competitiveness (Gibbon and Ponte 2008).

This is the general environment within which the seven RED companies examined here operate.[13] All seven are high-profile branded manufacturers[14] (or providers of services). They are all subject to extreme competition in the segment in which they operate. Despite the fact that a number of these companies have their own retail outlet chains (Armani, Apple, Converse/Nike, Hallmark, and Gap), some of them are under growing pressure to deliver higher volumes at lower prices, and with more "content," to large retailers (or phone carriers in the case of Motorola), as more of their products are being sold through them. With the exception of Hallmark and American Express, RED companies' operations are labor intensive, and depend on a low-skilled, low-paid workforce, largely based in developing countries, to function profitably.[15] All of them are headquartered in the United States (with the exception of Armani) and are quoted on the New York Stock Exchange (with the exception of Armani and Hallmark), and thus are subjected to the pressure of delivering "shareholder value" (that is, increase dividends to shareholders and maximize returns over capital employed).

At the same time, they are at the receiving end of retailers' pressures to deliver more (volume, specifications) at lower prices.

Within this framework, it seemed logical for these companies to choose RED as part of their CSR portfolio: it does not address the fundamentals of "hard commerce" and at the same time can help increase sales, visibility, and brand equity. Another scenario, applicable to companies quoted on the stock exchange, is that they may be responding to a perception of increased vulnerability—however large, they can be taken over rapidly by private equity funds and sovereign wealth funds, and they can and are stalked by activist investors. RED may be considered a defensive posture against such threats, a possible way of shoring up loyalty in a political sense.[16] At the same time, each company operates in a different industry and faces different challenges. How much RED can help them in tackling these market and "take-over" challenges varies dramatically. At the time of writing, it was still too early to assess the impact of the financial and economic crisis that started in 2007–8 both on these companies and on the RED initiative as a whole; however, the number of companies becoming RED continues to grow.

The following chart summarizes the main features of the seven RED companies in the period immediately preceding the onset of the financial and economic crisis, including essential information on location and main sectors of operation, whether they are "public" or "private" (quoted on a stock market or not), core financial data, market share, main competitors, retail strategy, value chain structure, and whether or not they have a presence in Africa (the beneficiary region of funds raised by RED). Out of seven, four are large companies with revenue ranging from $16 billion to $43 billion (AmEx, Apple, Gap, and Motorola) and two have sales in the range of $1.9 billion to $4.1 billion (Armani and Hallmark). Converse revenues are not public, but sales were $205 million in 2002, the year before it was taken over by Nike. Nike, a $15 billion company, does not disaggregate Converse financial data, but indicates that revenue has increased significantly since 2002. Interestingly, net income for three of the four big companies (AmEx, Apple, and Motorola) was almost identical (around $3.6 billion) in 2006–7, while the only two others for which data are available netted $335 million and $778 million (Armani and Gap, respectively).

Company name	American Express	Apple	Armani	Converse	Gap	Hallmark	Motorola
Type of company	Public (NYSE: AXP)	Public (NYSE: APL)	Private	Public (NYSE: NKE)	Public (NYSE: GPS)	Private	Public (NYSE: MOT)
Founded	1850	1977	1975	1917	1969	1910	1928
Headquarters	New York	Cupertino, California	Milan, Italy	North Andover, Massachusetts	San Francisco, California	Kansas City, Missouri	Schaumburg, Illinois
Main sector(s)	Financial services	Personal computers, digital music players; online music sales	Fashion clothing and accessories	Sport shoes	Casual clothing and accessories	Greeting cards	Mobile phones
Parent company	—	—	—	Nike (since 2003)	—	—	—
Slogan	Are you a card member?	—	—	—	Peace. Love. Gap.	When you care enough to send the very best	Intelligence Everywhere
Revenue	$27.1 billion (2006)	$24 billion (fiscal 2007)	€1.5 billion (2006) ($1.9 billion)	$205 million in 2002, just before Nike's takeover	$16 billion (2005)	$4.1 billion (2006)	$42.8 billion (2006)
Net income	$3.7 billion (2006)	$3.5 billion (fiscal 2007)	€267 million (2006) ($335 million)	Not available	$778 million (2007)	Not available	$3.7 billion (2006)
Market share	20% (2008)	8.1% of U.S. personal computer market; 82% of hard drive digital music players; 87% of U.S. legal digital music sales (2007)	Not available	1% (2004)	9.5% (2003)	Over 50% (2005)	21.8% (2006)
Main competitors	Visa, MasterCard, Discover	Hewlett-Packard, Dell	Prada, Gucci, LHMV group	Reebok, Adidas	Abercrombie & Fitch, American Eagle, J. Crew	American Greetings	Nokia, Samsung, Sony Ericsson
Employees	65,800	Approximately 18,000; plus 2,400 temps	5,000	260	152,000	18,000, of which 17% are in the United States; 1,000 writers and designers; 10,000 part-time "retail merchandisers" stocking cards in retailers	66,000, of which 41% are in the United States
Retail strategy	Focus on affluent card-holders and business	Online store; own retail stores; direct sales force; third-party wholesales, resellers, retailers	420 boutiques, approx. 150 directly owned	12,000 athletic specialty shops, sporting goods shops, specialty department and national chain stores in the United States and Canada; international sales through 42 licensees in over 100 countries	3,139 stores in the United States, Canada, Mexico, France, Germany, Ireland, Japan, Malaysia, Singapore, Indonesia, and the UK	43,000 retail outlets, of which 30,000 are mass retailers; Hallmark Gold Crown: 3,700 stores in the United States, 480 owned, the rest franchise; the proportion of sales through mass retailers increasing (from 45% in early 1980s to 65% in late 1990s)	Through retailers and phone carriers

Product lines and subsidiaries	Credit and debit cards; expense management services; 2,220 travel agencies; lifestyle publishing	Apple personal computers; AppleTV; iPod, iTunes, iPhone	Giorgio Armani, Emporio Armani; A/X Armani Exchange; Armani Jeans, Junior, Accessori, Casa, Occhiali, and Hotels	Sport shoes, especially for basketball	Gap, Banana Republic, Old Navy	19,000 new and redesigned cards and related products per year; Hallmark Magazine; Hallmark Music; the Hallmark channel; Hallmark flowers; Binney and Smith (makers of Crayola, LLC); Rainbow Brite (franchise of children's toys)	Mobile phones and accessories; broadband home networks; data and information solutions for governments and business
Value chain and operations	American Express runs its own card networks, but also issues cards, sends out bills, and charges customers interest on their unpaid balances. (In contrast, Visa and MasterCard's cards are issued by banks; Visa and MasterCard run the networks that allow purchases to be made with the cards. They collect a fee on every transaction, but not interest or finance charges.)	Manufacturing done mostly in China (computers) and Taiwan (iPods); components made in China, United States, Taiwan	Controls much of manufacturing; against trends in the industry, has bought up many previous contract manufacturers; all own contract manufacturing plants based mostly in Eastern Europe	All manufacturing done in Asia via Nike's contract suppliers; Chuck Taylors are made in Indonesia	3,000 contract factories around the world	Gift-wrap and greeting-card manufacturing facilities in Topeka, Lawrence, and Leavenworth, Kansas; moved some production facilities overseas; the only subsidiary Hallmark currently has in Asia is in Japan. For other Asian countries, it primarily licenses production to local firms	Over 32,600 suppliers and contractors; but 6 main ones (Celestica, Flextronics, Hon Hai/Foxconn, Jabil Circuit, Sanmina-SCI, Solectron); 55% of product manufacturing operations are owned, 45% contracted out; direct materials spend: over $24 bn, 39% in Asia-Pacific, 31% in China, 21% in the United States
Presence in Africa	Offices and charge cards offered in South Africa	Selling own products there; e-waste ending up in Africa, especially in Nigeria	Some sales	Some sales	Contract manufacturers in Kenya, Lesotho, Madagascar, Mauritius, and South Africa	Hallmark Flowers is selling flowers "picked by African farmers" under its RED line	Motorola announced plans in 2006 to set up a plant in Nigeria to assemble phone handsets and accessories; some of the RED phones are apparently assembled there

Main characteristics of companies involved in RED as of December 2007. Sources for individual entries are available from the authors.

All companies are important, if not dominant, in their respective industries (with the exception of Converse). Hallmark controlled over 50 percent of the greeting card market in 2005; Motorola had a 22 percent share of the mobile phone market in 2006; and Apple controlled 87 percent of legal digital music sales and 8 percent of personal computer sales in the United States in 2007. At the time of joining RED, only one company was not performing well (Gap had been experiencing declining sales), although in 2007 it still made $778 million in net income.

Four of these companies own, operate, and/or franchise chains of branded retail outlets (Apple, Armani, Gap, Hallmark), although some are increasingly dependent on sales through mass and specialty retailers, which is the main retail channel for two of the other companies as well (Motorola, Converse). Manufacturing is outsourced to a high degree, or even completely, by Gap, Converse, and Motorola. Hallmark still maintains some production facilities in the United States, while Armani has gone against industry trends and has actually increased its direct control over manufacturing. AmEx's business model is based on its own operation of billing and debt collection, while its main competitors (Visa and MasterCard) leave those functions to the banks that are issuing the credit cards.

The business challenges that these companies faced at the time of joining RED, in addition to the general ones highlighted above, and the new opportunities that they could exploit are quite diverse. *American Express* was probably the company that had least to fear from the market among the seven at the time it joined the initiative. Credit card interchange fees are levied as a percentage of each transaction—sometimes accompanied by a flat fee. "Credit-card transactions are growing 10% to 12% annually, and debit-card usage is growing even faster. . . . Every time a card is used, the credit-card network takes a small percentage."[17] Although MasterCard and Visa are accepted at a larger number of businesses worldwide, AmEx is still dominant among "high spenders"—its main business challenge is to maintain such a position.

Apple also joined RED from a position of strength. It had been riding a wave of increasing sales and profitability throughout the 2000s, on the back of iPod and iTunes sales but also of its new generations of personal computers. Margins on iPods are very healthy for the company.[18] In 2005, Apple made a 35 to 40 percent profit on each iPod Shuffle player sold.[19] The computer maker's margins on other products tend to be slimmer but are still substantial.[20] Not only is its position strong; its products are highly esteemed for their sleek design—this makes Apple a natural fit for the "cool profile" of the RED initiative. Anecdotal evidence suggests that it was Steve Jobs's personal enthusiasm for Bono's initiative that brought the company into RED. Apple's involvement with RED, however, took place in a more discreet way than for other companies—expressing support without excessively publicizing the co-branding arrangement.

Armani, the only non-U.S.-based company to join RED at the time of our analysis, and one of two that are still private, operates an unusual business model in the fashion business. It is still in the hands of its founder, Giorgio Armani; it has taken over production facilities, instead of outsourcing them; it has avoided being purchased by one of the fashion conglomerates; and, contrary to many others in the industry, it has maintained healthy profitability all along. Giorgio Armani joined RED because of his history working with the Shriver family and Bono, according to Caroline Brown of Armani marketing and communications.[21] According to Armani's director of communications, Robert Triefus, "Giorgio wouldn't claim to be a pioneering cause-related person. Bono is a very persuasive individual."[22]

Converse, after changing hands a number of times in the last few decades, and going through a severe crisis in the late 1990s, was purchased by Nike in 2003. It has seen sales growing again, riding on the wave of its "retro" Chuck Taylor basketball shoes, a version of its canvas All Star shoe originally designed in the 1910s. Nike is thriving even though the athletic shoe industry appears to be leveling off after explosive growth in the 1990s. Nike's flagship brand "Air Jordan," for example, has seen sales drop by more than 20 percent.[23] Converse has brought its "make your own shoe" concept to RED. Customers are encouraged to be "artists" and design their own RED shoes through a rather extensive online platform.

The last three companies in the RED list (as of December 2007) are the ones that came into the initiative with more serious and immediate business challenges at hand, and where perhaps the expectation was that RED would help them revamp their fortunes. *Gap* joined RED on the back of exposed labor disputes in the 1990s and diminishing sales and profitability in the 2000s. There was even talk about a take-over by the Swedish clothing retailer H&M in early 2007. Increasingly short life cycles for seasonal garments (Cela Díaz 2005) and cutthroat competition from mass-merchandise discounters have affected Gap's profits.

Also, U.S. consumers in the mid-2000s were buying less clothing ($11 billion less annually) than in the early 1980s. They are buying clothing from different retail outlets, depending on their income group. Workers with falling wages are shopping at stores like Walmart, while upper-income groups buy from specialized outlets. This leaves Gap in a disappearing middle. As private labels grow, clothing manufacturers are trying to shift competition toward branding, innovation, and a better shopping experience (ibid.). Gap's struggle to improve profits and its inability to retain its top staff are both well known in the industry. This may explain Gap's wholehearted embrace of RED and its willingness to engage in such an ostentatious launch of its RED products (see the Introduction).

On the surface, *Hallmark* looks like a dominant player in the greeting-card industry, as it controlled over 50 percent of the market in 2005. But the sale of greeting cards has become a mature industry, and sales volume has been flat or down for several years. The e-card business is much less concentrated, and younger consumers have increased their usage of e-cards in lieu of traditional cards.[24] In addition to the challenges of e-cards, Hallmark has to comply with the increasingly stringent demands of multiple retailers (including the leading super-market chains).[25] Within this framework, RED provides a new entry point to a different demographic, a new positioning device, and a possible escape route from the tight embrace of discounters.

As for *Motorola,* the global mobile-telephone handset industry has entered a transition phase. The market is expected to "continue to grow in terms of units, but the average price per unit seems likely to decline. The majority of units . . . will be priced low in order to gain market share in emerging markets like China and India" (Wilde and de Haan 2006,

18). A major problem for Motorola is the relatively low profitability of its mobile phones.[26] Mobile-phone manufacturers also need to deal with giant mobile network operators, who are large-scale resellers of mobile handsets. In the United States, phones are offered to consumers for free or at a greatly reduced price on the condition that they buy a one- or two-year contract. This gives the carriers more control over pricing (and, to an extent, branding) than the manufacturers themselves (Wilde and de Haan 2006). Motorola, unlike Apple, has been characterized by its relative lack of "cool products," due to its focus on engineering and the legacy of its history as a semiconductor manufacturer. The company is now focusing more on branding and design.[27] As far as design and/or exclusivity are concerned, there seems to be a clear division between the seven RED companies analyzed here. AmEx, Apple, Armani, and Converse are clear "providers of cool" to the RED initiative. Gap, Hallmark, and Motorola are "demanders of cool."

A COMPARATIVE CSR PROFILE OF RED COMPANIES

The boundaries between CSR, corporate philanthropy, and cause-related marketing have become increasingly blurred over time. For this reason, we subsume all these activities under the broad umbrella of "CSR" in this chapter. Before examining in detail the engagement of companies in RED (in the next section), we first provide a brief comparison of their CSR "portfolio."[28] This is important because while RED may affect a corporation's CSR profile, their CSR profile may also affect RED and the other co-branded corporations that come together under the RED initiative.

In the following chart, we analyze the CSR profile of RED companies through five categories: (1) recognition in business ethics circles of the combined engaged/disengaged profile (ranking by *Business Ethics* magazine);[29] (2) degree and profile of "disengaged CSR"; (3) degree and profile of "engaged CSR"; (4) degree of exposure to negative profiling in the media and by NGOs in the past; and (5) known tricky CSR issues involving the company.

The first category of company emerging from this analysis is the "good performer-rebounder." These companies have been the target of

Company name	Ranking	Disengaged CSR profile		Engaged CSR profile		Degree of negative profile in media in the past	Tricky CSR issues	Qualitative characterizations
AmEx	36	High	One of the pioneers in cause-related marketing	Medium	Member of International Business Leaders Forum's "International Tourism Partnership and Business for Social Responsibility"	Low	Lobbied for new bankruptcy law in the United States and reaped benefits; benefited from subprime credit crisis	Muddler
Apple	Not available	Low	According to the company's 10-Q, they did not give away any significant amounts of money in 2007	Medium	Has a "Responsible Supplier Management" system, applies a "Supplier Code of Conduct" and has a "Supplier Diversity Program"; engaged with the "Electronics Industry Code of Conduct"	Medium	Alleged poor working and living conditions at one of the iPod final assembly suppliers in China; e-waste management not particularly good	Muddler
Armani	Not available	Low	Very few initiatives	Low	None apparent	Low	Some labor conditions allegations; found guilty of bribing tax auditors	Outside the public radar
Converse/Nike	3	High	Substantial donations (3% of pretax profits) through the Nike Foundation	High	Very advanced, sophisticated, and transparent audit system of suppliers; active on CO_2 emission reductions and environmental designs; original supporter of UN Global Compact	High	Numerous sweatshop allegations in the 1990s	Good performer—rebounder

Gap	25	Medium	Donated $8 million in 2006 (in the range of 1% of pretax profits)	High	Holistic supplier policy; subcontracting approval system; signatory or member of a range of CSR-related initiatives; lauded for "honesty" by *Business Ethics* magazine in 2004	High	Long history of sweatshop allegations	Good performer—rebounder
Hallmark	Not available	High	Donates substantial proportions of pretax profits through the Hallmark Corporate Foundation; company literature lists several initiatives	Low	Very simple code of conduct; no old growth in their products	Low	None apparent	Outside the public radar
Motorola	4	Medium	Involved in a number of initiatives; Motorola/Motorola Foundation charitable giving amounted to $30.8 million in 2006 (about 0.7% of pretax profit)	High	Comprehensive approach to CSR, including a sophisticated supplier policy; member of numerous initiatives; complies with EU "Waste Electrical and Electronic Equipment" directive (WEEE)	Medium	Coltan controversy; a few allegations of child labor and poor working conditions at some suppliers' factories	Good performer—proactive

Comparative CSR profile of RED companies. Data obtained from corporate reports, Web sites, and other publicly available materials; details available from the authors. Ranking from "Best 100 Corporate Citizens," Business Ethics magazine, 2007.

major allegations of misconduct in the past, but have addressed them in ways that are perceived as serious. Converse/Nike has the highest Corporate Citizen score, and a "high" score in our table in all three categories of disengaged CSR, engaged CSR, and past negative media attention—a sign that the company had encountered problems related to its operations (or those of its contractors) and has reacted. It is now perceived as a "good corporate citizen." Gap has a similar profile, but a lower score from *Business Ethics* and a lower "disengaged CSR" profile.

Motorola can be labeled a "good performer-proactive"; its profile is characterized by high "engaged CSR" standards and a medium degree of philanthropy involvement, both of which to a large extent have been the result of proactive initiatives rather than reactions to previous scandals. AmEx and Apple are labeled as "muddlers"; they have not faced a high degree of public exposure on their CSR record, although some of the tricky CSR issues they face are still unresolved. One is better at "engaged CSR" (Apple); the other is better at "traditional philanthropy" (AmEx). AmEx, incidentally, is the only company among the seven that had carried out high-profile cause-related marketing before. Finally, and in a sense in opposition to the first group, are those companies that have remained "outside the public radar"—Hallmark and Armani. They are private companies, have faced few or no scandals in the public sphere, and have very minimal or no engaged CSR profile; the only difference between Hallmark and Armani is the high disengaged CSR profile of the former. In more simplified terms, in our assessment, RED has engaged two "CSR model companies" (Motorola and Nike), three that are so-so (Gap, Apple, AmEx—with Gap closer to the model companies), and two that have been outside the radar of CSR (Armani and Hallmark).

INVOLVEMENT IN RED

The RED initiative was formally launched at the World Economic Forum in Davos in early 2006. Four companies can claim the title of "founding member": AmEx, Armani, Converse, and Gap. Their RED product lines were launched soon after, in March and April 2006. Motorola launched its range of products in May 2006, followed by Apple in October 2006 and Hallmark in October 2007.[30]

The following chart provides a general picture of the involvement in RED by the seven companies that had joined by December 2007. The table shows (1) when the first RED product was launched; (2) the range of RED products available, their prices, and their geographical markets; and (3) the portion of sales value or profit that is donated to the Global Fund from the sale of these products.

Product ranges co-branded with RED and market coverage vary substantially among these companies. AmEx has the most restricted offering: one RED card only in the UK. Apple offers two models of RED iPod and iTunes gift certificates in the United States, UK, Canada, and Japan or through its online stores. Motorola (despite having dropped out of RED in late 2008) still sold three models of its mobile phones with a RED logo and some accessories in early 2009, and these were available in at least ten countries in North America, Europe, and East Asia. Converse began with one model (the RED Chuck Taylor) but then expanded it to a much wider range, all of which are customizable online. These shoes are available at shoe stores in the United States and UK, and also at some Gap stores (in the United States). Hallmark offers a wide range of RED products, from flower bouquets to cards to wrapping paper, mostly in the United States. Gap and Armani offer a large range of RED clothing and accessories, with the former present in five countries in North America and Europe, and the latter at all its 124 Emporio Armani stores, located on all continents—except for Africa.

The RED product lines sold by these companies are not cheap trinkets, but are not prohibitively priced for Western middle-class shoppers. Most products range in price from $50 to around $200, with the exception of some more expensive Emporio Armani items and Motorola phones, and some cheaper Gap accessories, Hallmark cards, and iTunes gift cards. Both Hallmark and Converse allow customers to design and/or customize their RED products, aligning themselves with the "consumer participation" philosophy embraced by the RED initiative through its RED blogs.

Company name	First RED product launched	RED product range	Markets where available (as of December 2007)	Price range	Proportion of sales/profits donated	Further info	RED logo
AmEx	March 2006	American Express RED card	UK only	Typical 16.9% APR variable	1% of all money spent with the card	RED deals: cardholders get 50% discount at a Jermyn Street tailor, extra services at Hyatt hotels, 10% off at Jamie Oliver's restaurant in London, etc.	
Apple	October 2006	Special Edition (PRODUCT)RED iPod Nano and iPod Shuffle; iTunes gift cards	United States, UK, Canada, and Japan; elsewhere via online Apple stores	iPod Shuffle: $49; iPod Nano $199; iTunes gift card: from $25	Gift card: 10% of $25; iPod: not known		
Armani	April 2006	Emporio Armani (PRODUCT) RED: perfume, sunglasses, clothing, watches, accessories	In all Emporio Armani stores worldwide	$58–225	Average 40% of its gross profit margin; in 2006, it donated €400,000 ($500,000), raised through RED sales, to the Global Fund	Armani was the guest editor of a special RED issue of *The Independent*; "In developing his collection, Giorgio Armani collaborated with Ghanaian contemporary artist Owusu-Ankomah"	
Converse/Nike	April 2006	Converse (PRODUCT) RED Chuck Taylor All Star African mudcloth shoe; Converse (PRODUCT) RED collection	United States, UK; also at select Gap stores; available from online store and shipping to 29 countries	$67–75	15% of net retail price or 10% of net wholesale price, depending on the model	Runs a customization platform called MAKE MINE RED, where consumers can design their own Converse (RED) shoes	

Gap	March 2006	(PRODUCT)RED t-shirts, hoodies, jeans, tote bags, other accessories; also has kids and baby line	Online in the United States; at Gap stores in United States, Canada, UK, France, and Japan	$5–200	50% of profit	Gap spent $7.8 million on RED advertising during the fourth quarter of 2006; One t-shirt from the collection manufactured in Lesotho	
Hallmark	October 2007	(PRODUCT)RED flower bouquets of African roses, boxed holiday cards, photo cards; e-cards, wrapping papers, stationary; gift book	Online in the United States; at Gold Crown stores in the United States and Canada	$13–14 for boxed cards; $50 for bouquets	8% of net wholesale sales	Ran a PRODUCT(RED) greeting card design competition (January 2008)	
Motorola	May 2006	RED MOTORAZR, MOTOKRZR, and MOTOSLVR phones, BlueTooth headset, other accessories	United States, UK, Canada, Singapore, Malaysia, Australia, Switzerland, Japan, Portugal, Denmark	United States: The phone costs $269.99 without service and $29.99 with a two-year service plan, which costs around $30/month. Additionally, the phone is often free with the purchase of a two-year service plan; headset costs $69.99; UK: phone costs £150	United States: contribution by both Motorola and the operator is $8.50 per handset sold; UK: Motorola and the network operator contribute £5 each; the operator also contributes 5% of the customer's monthly bill	Studio RED: offers exclusive content, including limited edition wallpaper, ring tones, and video	

Involvement in RED by selected companies. Data obtained from corporate reports, Web sites, and other publicly available materials; details available from the authors.

Cause-related marketing campaigns do not always detail the specifics of their agreement to support the recipient organizations. In fact, it has also been documented that "some CRM campaigns rely on consumer misunderstanding about the donations" (Berglind and Nakata 2005, 450). In RED, the proportional contribution of sales/profits varies dramatically, with almost each company defining its help in a different way. For the AmEx card, the contribution to the Global Fund is 1 percent of money spent with the card. Gap and Armani contribute a portion of net profits (50 percent for the former, and an average 40 percent for the latter). Converse and Hallmark contribute a portion of retail or wholesale price. Motorola prefers set-amount contributions (depending on the end-market and model) plus a percentage of the customer's monthly bill (paid by the phone operator, only in the UK). Apple does not release what portion it donates from sales of RED iPods but states that 10 percent of the iTunes RED gift card is given to the Global Fund.

The only company from which the authors were able to get information on RED product sales and the amount contributed to the Global Fund is Armani. Our correspondence with Armani's press office reveals that, in 2006, Emporio Armani sold 44,000 RED sunglasses, 2,700 RED watches, and 70,000 RED ready-to-wear clothing items and leather accessories. In 2006, sales from RED products netted €5 million in sales ($6.3 million), out of which €400,000 ($500,000) was given to the Global Fund (equal to 8 percent of retail sales value). Armani's press office also clarified that all suppliers involved in RED production are based in Italy. The only other piece of information on Global Fund donations is its total size ($160 million as of December 2010). At the same time, Gap is reported to have spent $7.8 million on RED advertising during the fourth quarter of 2006 alone. RED headquarters has refused to provide a breakdown of contributions by company. Similarly, other companies have refused to divulge volume and value of sales of RED products (in stark contrast to calls for transparency and "responsibility").

But the (RED) Auction that took place in February 2008, organized by Damien Hirst (at Bono's request) and involving sixty other artists, may suggest that the benefits of RED's activities are located most heavily in building brand image and less in the actual boosting of sales of individual RED products. Thus, in the form of traditional corporate philanthropy, the pieces of art were donated by the artists (contrary to the RED rules for companies, which do not allow them to donate all profit to the Global Fund).[31] It raised over $42 million in one day (Valentine's Day 2008), compared to $60 million for almost two years of sales of RED products until then. The Sotheby's art auction provided a bump in the media profile of its curator, Damien Hirst, who was featured on mainstream television daily shows in the United States and the UK, and pushed RED contributions up to their target of $100 million. It appears to be much easier to raise large amounts of money in one lump sum from powerful corporations or foundations directly (the Gates Foundation has given $650 million so far). Also, as we have seen in chapter 3, however successful the RED campaign is in meeting its own goals for providing support, the Global Fund remains predominately an institution that exists because of public, not private, support. Public contributions (actually paid, not just pledges) to the Fund amounted to $18.2 billion as of December 2010, while private contributions amounted to $947 million, or 5.2 percent of total contributions. RED contributions amounted to $160 million at that time, $60 million more than in February 2008, suggesting only a limited level of slowdown given the onset of the financial crisis in late 2008.[32]

DISENGAGED AND DISTANT CSR

What does RED mean for the companies that are involved in Bono's initiative vis-à-vis their general CSR profile? And what does RED mean for CSR itself and the role of business in society more generally? In this chapter, we have shown that RED is a disengaged form of CSR—completely separated, with some exceptions, from the operations in which these corporations are involved. RED does not attempt to change or improve the normal functioning of business and trade. At the same time, RED's beneficiaries are distant—Africa, AIDS victims—constructed as "over there" and not likely to be part of the RED companies' core consumer group. This is important for the relations of Brand Aid that we discussed in chapter 2.

Some of these companies, as we have seen earlier in this chapter, are indeed involved in engaged CSR. Yet all have a low level of involvement with Africa in their day-to-day operations, thus their RED activities constitute what we call "distant CSR." American Express, Apple, Converse, Armani, and Hallmark have none of their production or procurement in Africa—and their final consumption markets in Africa are minimal. Motorola's sales in Africa are growing, but they are still small when compared to its markets elsewhere. Although no production of the components of mobile phones is done in Africa, Motorola has started some assembly operations in Nigeria. Gap has the clearest link to Africa, as it procures some of its clothing from contract manufacturers in Kenya, Lesotho, Madagascar, Mauritius, and South Africa.

Even when RED is factored in these operations, the picture does not change much: Gap manufactures one of its t-shirts in Lesotho (made of organic African cotton); Hallmark sells bunches of African RED roses (presumably from Kenya, the main African supplier of cut flowers); and Motorola started assembling some of its RED phones in Nigeria.[33] Even within this limited supply and manufacturing base, no explicit attempt is made through RED to implement better work, social, or environmental conditions of production. In other words, RED is focused on the welfare of Africans with AIDS in selected countries, not of workers in factories producing RED products.

At the same time, RED differs from traditional forms of cause-related marketing in a number of important ways. First, it is based on co-branding rather than on enhancing the visibility of one brand alone—RED provides the "umbrella" brand under which the other brands are embedded. Second, the RED brand is built around the notion of continuity, ongoing support, and the buzzword popular in the international development arena, "sustainability." This is in direct contrast to the cause-related marketing strategy of time-limited impact. "The idea is to make an impact, not to become just another accepted but ignored addition to the marketing clutter out there. Every promotion should have a clearly defined point of closure" (Welsh 1999, 2).

Third, the RED brand links corporations with seemingly diverse business and CSR profiles. Finally, RED seeks to support a social cause that is removed from the everyday lives of most of its consumers. Product RED turns cause-related marketing into the vector of saving distant others.

Bono explicitly distinguishes RED from philanthropy, stating that "philanthropy is like hippy music, holding hands. RED is more like punk rock, hip hop, this should feel like hard commerce."[34] Yet RED as a form of "distant and disengaged CSR" resembles an older form of societal engagement—corporate philanthropy—but one with a direct link to and clear dependence on increasing profit. Thus, RED can be understood as a force that could also constrict the meaning of CSR. RED pushes CSR back toward the disengagement that characterized the "old-style" philanthropy it is framed against—but with a new funding mechanism based on consumption and co-branding.

But from another perspective, RED differs considerably from corporate philanthropy as well. In traditional philanthropy, the act of giving is formally independent from the act of profit accumulation: "normal business practice" leads to profits, and accumulation of profits, assets, and capital is used ex-post for purposes that have little to do with the operations in which the company is involved. In RED, on the other hand, companies use "doing good" to sell a particular set of products—profit is generated and donation is given at one and the same time. The additional twist is that "giving" is channeled through a reputable international agency (the Global Fund) to engage business in the fight against AIDS. This adds an additional layer of legitimacy, and distance. If it were "engaged CSR," we would find pharmaceutical companies as RED "partners" providing ARV drugs on highly concessional terms.

In this chapter, we have shown that RED is a manifestation of CSR that does not question the core objective of profit maximization. RED improves a company's brand without challenging any of its actual operations and practices, and increases its value and perception. For these companies, RED achieves a double capitalization: capitalization via sales and profit; and capitalization via improvement of brand image, another asset. The ( )^{RED} embrace that envelops the logos of these seven companies is itself a good investment. As brand equity has come to incorporate ethical values and reputation, and as brands are increasingly more about lifestyles than products themselves, the actual sales figures and coverage of RED products are less important than the media attention that they generate. As RED and initiatives like it gain ground as legitimate CSR, the products and the circumstances of their production and exchange are swept aside in the haste of emergency.

(5) DOING GOOD BY SHOPPING WELL
The Rise of "Causumer" Culture

Corporate giving, powered by consumption of branded products, takes center stage in RED. The credibility mechanism put in place by RED is quite different from the one that emerged, in the last two decades, through certification systems and labels on social, economic, and environmental sustainability. These now popular certifications, standards, and codes of conduct are based on bureaucratized, systemic, and detail-oriented third-party verified procedures. RED, on the contrary, relies on aid celebrity verification processes, a personal charismatic guarantee. While charismatic guarantee assures consumers of the positive impact of buying RED products, the brands under the RED umbrella guarantee quality and design. Those brands that achieve iconic status (Holt 2004) can even promote a brand profile that builds more on culture than on the product itself.

Both celebrity and brand can transmit trust in essentialist, shortcut ways, without getting consumers lost in detail. Although labels are also simplification devices, with RED, consumers can become "causumers" (shoppers that seek to make the world a better place) without knowing much about the social and environmental relations behind the products on offer; they do so just by knowing more about the people they help by buying RED products. RED products ride on the double guarantee that they are "good" both for consumers and for recipients of help. The RED brand achieves iconic status as it enacts the myth of "just capitalism." Within "causumerism," the use of AIDS treatment as a totem of signification stimulates "compassionate consumption" and detached action, rather than "conscious consumption."

Causumerism (shopping for a better world, effecting change through the marketplace) is the other side of the coin of the cause-related marketing campaigns we highlighted in chapter 4. The term seems to have been first coined by Ben Davis, cofounder of "buylesscrap,"[1] a Web site critical of the RED campaign that promotes direct donations to the Global Fund in place of purchasing RED products.[2] But other terms have been used in the literature, such as political and/or ethical consumerism, essentially to denote the same phenomenon.[3] Holtzer (2006), for example, highlights how political consumerism is the collectivization of private consumption choices, guided by a "social movement." Individual consumers "lend" their purchasing power to social movements to enable them to effectively voice their concerns and leverage positive or negative sanctions.

Our focus in this chapter is on the "Western consumer" and his/her approach to brands and "good causes," not because we think consumers in the South are not important, but because RED explicitly targets consumers in wealthy societies. No RED products are available for sale in Africa at the time of writing. We neither seek to glorify nor to vilify consumer culture (the culture of consumption) or causumer culture (doing good through shopping) in this chapter. We do not seek to adjudicate how much power consumers have overall, or how reflexive they are. We observe the processes of enrollment that celebrities perform in linking branded consumption to aid for AIDS in Africa, and argue that by placing priority on disease, RED obscures the social and environmental relations that underpin the production and trade of the goods that are sold under its umbrella.

In the previous chapter, we have argued that RED is a form of corporate social responsibility (CSR) that solves the problems of distant others. RED does not address the day-to-day business practices of RED companies, or the social and environmental impact of their operations. This process, first highlighted by Marx as "commodity fetishism," has been used repeatedly in the literature to show how companies conceal labor abuse and environmental damage. What is new in our use of the term is that RED commodity fetishism conjoins consumption and giving through celebrity mediation and iconic branding. The masking of social relations behind the production of RED products is paired with showing off another set of social relations, in which Western causumers save the lives of African AIDS patients.

CONSUMPTION

The material and cultural aspects of consumption, the role and limitations of consumer activism, and consumption politics have been the focus of a large body of literature over the last two decades. The classic critiques of conspicuous consumption date back to the early twentieth century (Simmel 1930; Veblen 1912). Rather than providing a detailed review of the large consumption literature in this chapter (for such reviews see, among others, Aldridge 2003; Fine 2002; Trentmann 2006), we briefly highlight some broad tendencies and focus on how commodity fetishism, via celebrity mediation and branding, successfully marries branded consumption and giving.

Characterizations of consumers in the literature vary according to how much power is placed on consumer agency and how material or symbolic the act of consumption is thought to be. In very simplified terms, both rational choice models based on *homo economicus* and much of the contemporary cultural/symbolic approaches to consumption see consumers as empowered and dominant actors. The Frankfurt school of sociology (see, among others, Adorno 1991; Marcuse 1973 [1969]) and political-economy/regulation approaches (see, among others, Marsden, Flynn, and Harrison 2000; Trentmann 2006; Wrigley and Lowe 2002) have portrayed consumers as dominated—either through subtle manipulation (Finkelstein 1989) or sheer retail and advertising power. Similarly, Bourdieu (1976) posits that consumption behavior is an expression of class position and that consumer choice and agency are severely limited by habitus—the set of appropriate tastes that are learned within a specific class culture. Extreme postmodernist positions have moved beyond the issue of agency and see consumption as entirely symbolic (Baudrillard 1998). Other postmoderns see society as a "spectacle" where everything and everybody can be objectified and commodified, including all forms of contestation; the spectacle unfolds without meaningful participation, activity, or involvement (Debord 1967).

Condemning accounts of consumption still abound in the literature—from critiques of commodity culture as "debasing" (Featherstone 1991) and of consumerism as the "economics of deception" (Bauman 2005), to accounts of the so-called processes of McDonaldization (Ritzer 1996) and Disneyization (Bryman 1999). But much of the recent consumption literature has underlined the reflexivity and multiple identities of consumers (Gabriel and Lang 1995), the complexity of acts of consumption, consumer politics, and consumer agency (Fine 2002; Miller 2001; Warde 1997), and the tensions between consumption and citizenship (Aldridge 2003).

Causumerism relies on changing behavior of consumers, so it is important to examine how existing scholarship on consumption interprets *change* in consumer behavior. Warde (1997) highlights four main interpretations. A first is that diversity in consumer behavior has increased as a result of the decreasing constraints deriving from social group approval (Beck 1992). From this point of view, the consumer is seen as a "hero" engaging in "a conscious project of autonomous, reflexive self-creation" (Warde 1997, 15). As stated by Featherstone, "the new heroes of consumer culture make lifestyle a life project and display their individuality and sense of style in the particularity of the assemblage of goods, clothes, practices, experiences, appearance and bodily dispositions they design together into a lifestyle" (1987; cited in Warde 1997, 15).

A second interpretation of changing consumer behavior is that the disembedding from traditional social networks does not lead to individualization and the total disappearance of regulation, but to more specialized and small-group (neotribe) formation (Bauman 1991). These are groups where "people are intensely, if temporarily, attached to each other by means of shared self-images. . . . Lifestyle groups proliferate, visible through their differences, but not grounded in a social or material substratum" (Warde 1997, 16).

A third interpretation is that uniformity and apathy characterize the sphere of consumption. Mass culture feeds uniform and soothing cultural products to consumers who accept them passively in private (Adorno 1991; Ritzer 1996). This leads to greater conformity of consumer behavior, not individualization as in the first interpretation above. A fourth interpretation, according to Warde, is that consumer practices are in fact increasingly differentiated along structured social principles, such as class, ethnicity, or nation (Bourdieu 1976).

Our own take on the consumption debates for Brand Aid is that consumers are neither duped nor completely in control of their agency. Following Slater's (1997) characterization of contemporary consumption, we argue that consumer culture is neither just a consumption of signs nor just a reflection of an existing social order. Consumer culture is a site of contestation playing out in three fields, as Slater elaborates.

First, it is a struggle over social (and cultural) arrangements that underpin the mobilization of material resources. Thus, for us, it is important to examine how access to the objects of consumption is regulated and what specific productive arrangements, technologies, and labor relations underpin the provision of goods (as we discussed in chapter 4) (see also Fine 2002). Second, consumption "animates public and social systems of signs, not necessarily in the sense of public display [as in "conspicuous consumption"] . . . but more fundamentally through the process of cultural reproduction. . . . As consumption has become an ever more central means of enacting our citizenship of the social world, struggles over the power to dispose of material, financial and symbolic . . . resources have become central to the cultural reproduction of the everyday world" (Slater 1997, 4–5). Third, struggle plays out over ethical questions, "the scale, nature and social ordering of consumption . . . [that underpins the] social, moral or religious regulation of the self" (ibid., 5).

The case study of RED confirms the characterization that consumer culture is a culture *of* consumption, where the values of society are organized through and derive from consumption. It is a culture portraying freedom of choice and consumer sovereignty, and a culture of needs that are in principle unlimited and insatiable. Furthermore, in contemporary consumer culture, values expressed through consumption spill over to other areas of social action such as health provision or, as in RED, the financing of giving (see Slater 1997, 24–25). As the value of goods depends increasingly more on their "sign" than on their functional or economic value, advertising, marketing, and branding become central functions on their own, not subordinate to production. In the Global North at least, material satisfaction is increasingly subordinate to the consumption of culture, signs, representations, services, and "experiences" (ibid., 32).

RED AND "CAUSUMER" CULTURE

The consumption of signs and experiences can be the vehicle for the mobilization of "meaning," political action, and belonging to a "community." Citizen-consumers are increasingly seen as exercising their rights to demand social and environmental change via individual acts of "conscious consumption"—backed up by systems of certification, labeling, and codes of conduct (Klooster 2005; Ponte 2008). In this operating environment, citizen-consumers are portrayed as ever more informed, reflexive, active, sometimes socially and environmentally conscious, and empowered to make a difference with their purchasing power (Trentmann 2006). This is a far cry from the duped and victim consumer depictions presented earlier in this chapter. But while consumer agency may take the form of collective action through campaigns and consumer organizations' pressure, in RED the focus is on the individual act of consumption. Depictions of RED consumers as fashion conscious yet actively engaged, reflexive, and therefore INSPI(RED) are part and parcel of this trend.

The engagement of consumers may go beyond their responsiveness to received information about the products upon which they will make a shopping decision. They are increasingly involved in product formulation and customization as well. The Converse (RED) series of sneakers, for example, can be customized by consumers with a wide array of designs of both shoe and canvas through a platform called "Make Mine (RED)."[4] On the Converse Web site, consumers are invited to "Pick a Shoe. Make it Yours" in which a series of choices from shoe type, style, and material are all up to the consumer's click. On the introductory Web page, together with the choice of diverse shoelace colors, consumers can click a link labeled "You like shoes, you buy them, you help people."

But this involvement can be far less empowering than it appears to be. Banet-Weiser and Lapsansky show how RED delimits the space for consumer participation and how it "has appropriated the language of social action and rebellion, and mixed it with a neo-liberal economic model of consumption in a way that... strengthens the pillars of... consumer culture on which it is premised" (2008, 1254).

More generally, Callon, Méadel, and Rabeharisoa (2002) have suggested that one of the main concerns of business is to prompt consumers to question their preferences and, indirectly, their identities. What Callon and colleagues define as an "economy of qualities" is based on the "formatting of socio-technical devices which, distributing and redistributing the material bases of cognition, format the bases of calculation and preferences" (ibid., 213). Business is increasingly trying to steer so-called spontaneous and gradual processes of qualification and requalification of products to their advantage. They do so, inter alia, by setting up and steering forms of organization promoting collaboration between suppliers and consumers in the qualification of products.[5] In this way, competition is shifted from price to "the attachment of consumers to products whose qualities have progressively been defined with their active participation" (ibid., 212; see also DuPuis 2000).

In RED, "causumer culture" is mobilized by celebrities and rests on the engagement of discourses of transparency, consumer participation, and the creation of an image of social movement-cum-brand community. But, as argued in chapter 4, there is no transparency on the social and environmental relations that underpin the production and trade of RED products. In RED, transparency is restricted to the constructed "impact" of purchase—the number of doses that will be provided to AIDS patients and the number of people "saved." In some cases, impact becomes the totem worn by the causumer: the Gap's RED "two-week" t-shirt indicates that its purchase enables the provision of two weeks of antiretroviral (ARV) medication (Sarna-Wojcicki 2008). Lost is the irony that two weeks are indeed a very short time. It would take the purchase of twenty-seven t-shirts to ensure the survival of one AIDS patient for only one year. It would take many more to provide the necessary drugs every day for the rest of that patient's life.

The "brand community" is created via blogging on the RED Web site and in networking sites such as MySpace and Facebook and perhaps meeting at (RED) Nights concerts in places like Carnegie Hall in New York.[6] It is a community of Western causumers, whose voice is "limited by what items and ideas the brand puts on the market, such that the agency of choice can only operate in a narrow sense" (Sarna-Wojcicki 2008, 15). "The formation of the brand community of (RED) relies on a set boundary that does not arise organically, but rather is shaped in marketing and produced by consumers' definition of self against a dialectical other" (ibid., 27). There is no African agency in RED causumerism beyond the representations of needy Africans in pictures (see chapter 2).

We argue that it is important to analyze the interplay between cultural forms of causumerism and their material links. The previous descriptions of RED's consumer-based customization, participation in the design of products, and the creation of brand communities can be understood as extensions of the trend toward product differentiation that came alongside the general passage from a Fordist to a post-Fordist organization of capitalism. These two different overarching organizational forms are based on distinct social contracts. Fordism characterized a system of large-scale production of undifferentiated products for mass consumption that lasted from the early twentieth century to the 1970s (Aglietta 1979). Fordism was associated with economies of scale, technologically inflexible factories, firms with high degrees of functional specialization, and large concentrations of semiskilled labor. The regulation of such a system was based on national collective bargaining agreements between labor, business, and the state. In exchange for maintaining labor discipline for business, unions obtained rising wages that in turn stimulated consumption and provided demand for the goods produced. Government obtained full employment and relative political and industrial peace.

By contrast, the term post-Fordism has been used to designate a post-1970s system of batch production of differentiated products for niche markets, smaller but more technologically versatile factories, and firms with competence in design, marketing, and branding and with higher- and more multi-skilled labor. Marketing, instead of reaching the mass consumer, disaggregates consumption into life-styles and market segments, not defined by broad demographics but by cultural meanings (including "political participation"). In post-Fordist times, the immaterial value of a product surpasses its material worth. Arvidsson describes how brands must change radically in the post-Fordist context to create valuable immaterial resources or "buzz": "Since mass intellectuality cannot be directly commanded, you cannot order someone to be 'creative,' 'cool,' or even sympathetic to your cause, management instead must proceed by designing particular kinds of affective environments, or 'platforms' where these effects are likely to arise spontaneously" (2007, 16–17). Culturally constituted lifestyle categories based on consumption replace, or increasingly displace, forms of association based on work or citizenship (Slater 1997, 191–92). The state retrenches into deregulation rather than being directly involved in negotiations between the parties. Thus, the state only provides a form of external guarantee while NGOs and corporations are left to hammer out the social contract(s). Causumerism and civil society engagement by individuals increasingly replace organized political action. In the case of RED, the social contract between consumers and corporations is mediated by the celebrity in the name of receiving Africans. The celebrity substitutes the state as the external guarantor of welfare, a new form of the social contract that underpins Brand Aid.

ETHICAL TRADE: SUSTAINABILITY LABELS AND CERTIFICATIONS

RED is far from the only initiative trying to canvass causumer culture. For this reason, in this section we place RED against the background of the evolution of selected labels and certifications that attempt to improve the social, economic, and environmental impacts of production and trade of specific commodities, also known collectively as "ethical" or "sustainable" trade.

"Sustainability" labels and certifications are available for a large range of products available to Western consumers. They allow consumers to choose products that are putatively "better" for the environment, trade relations, producers, or workers. Via a label or logo placed on the product, consumers can identify which products have such characteristics and thus promote sustainability or ethical trade via a market-based (rather than regulation-based) mechanism. A survey and discussion of the range of sustainability labels and certifications is out of place here. However, there are several lessons to be drawn from specific experiences that have implications for RED.

In the realm of food and agriculture, in the last two decades or so, more awareness of the socioeconomic plight of developing country farmers, increased interest in the health and safety of food, and recognition that expansion of agricultural and fishing "frontiers" constitutes the greatest threat to global biodiversity have popularized several sustainability initiatives. As a result, these initiatives have enjoyed a much greater recognition and a fast-growing market value. The concept of sustainability in agriculture usually refers to aspects variously referred to as "economic viability for farmers" (or wage earners), "environmental conservation," and "social responsibility." Both existing and emerging labels and certification systems seek to meet some or all of these needs (Giovannucci and Ponte 2005).

The example of coffee is particularly instructive as it was one of the first internationally traded products where collective efforts were undertaken to develop standards and labels on processes that address socioeconomic and environmental concerns. By developing "sustainability" labels, social and environmental movements (later on in collaboration with industry) were able to give consumers the possibility of making informed choices that directly influenced the way coffee was grown and traded. Labels, in other words, helped turn consumers into causumers. While such initiatives started as niche marketing in the late 1980s, they have now moved into the mainstream as well. Some sustainable coffees are sold as certified coffee, such as Organic, Fair Trade, Bird-Friendly, Rainforest Alliance–certified, and Utz-certifed "Good Inside." Others are sold under initiatives that are designed by private companies, with or without third-party monitoring and verification. The largest private initiative with third-party monitoring is Starbuck's Coffee and Farmer Equity (C.A.F.E.) practices. Certified sustainable coffees (including Starbuck's C.A.F.E.) represented only 1 percent of total coffee trade in 2003. In 2006, they had jumped to 4 percent of global coffee exports by volume and nearly 8 percent of North American imports (Giovannucci, Liu, and Byers 2008). By 2007, sustainable coffees reached 5.5 percent of total exports by volume.[7]

Two points relevant to Brand Aid should be kept in mind here: first, what started as niche marketing (like RED) can become mainstream in a relatively short time; and second, the performance of different initiatives in terms of delivering to their beneficiaries is quite different. It is indeed possible to do good via causumerism, but the spread and depth of "good" varies, as well as the power relations between giver and taker. Taking coffee as a case study, for example, several studies have shown that traders, roasters, and retailers engaged in the global coffee market earn higher margins on sustainable coffees than on regular coffees (Daviron and Ponte 2005; Giovannucci, Liu, and Byers 2008). This suggests that there is a business case for ethical trade. However, the price premiums paid to beneficiary farmers vary considerably, with fair trade paying the highest premium at times of low international prices (such as during the coffee crisis of 1999–2003), followed by organics. Some supposedly ethical initiatives provide no guarantee of a price premium to farmers, yet the farmers may benefit nonetheless. Some of the most significant benefits of sustainability certifications may be indirect. For example, fair trade involvement usually improves local community organizations and their networks. In matching requirements such as traceability and process-management standards, farmers prepare to meet the demands of modern agricultural export trade. Finally, certification processes may also have spill-over effects on adjacent communities (Giovannucci and Ponte 2005).

In short, with the right dynamics, the efforts needed to meet sustainability standards required by ethical trade initiatives can create a virtuous circle of empowerment and organizational strengthening among beneficiaries. But in other cases, farmer organizations find it difficult to maintain cohesion if the expected benefits do not materialize in the short term. For many producers, the hidden costs of marketing, coordination (e.g., time spent in meetings, transport), uncertainty, and the limitations of collective action may significantly decrease the overall net benefits of certification efforts and threaten the existing governance structures in cooperatives or associations (ibid.). In other words, the world is messy—and no ready-made RED impact calculator is available for any of these initiatives.

More broadly, "sustainability" labels and certifications for food required for ethical trade include some beneficiaries and exclude others, and the costs and benefits of inclusion vary.[8] Sustainability certifications can indeed marginalize smaller producers and producers in poorer countries (Daviron and Ponte 2005; Klooster 2005; Morris and Dunne 2004; Muradian and Pelupessy 2005; Pattberg 2006; Ponte 2008; Taylor 2005) even though they were designed with the best intentions. The divergent performance of sustainability initiatives has an important historical dimension as well, which is particularly relevant to RED and other forms of Brand Aid. In an analysis of fish, timber, and coffee sustainability initiatives carried out elsewhere, one of the authors (Ponte 2008) showed how "old wave" initiatives (established before 1990) such as organics and fair trade are the only ones paying regular and predictable premiums to producers, and are the only ones where certification costs are not fully paid by producers in Third World countries (see the following chart).[9] Old initiatives tend to be more radical in their objectives: for example, fair trade attempts to address some of the inequalities that are built within the trading system itself, and the organic movement questions the nature of an industrial approach to agriculture. In both cases, however, these "radical" challenges seem to be on the wane in the name of commercial success (Guthman 2002; Raynolds 2004; Raynolds, Murray, and Taylor 2004; Mutersbaugh 2005; for a dissenting view, see Gibbon 2008).

But in "new wave" initiatives, the imperative of commercial success has been "built in" from the beginning. This commercial drift is shown clearly in the Forest Stewardship Council (FSC) certification for sustainable timber. Klooster (2005) argues that large buyers, such as IKEA and Home Depot, demand not only certification from their suppliers, but also high volumes, uniform characteristics, and a competitive price (see also Morris and Dunne 2004). "These commercial

Product	Certifications and labels	Old wave/new wave (O/N)	Corporate involvement in formulation?	Stakeholder-driven?	Regular and predictable premium paid to the producer?	Producers bear cost of certification?	Special flexibilities for small-scale producers?
Coffee	Fair trade	O	N	Y/N	Y	Y/N	Y
	Organics	O	N	Y	Y	Y/N	Y
	Utz Kapeh	N	Y	N	N	Y	N
	Rainforest Alliance	N	N	N	Y/N	Y	N
	Bird-friendly	N	N	N	Y/N	Y	N
Timber	FSC	N	Y	Y	N	Y	Y
Fish	MSC	N	Y	N	N	Y	N

Sustainability certifications in coffee, timber, and fish. Regarding fair trade coffee, FLO recently started to charge cooperatives for certification, with reduced fees for very small producer organizations. For organic coffees, many organic certification schemes are subsidized either by governments or aid agencies. Adapted from Ponte (2008).

values condition the ability of other actors to fully realize the social and environmental values of environmental certification of forests" (Klooster 2005, 404). Similarly, in the case of sustainability certification of fisheries, the commercial imperatives of certifying large fisheries under the Marine Stewardship Council (MSC) label trumped the environmental protection objectives (Ponte 2008).

It is important to compare different kinds of ethical initiatives to understand how the standards for "who benefits" may shift. In "new wave" initiatives (started in the 1990s and beyond), it is mainly a "preferred supplier" status that retailers and importers offer to certified suppliers. In no case where corporate involvement was heavy at the time of formulating a labeling initiative is a premium paid to producers on a regular and predictable basis. In time, the standards that underpin "new wave" initiatives may actually become the new minimum standards for mainstream products as well, effectively redesigning the nature of market access. This has already happened to food safety and good agricultural practice (GAP) standards in fresh fruit and vegetables (Hanataka, Bain, and Busch 2005; World Bank 2005). If a standard becomes the de facto purchasing criterion, then most farmers will have to comply with it and incur the related costs. Furthermore, as these criteria become a widely accepted standard, there may be growing unwillingness amongst buyers to pay extra for such achievements—leaving farmers with higher costs of production and no direct financial incentive.

RED can be seen as an extension of the trend illustrated here— one signaling less concern with the beneficiaries of sustainability initiatives and more concern with commercial imperatives. The radical difference with RED is that in order to do good it has severed the link with producers (or workers) completely. The problem with the product (e.g., low prices paid to producers) is substituted with the problem with the people who benefit from RED profits (women and children with AIDS).

In addition to this, in RED, third-party certification against a set of (more or less) negotiated standards is substituted by celebrity validation and brand assurance of "quality." All is served in simple terms on the plate of consumers, who do not have to sacrifice anything to achieve the good of others. While some labeling initiatives do leave space for NGOs and consumer organizations to engage with standard setting and revision via civil society groups, in RED, participation is limited to shopping (and to some extent blogging or concert-going). Sustainability certifications and labels have had a mixed record, as we have elaborated here, in delivering to their putative beneficiaries. But at the very least, the beneficiaries of better economic returns and/or positive social or environmental dynamics have an active role in the process—they produce, process, and trade such commodities. In RED, beneficiaries are passive recipients, in line with old-style paternalist charity, not the workers of the factories that produce RED t-shirts and mobile phones.

BRANDING AND VULNERABILITY

As we have seen so far, much of the success of causumerism is based on the visibility and wide recognition of labels that tell the consumer how a good or service has been produced or traded, and on the increased importance of consuming signs and experiences. Branding is essential for causumerism and for ethical trade at the global scale. Causumerism targets mainly branded products because it is on the basis of the vulnerability of brands to negative media exposure that consumer action is possible. After a brief discussion of branding and brand vulnerability, we examine how RED, as both an iconic and an umbrella brand, can help RED companies manage brand vulnerability.

Branding is about leaving "an indelible mark in . . . the corner of a 'consumer's mind'" (Conroy 2007, 6). A brand is a promise to deliver satisfaction and quality. It is a collection of perceptions in the mind of the consumer. "The brand tells us first about the standard qualities of a product: how well it will work and how long it will last. . . . The purpose of branding is to create a name or symbol that consumers associate positively with products and services." Major brands have some common characteristics: they are visually distinctive, create an "indelible impression" on consumers that allows them to "shop with confidence," and carry with them "underlying appeals," embedding specific lifestyles and values (ibid., 7).

"In companies with powerful brands, the brand and the business are all bound up together.... [The brand] shapes the idea of what the company is, at its core.... [The] more bound up the brand and the business are, the harder they are for rivals to emulate,"[10] to the point that corporations are now referring to brands as distinct from products, not simply as the marks of products (Arvidsson 2007). But brands are not only important for corporate management, to foster innovation, and to rally employee loyalty. They are also enormously valuable on their own. Interbrand's ranking, "100 Most Valuable Brands," in 2008 estimates the value of the Coca-Cola brand, the most valuable, at $66.7 billion.[11] The market capitalization value of the Coca-Cola company at the end of the period considered in the Interbrand study (June 2007–June 2008) was $117 billion. This means that the brand itself was worth 57 percent of Coca-Cola's market value at that time. This is not uncommon—almost one quarter of companies ranked in the top one hundred had a brand value that constituted more than 40 percent of market value in 2005 (Conroy 2007, 7). Brand value is not only built on estimates of sales, but also incorporates estimates of the attention, buzz, loyalty, and social standing that the brand can generate, what Arvidsson calls "the affective and relational complexes that arise as commodities circulate in the social" (2007, 15).

What about the brands sitting under the RED umbrella? According to the 2008 Interbrand report, four of the seven RED brands make it to the top one hundred:[12] Apple ranks twenty-fourth with a brand value of $13.7 billion (and a market capitalization value of $55.4 billion as of June 2008); Nike/Converse is twenty-ninth (with a brand value of $12.7 billion and market cap of $28.8 billion); Gap is seventy-seventh (brand value $4.4 billion and market cap $11.7 billion); and Armani ninety-fourth (brand value $3.5 billion, no market cap because it is a private company).[13]

But as brands can become valuable assets when they are recognized widely, they can also turn into liabilities when they are linked to negative characteristics of products or production processes. Because brands represent a substantial portion of market capitalization of major corporations, they need to be managed carefully. Brand management is then about organizing relations between the brand

and its customers; it is about "managing the affective dimension of social interaction, making sure that a desired modality of interacting and relating arises" (Arvidsson 2007, 10). This includes the way a brand's image, as a set of symbolic meanings and affective relations, is portrayed in the media.

Perhaps, ironically given the "no logo" (Klein 2000) calls from the antiglobalization movement, it is brands that lie at the heart of ethical trade initiatives. Ethical trade can be one way that corporations attempt to build up their brand value. According to Conroy (2007), brand vulnerability to possible negative repercussions on stock market value is what made the birth of a large number of codes of conduct, labels, and certification systems possible in the last two decades. Conroy argues that, as a result of this "revolution," corporations are changing their practices substantially. At the same time, some industries (e.g., timber) are more advanced than others (e.g., mining) and some companies react to immediate exposure without building a long-term commitment to "ethical" practices (ibid.). Negative exposure in the media can tarnish a hard-built ethical profile of a brand. Moreover, reactive measures that aim at addressing the problems at the root of such exposure do not necessarily restore such reputation. The story of Starbucks (one of the companies that joined RED in 2008) is one example of how this can happen.

CAN RED SAVE STARBUCKS FROM THE AFRICANS?

Since 2002, Starbucks has been running what is now the largest sustainability initiative in the coffee industry. Its C.A.F.E. practices are third-party certified and in 2007 covered 102,000 tons of coffee that the company purchased, 9,000 more tons than the second largest volume of certified coffee (organic), and 42,000 more than the third (fair trade).

In 2004, the intellectual property rights (IPR) office of Ethiopia, with NGO support, started to explore ways in which Ethiopia could benefit from the rights for high-quality coffees originating from the regions of Harrar, Sidamo, and Yrgacheffe. A decision was made to apply for the registration of these coffee names as trademarks in various countries. Registering a name as trademark means that coffee retailers, in order to use a trademarked name, would have to obtain a licensing agreement and pay a licensing fee to the Ethiopian IPR office. If managed properly, these funds could have been either channeled to the producers of these coffees or used for community or coffee-related projects. Applications were successful in the European Union, Canada, and (partly) Japan. However, in the United States the process became more complicated because Starbucks had already registered two of the Ethiopian coffee names for itself and was using them on retail packages. In 2005, the Ethiopian embassy in the United States contacted Starbucks offering an amicable solution to this potential conflict. It received no response from Starbucks. Oxfam was then brought in to mediate between the two parties. In February 2006, Ethiopia asked Starbucks to forego their trademark rights and offered in exchange a free licensing agreement—this meant that Starbucks would not have to pay any royalties to the Ethiopians.

But Starbucks refused to sign the agreement and mobilized the National Coffee Association (NCA) of the United States to file a letter of complaint to the U.S. trademark office. The NCA letter claimed that Sidamo and Harrar are "generic" names for coffee rather than distinctive and valued trademarks. The Ethiopian application was refused (Yrgacheffe went through because it had not yet been trademarked by Starbucks). Yet Sidamo and Harrar are so "generic" that they are used by Starbucks in their luxury "Black Apron Exclusives" product line, which sells at $23–26 per pound in the United States, instead of the $10–13 per pound for regular whole beans. Also, leading Ethiopian coffees have been a key ingredient in building Starbucks's brand, which is based on the idea of consumers as cosmopolitan connoisseurs and of Starbucks's coffees as handcrafted products coming from exotic places. This is contrasted to "industrial" and "anonymous" coffees, sold by mainstream roasters to consumers of generic commodities.

In September 2006, Ethiopia went back to Starbucks, again with mediation from Oxfam, to start a new round of negotiation—but nothing came of it at that time. But Starbucks's brand equity is partly based on its ethical sourcing guidelines and an image of a sophisticated, well-meaning business catering to educated consumers. Following press coverage of the conflict with Ethiopia (and combined with other factors), Starbucks's stock value fell from a high of almost $40 in mid-November 2006 to barely over $25 in mid-June 2007. In late June 2007, Ethiopia and Starbucks finally reached an agreement: Ethiopia was granted trademark rights over the names of its specialty coffees, and Starbucks a royalty-free license to use these names on its retail products.

The Ethiopia saga was certainly a contributing factor in the Starbucks stock-price fall of 2007. Return on equity and net income had increased both in 2005–6 and 2006–7.[14] Starbucks's stock price had hovered at the relatively stable level of $30–37 in the year previous to November 2006, the start of media coverage of the issue. Following the agreement with Ethiopia in June 2007, Starbucks's stock price stabilized at around $25 for about five months, before taking a further slide following the onset of the U.S. subprime crisis. Following bad fundamentals in the first half of 2008 (lower net income in the first quarter and even negative in the second), Starbucks's stock price was already as low as $15 at the start of the full-blown financial crisis in September 2008. Interestingly, in November 2008, Starbucks joined the RED initiative. Whether RED will help Starbucks in its financial woes and in reestablishing an "ethical aura" remains to be seen.

ICONIC BRANDS

In addition to ethical trade engagement, another way of minimizing brand vulnerability is to build up a brand profile that is based on culture, not on the product itself. These culture-heavy brands are what Holt (2004) calls "iconic brands." Holt argues that "cultural icons are exemplary symbols that people accept as a shorthand to represent important ideas . . . or values that a society deems important" (ibid., 1). Icons perform particular myths charismatically, and their consumers use them to "address identity desires and anxieties" (ibid., 2). "Iconic brands address cultural anxieties from afar, from imaginary worlds rather than from the worlds that consumers regularly encounter in their everyday lives" (ibid., 8).

Holt applies this analytical framework to show how brands such as Coca-Cola, Corona, Snapple, and Mountain Dew became "iconic" in specific historical and social circumstances because they were able to exploit identity myths that "stitch back together otherwise damaging tears in the cultural fabric" (ibid., 8) of American society. Such brands did not remain "iconic" on the basis of an unchangeable set of product characteristics, as argued in much of the branding literature, but only if and when they were able to adopt (and adapt) other appropriate myths in time. Holt argues that Mountain Dew, for example, was able to exploit the hillbilly myth in the 1950s and early 1960s, the redneck myth in the late 1970s and early 1980s, and the slacker myth from the late 1980s. Mountain Dew based its iconic branding on ads that were playful reactions to threats emerging from "national ideologies." In the case of the redneck myth, the ideology was the so-called Wall Street Frontier (a Reagan-era reenactment of the classic Western Frontier myth) and the rise of Yuppies, paired against increased unemployment and falling real wages especially among working-class men. This generated the myth of redneck resistance (incorporated in cultural products such as Southern rock as a music genre and the TV series *The Dukes of Hazzard*) that was used by Mountain Dew in ads generally featuring Dukes of Hazzard–style "boys peacocking for girls by taking exciting, watery plunges" (ibid., 48). Other iconic brands, such as Corona, after exploiting the American myth of the "Mexican spring break," were unable to adapt to new social contradictions and went into a crisis, only to come back by hitting the right myth again—in this case the myth of relaxation on a Mexican beach as a response to the "rat race" and work-related stress of middle-class white-collar workers in the 1990s. In sum, most of the iconic brands have remained durable over time on the basis of reconfigured cultural appropriation, not of radically changing products. This "same product, different myth" pattern holds some explanation for the power of the RED co-brand and other potential Brand Aid interventions to come.

What does cultural branding and the possibility for a brand to become an icon mean for RED? We argue that RED is an iconic brand in the sense that it seeks to enact the global myth of "just capitalism."

Such a myth tries to reconcile the contradictions of global wealth and poverty by portraying the idea that capitalism can be fixed to rein in its excesses and target its creativity and resources to help groups of "deserving others" (in the case of RED, these are women and children, Africans, and affected by AIDS). The rise of the antiglobalization movements from the late 1990s and of social and environmental labelling earlier in that decade opened new possibilities for the myth of just capitalism to be exploited by the time RED was launched in the mid-2000s. With RED, unlimited consumption, the harnessing of viral marketing, and the hunting of "cool" are used to save Africa with technology (ARVs)—a neomissionary, civilizing myth (see chapter 2). The charismatic performances of Bono are embedded in the iconic RED brand—salvation and excess are reconciled. The co-branding modality can be seen as a "marriage," providing the brands under the RED umbrella with a new beginning, bringing salvation not only to Africans but also to some of the brands' past sins of exploitation and environmental damage. And in a period of crisis such as the current one, RED can still exploit the myth of "just capitalism" by portraying itself as a workable alternative to "casino capitalism," and as a modality where consumption and cool can be channelled toward a good cause.

Given the vulnerability of brands and the need to manage brand risk, RED becomes an attractive vector for building the ethical component of brand reputation and for turning brands into icons. RED does not question the fundamentals of "hard commerce" and at the same time can help increase sales, visibility, and brand equity. It also helps to shift attention from the product to a cause by enacting the myth of just capitalism, which can fix the social and economic contradictions of capitalism at large. Finally, the fact that RED is a co-branding exercise helps manage individual brand risk by spreading the risk of failure or of negative repercussions among several brands and especially externalize it to the nonproduct brand, RED itself.

In the end, the co-branding exercise of the seven companies involved in RED is a good investment. As brand equity has come to incorporate ethical values and reputation, and as brands are increasingly more about lifestyles and culture than products themselves, the actual sales figures and coverage of RED products are less important than the media attention and buzz that they generate. Although AIDS patients may suffer from a drop in sales, the ethical content of the RED brands would not necessarily suffer.

MI(RED) IN COMMODITY FETISHISM?

In this chapter, we have argued that RED, in its positive spin and effort to achieve iconic status, helps mask the social and environmental relations of trade and production that underpin poverty, inequality, and disease—a process also known as "commodity fetishism." Commodity fetishism describes "the necessary masking of the social relations under which commodities are produced from which capitalist commodity production gains much of its legitimacy" (Guthman 2002, 296). In Marx's formulation (Marx 1976), under capitalism commodities appear to have value to each other or in relation to money, while the true source of value, labor, is not visible. This means that as consumers (and even as causumers), we do not "see" labor relations and class divisions that are behind their production. The process is "fetishistic" because it translates the product of labor into a "social hieroglyphic" that needs to be deciphered. The totem of commodity encloses intrinsic powers, values, and meanings (Slater 1997, 112). But what for Marx is mystification, for Durkheim (1915) is essential to solidarity. Consumption rituals, in this light, are akin to religious rituals (see also chapter 2), which are essential to social solidarity and "moral remaking" (Rojek 1985). In other words, "goods and rituals make social order both visible and effective" (Slater 1997, 149). Consumption goods and rituals constitute cosmologies that order a moral universe (Douglas and Isherwood 1980), but they do this in ways imagined from the Western capitalist viewpoint.

In contemporary debates on trade and development issues, the concepts of commodity fetishism and totemism are used to distinguish between what is hidden and what is communicated about the composition of products and their origins (Guthman 2002; Raynolds 2002; Taylor 2005). According to these accounts, transparency in trade suffers when there are discontinuities in the distribution of knowledge and creations of mythologies (Appadurai 1986). Appadurai argues that commodities represent complex social forms and distributions of knowledge at the levels of production, exchange, and consumption. Technical knowledge at the sites of production, applied within cosmological, social, and ritual boundaries, is mediated by degrees of knowledge of markets, consumers, and destinations of things. In this process, "[l]arge gaps in knowledge of the ultimate market by the producer . . . [may lead] to high profits in trade and to the relative deprivation of the producing country or class in relation to the consumer and the trader" (ibid., 43).

Read through these lenses, the "sustainable" products (i.e., Fair Trade coffee, Forestry Stewardship Council wood products, and Marine Stewardship Council fish) we mentioned previously in this chapter should provide, via a label, transparent information about the processes that lie behind the products. Consumers and trade operators are supplied with much more information on the "where, when, how, and whys" of the product, production processes, and conditions of exchange. Information is supplied not only in relation to social relations but also to society-nature relations that are otherwise concealed in commodity production (Allen and Kovach 2000; Guthman 2002; Hartwick 1998). In this context, consumer and NGO demands on transparency in production and trade could be seen as "lift[ing] one corner of the veil of commodity fetishism" (Goodman 2004, 4) because they provide information on ecological and production relations that would otherwise be concealed from distant consumers.

But other interpretations have moved beyond the fetishist argument to highlight that the political meaning of ethical foods derives from the visibility of material claims (no child labor, environmentally sound practices), rather than in its concealment (commodity fetishism) (Guthman 2002, 306–7). In this guise, "sustainability" initiatives are imbued with symbolic values meant to show solidarity, responsibility, and care for environmental and socioeconomic concerns. At the same time, work on standards in agro-food products also suggests that some of these "transparency" demands themselves may conceal as much as they reveal in terms of socioeconomic relations of production and trade (Raynolds 2004; Guthman 2002, 2003). Freidberg, in particular, claims that the increasing codification of social and environmental

concerns through standards, codes of conduct, and labels actually results in a "double fetishism"—the masking of social relations of production combined with the commoditization of the knowledge about
the commodity itself (2003; see also Bonanno et al. 1994; Cook and
Crang 1996; Freidberg 2004).

From this point of view, one could argue that sustainability certifications are similar to RED. RED is indeed fetishist in the sense that
it embeds information about the "quality" of the product in the most
powerful instrument of codification—branding—without actually re-
leasing significant information on the trade and production relations
that are behind these products. As the example of the Converse RED
shoes from chapter 4 suggests, RED consumers cannot actually know
how much of the purchase price of their "Manamela RED shoes" goes
to support the Global Fund because they are not privy to the "net wholesale price" of the shoes. Nor can consumers look at the public reporting
of the Global Fund's contributions to know how much Converse, or
any individual RED company, contributed through the RED track, as
we describe in chapter 3. Thus, the RED fetish links causumers and
caring products though iconic branding.

But RED's reliance on the celebrity makes the verification *process*
different from the current spate of certifications, labels, and codes of
conduct. It is contradictory to the "audit culture" that underpins these
processes (Power 1997; Gibbon and Ponte 2005) and that aims at "impersonal" and systemic solutions to problems of quality, food safety,
environmental impact, and social conditions of production (Ponte
2007, 2008). RED, backed by iconic brands, is based on "celebrity validation," which is based on personal capacity. This allows RED both to
achieve commodity fetishism and at the same time to use aid celebrities as a totem of care for AIDS victims in Africa (as opposed to a totem
of care for the social and environmental relations of production of RED
items). Brands guarantee "quality," design, and the replicability of the
experience of consumption. Because RED does not challenge their
"normal" business practices, brand risk management is also assured.
RED switches attention from the possible negative social and environmental impact of production and trade toward solving the problems of

distant others. This way, brand vulnerability to negative exposure is minimized.

What we are witnessing with RED is the subtle passage, within causumer culture, from conscious consumption (making choices based on information embedded in labels, for example) to compassionate consumption (making choices based on emotional appeal). Celebrities manage and negotiate this affective element of international development and thus link consumers with their causes through iconic brands.

CONCLUSION
Celebrities, Consumers, and Everyone Else

What we have described in this book as "Brand Aid" is a double process. It is aid to brands, a mechanism that helps selling products, profiling a brand in the media, and building brand value. It is also aid financing that is provided through branding. Corporations attach their name to a good cause and donate a portion of the profits that arise from the sale of specific products. Celebrities mediate the communication between brands, consumers, and international development aid. In the case of RED, an umbrella brand is created to provide a common framework under which a diverse group of companies is united. The RED co-brand magnifies the contribution of any single brand and also provides a buffer against negative profiling of individual companies in case anything goes wrong.

The profit and brand-management motives of corporations that are willing to be part of Brand Aid are multiple. Brands are key assets and are increasingly about lifestyle, culture, and identity, yet negative media exposure can quickly tarnish a company's image. As a result of having been profiled for negative labor and environmental practices for over two decades, large corporations are developing "responsible practices." Brand Aid, by focusing attention on the plight of "distant others" (Africans smitten with AIDS in the case of RED), helps deflect attention away from the day-to-day practices of these corporations within their organizational structure and in relation to their suppliers, many of whom are based in developing countries. Through RED, corporations become responsible for saving suffering strangers.

The need for international aid to be "branded" comes not only from the perception that more funds need to be raised to support successful development interventions. Development aid itself has been in dire need for "rebranding," in the sense of changing its perception from the public. For decades, aid has been under attack from right-wing political constituencies in the United States, and it is now coming under attack even in European countries that have long been ardent aid supporters. Aid, it is argued, is ineffective and wasteful, and business is better at delivering development than traditional aid mechanisms. The international aid community has responded by developing new public-private partnerships, by attempting to reform its delivery mechanisms, and by arguing that given the right conditions, including sufficient funding, aid can make a difference. The involvement of Bono and other celebrities in pressuring politicians to deliver more and better aid, especially to Africa, has also been part of this response.

Brand Aid is a manifestation of the need to do something radically new in how development is financed and how it is understood. Its relevance, therefore, is not merely related to the amount of funding that one initiative such as RED raises, but to the kind of impact through media exposure that Brand Aid will have on aid more generally. Therefore, Brand Aid's changes in the representations of consumers as citizens, of "good" corporations, of Africa, and of AIDS are as important as determining whether it raises enough money for aid.

CELEBRITIES

The celebrity is a central element of Brand Aid. Celebrities have become proxy philanthropists, statesmen, and executives. At the same time as celebrities are endowed with expertise, experts are reshaped as celebrities. As development aid is perceived as increasingly complex and ineffective in the public sphere, celebrities are the new vectors for making aid more attractive, simpler, and better able to solve problems. Celebrities are able to use narratives of justice and social change without considering the inequalities in global social systems that make "celebrity" possible. Raising consciousness about social justice does not necessarily entail sharing responsibility for the cause of inequality or for its perpetuation.

In this book, we have concentrated on the role of one type of celebrity—the "aid celebrity." We have avoided discussions of whether celebrity involvement in aid-related activities is authentic, whether aid can help the celebrity, and why celebrities choose specific aid interventions. Rather, we have concentrated on the process of celebrities becoming increasingly involved in international development aid, and how that involvement has made the mechanism of celebrity itself more legitimate, leading to the formation of aid celebrities. These are development "experts" (whether they were celebrities in the entertainment business to start with or not) whose identity has been made inseparable from their aid work, but whose claims to expertise extend beyond their formal qualifications.

Rather than arguing that celebrities are taking over aid, we have shown that celebrity mediation dominates new forms of aid like RED. Aid celebrities are forming the new features of the international aid system. In this context, celebrities are the faces of doing good. They add not only media exposure, but also to the credibility and believability of international development in the eyes of the public. In the process, they may also lend credibility to other kinds of celebrities who might still be involved in traditional development interventions or humanitarian causes.

In RED, celebrities operate in ways that could be seen as antithetical to the many certifications, labels, and codes of conduct that characterize ethical and sustainable trade initiatives and corporate social responsibility. Celebrity validation is indeed contradictory to the impersonal, systemic, and audit-based procedures that guarantee quality, food safety, environmental impact, and social conditions of production. However, from the consumer point of view, both labels and celebrities simplify complex socioeconomic and environmental processes. But, instead of being based on an aura of science and standardized procedure, validation through celebrity is based on affect and the performance of persona.

CORPORATIONS AND BRANDS

Brand Aid operates under the principle that "hard commerce" can be an appropriate vector for raising funds for good causes. In this book, we placed the corporate activities carried out under the umbrella of the RED initiative against the background of the "normal functioning" of the industries in which the RED companies operate, and in relation to activities broadly portrayed as part of corporate social responsibility (CSR). We examined how corporations build up their brand profiles, sell products, and/or portray themselves as both "caring" and "cool" under RED. We also showed that, more than simply another example of cause-related marketing, RED engages corporations in profitable "helping" while simultaneously pushing the agenda of CSR toward solving the problems of "distant others."

We have shown that RED is a "disengaged" form of CSR—companies do not attempt to change or improve the normal functioning of business and trade. At the same time, the beneficiaries of RED are "distant"—they are African AIDS victims, not workers in plants producing RED products or even other products for the RED companies. RED corporations have a low level of involvement with Africa in their day-to-day operations anyway. From these points of view, RED constitutes a form of "distant and disengaged" CSR. It pushes CSR back toward the old-style philanthropy it is framed against—but with a new funding mechanism based on consumption and co-branding.

But from another perspective, RED differs considerably from corporate philanthropy as well. In traditional philanthropy, the act of giving is formally independent from the act of profit accumulation: normal business practice leads to profits, and accumulation of profits, assets, and capital is used ex-post for purposes that have little to do with the operations in which the company is involved. In RED, on the other hand, companies use a good cause to sell a particular set of products—profit is generated and donation is given at one and the same time.

But just as brands can become valuable assets when they are recognized widely, they can also turn into liabilities. Because brands represent a substantial portion of market capitalization of major corporations, they need to be managed carefully. Negative exposure in the media can tarnish a hard-built ethical profile of a brand. In this context, RED becomes an attractive vector for building the ethical component of brand reputation. The fact that RED is a co-branding exercise also helps manage individual brand risk by spreading the risk of failure or of negative repercussions among several brands and especially externalize it to the nonproduct brand, RED itself. RED does not question the fundamentals of hard commerce and at the same time can help increase sales, visibility, and brand equity.

As brand equity comes to incorporate ethical values and reputation, and as brands are increasingly more about lifestyles than products themselves, the actual sales figures and coverage of RED products are less important than the media attention that they generate. Although AIDS patients may suffer from a possible drop in sales, the ethical content of the RED brands would not necessarily suffer.

CONSUMPTION

Brand Aid rests on celebrity validation but also on consumer culture, a culture *of* consumption where not only are the values of society organized through consumption, but they also derive from it (Slater 1997). It is a culture of choice and consumer sovereignty, where values expressed through consumption spill over to other areas of social action.

The consumption of signs and experiences can be a vehicle for the mobilization of meaning, political action, and belonging to a real or imagined community. Consumer-citizens are now exercising their rights to demand social and environmental change via individual acts of consumption. In this book, we borrowed the term "causumerism" (or shopping for a better world, effecting change through the marketplace) to denote the collectivization of private consumption choices guided by a "social movement." Individual consumers lend their purchasing power to a social movement to enable them to effectively voice their concerns and leverage positive or negative sanctions. In Brand Aid, causumerism rests on the engagement of discourses of transparency, consumer participation, and the creation of an image of social movement/brand community. But in the case of RED, transparency is restricted to the impact of purchase (the number of antriretroviral

[ARV] doses that will be provided to AIDS patients, and the number of people "saved") and consumer participation through blogging is placed within narrow confines.

In Brand Aid, consumers can become "causumers" without knowing much of the social and environmental relations behind the products on offer. They do so just by knowing more about the legitimate beneficiaries that they help by buying the "good cause products" (and services). Here we see the resemblance between Brand Aid and traditional discourses of philanthropy in which there is a fundamental "assumption that quick, convenient, and relatively inexpensive acts of giving have nonetheless powerful effects and deep spiritual meaning" (King 2006, 73). RED products ride on the double guarantee that they are "good" both for consumers and for recipients of help. Brand Aid may be the start of a new phase in which the contradictions of capitalism are resolved through shifting focus from products onto the "people with the problem." Within the emerging realm of causumerism, Brand Aid shifts the focus from conscious consumption to compassionate consumption.

AFRICANS WITH AIDS

Brand Aid stimulates changes in representations of consumer agency, the positive role of business in development, and the attractiveness of international aid more generally. But it does this on the basis of other kinds of representations of the "need" for which aid, business, and consumers can "help." In specific relation to RED, existing maps of understanding of who is in need of what kind of help are consulted to lead to a depiction of AIDS that can be solved by proper shopping. These common understandings draw on nineteenth-century stereotypes of Africa. From these scripts, Brand Aid is able to alleviate suffering and bring development. Aid celebrities embody this recycled ideal of Christianity, Civilization, and Commerce (Magubane 2008). In RED, celebrities and images embrace religious metaphor to emphasize a cross-cultural responsibility for helping those in need, while simultaneously reinforcing stereotypes of gender, race, and culture in defining who the needy are. The explicit referencing to a general cultural Christianity throughout the campaign is used as a foil for the promotion of material values and perpetuation of stereotypes of African AIDS. RED benefits from the assumption on the part of Western consumers that Africans need their help. By wedding a vague but powerful recognition between Western consumers and cultural Christianity, the RED virtualism of treatment allows the possibility of believing that conscious consumption and ARV pills will save Africa.

RED's representations of AIDS in Africa as something that you can know from a distance are deeply problematic. Most Western consumers have firsthand experience neither with living with HIV and AIDS nor with Africa. Most do, however, own something that contains components from Africa and consume food that was grown by Africans in African soil. Yet Africans in RED are characterized only by their "need" for international development interventions, not by their multiple roles, varying forms of agency, and positionality in the global economy of production and consumption. RED's pictures of AIDS show us Africans as deserving, suffering, and persevering in places that are distant and disengaged from the consumption that is meant to help them. The many ways that various forms of power condition the entry of RED, its pictures, and its products into the global marketplace of ideas and objects are eclipsed by the urgency of the emergency.

The possibility that while you are designing your own sneakers, you are contributing money that will save the lives of African women and children is constituted by the virtualism of ARV treatment in RED. This virtualism is the simple intervention of doctors prescribing pills in an African clinic, and patients swallowing "two pills a day" for the rest of their lives. The component that is missing to save Africans with AIDS, according to RED, is the provision of ARVs. While drugs are an essential component to treatment, the RED virtualism omits even the most basic, and still unresolved, problems in most highly affected African countries caused by the lack of a functioning health system. Even if one were to support an intervention whose exclusive focus was on ARV treatment in African countries, issues of resistance must be addressed through continual treatment upgrades, adequate nutrition must be maintained for the medicines to work, treatment of opportunistic infections and coinfections with TB must be effective, and given the unfortunate lack of evidence that a cure will be forthcoming, treatment regimens will be required for a long time to really "save Africans with AIDS" even in the strictly medical sense.

While RED explicitly claims to link development goals with business methods, to constitute shopping "at home" as an effective means of combating AIDS in Africa, the gendered and racial tensions that underpin such an approach are tapping into traditional discourses of power. And, as a regular *Financial Times* columnist writes, "who is setting the agenda? Look no further than an Irish musician in wraparound shades—perfect for those hot African days" (Rachman 2007). Bono stated in an interview with the *New York Times*, "Africa is sexy and people need to know that."[1] Yet, as even the more potentially progressive "body map" intervention that aimed at changing the ways that Africans living with AIDS were perceived was forced to confront, "disrupting the codes of connotation through which images of HIV-positive black women's bodies are read requires something more radical than replacing a 'negative' image with a 'positive' one" (Thomas 2008, 220).

While RED's aid celebrities redeem sex in "sexy" Africa on behalf of causumers, they never challenge the global inequities of masculinity, the racialization of sexuality, or the social hierarchy where cool, rich, white men save poor African women and children. The aid celebrities make it possible for Western shoppers to feel empowered through the purchase of RED products. All of this is managed within a discourse of concern, care, and ethics. Public, Western, and masculine agency is called forth to save intimate, African, and feminine beneficiaries. Subtle yet stereotypical depictions of gender relations throughout the campaign, from the insidiously gendered linking of women and shopping (see King 2006, xxv) to the framing of African women and children as passive yet worthy recipients and aid celebrities as powerful and effective, do nothing to thwart the existing "unequal relationships between men and women" or the "gender stereotypes" to which the international community returns when continuing to try to understand HIV and AIDS (see UN 2008, 25). The proximity and distance of RED's virtualism of AIDS treatment distracts our attention from critical issues of gender relations in either African recipient societies or Western consumption ones. In spite of the fact that the biggest global health initiative in history is to target Africans for AIDS treatment, we still know very little about who is living or who is dying or why.

BETTER (RED)™ THAN DEAD?

In this book, we have used the case study of RED to epitomize the rise of "Brand Aid." Within the emerging realm of causumerism, RED facilitates at least three shifts: from conscious consumption to compassionate consumption; from attention to the product and its production process toward the medical treatment of the "people with the problem" (AIDS patients in Africa); and from addressing the causes of problems to solving their manifestations.

Branding, commerce, and marketing are key elements in operationalizing compassionate consumption. Bono explicitly recognizes this strategy for RED: "In the 21st century, commerce is the catalyst of change, good and bad. Marketing people, marketing brilliance, marketing budgets; we wanted to work with them. We wanted to make the fight against HIV/AIDS sexy and smart."[2] If the focus is on solutions, and if one sets aside corporations' profit-maximizing objectives, the negative externalities of their production processes, and their short-term perspective, then corporations can be seen as efficient and effective problem solvers.

Successful businesses are also good at stimulating consumption. The cultural insecurity of Western consumers vis-à-vis their own standing among their peers paves the way for compassionate consumption as a vector for empowering them within an imagined global community of the needy. You can look chic enough in Armani, hip enough in Converse, pay for your goods with AmEx, and feel good about yourself ethically. If consumption cannot address exploitation and inequality, at least it can do something about tackling disease. "Shameless exploitation in pursuit of the common good," the slogan of Newman's Own company, might be a perfect slogan for Brand Aid more generally.[3]

But can one benefit from and challenge exploitative relations at the same time? The representative from American Express launched the RED card at Davos noting: "It starts with building a profitable and sustainable product for the consumer, and ultimately that's where our success will lie."[4] One of the only voices to have spoken critically of the RED launch in Davos was a professor of marketing from the Said Business School at Oxford University who suggested that such efforts "build awareness, but what we need is a new social movement" that makes direct contact between the consumer and the producer.[5] RED in fact does the opposite: as an umbrella brand, it shifts the consumer's focus away from the producer and onto the African AIDS victim.

RED, a lean, network solution to aid financing, takes funds from consumption—not taxation. It is an individual effort, the result of consumer power—not of public will. It can also be tailored to individual significations and coproduced with consumer feedback through blogging[6] and focus groups. It shapes and is shaped by a community of cool, educated, and compassionate consumers. RED brings together AIDS activists and businesspeople, rockers and doctors, but its relations to the producers, unless they are Africans smitten by a deadly disease, remain opaque.

Ethical labels and certifications are also about consumption—they are instruments to guide consumers to make better decisions, but not necessarily to consume more. Coffee that is fair trade labeled is expected to return higher prices and better organizational support to producers than its non–fair trade equivalent. An organic apple is expected to have been grown with methods that are better for the environment and healthier for the farmer and the consumer. At least for fair trade and organics, a price premium is charged to the consumer to pay for the extra costs that are involved in improving procedures and obtaining better impacts. In other, more mainstream, initiatives, however, this is not the expectation anymore. Putatively "better" products are offered to consumers at the same price, while costs are transferred upstream toward producers (so they are not really "better off" from a point of view of financial returns).[7] But in theory at least, the consumer's decision has a potential impact on the conditions of trade and production and on societies and environments.

In RED, the consumer is implicitly asked to consume more, not differently. RED is at pains in explaining that the RED co-branded products are the functional and quality equivalent of non-RED products that the partner companies provide (e.g., the RED iPod is the same as a normal iPod). The push is to consume more because, as beautifully expressed by the RED "impact calculator," the more RED products you buy, the more ARV treatment doses you provide for free to Africa. Not only can one help Africa, he/she will be able to buy a RED product at the same price as its equivalent non-RED version. In so doing, RED, and those ethical labels that do not charge more to consumers, can solve what Daniel Miller (2001) calls the "dialectics of shopping."

According to Miller, there is an innate contradiction in shopping between the moral activity of saving money on behalf of the household at large and the ethics of considering the concerns of distant others (which would entail paying a higher price). In other words, buying cheaper maximizes returns to immediate others in the household, while paying more to buy ethical products maximizes returns to the distant others at the point of production. With RED, the shopper pays the same price and can help distant others too. There is no sacrifice involved in being "ethical"—not only is the price the same, but the product looks and feels good as well. RED explicitly plays against earlier trends in ethical consumption of the "old days," when organic produce looked ugly or Peruvian handmade sweaters felt rough, and raises the cool standards for "good" products. The RED message is coated with positive spin and emergency talk at the same time. Bono explicitly stated at the RED launch that labor issues are of secondary importance to people dying with AIDS: "We do not think that trade is bad. We are for labor issues. Labor issues are very serious but six and a half thousand Africans dying is more serious."[8]

Pre-1989 critiques of capitalism from the left were occasionally counterargued from the right with the catchy proposition of "Better dead than red." Thereafter, much of the critical argumentation on capitalism has been focused on how to soften its rough edges, rather than on how to get beyond it as a system. In this context, the implicit slogan "Better (RED)™ than dead" captures the spirit of a moderate project of "soft capitalism." Through RED branding, something can be done against deadly disease without undermining the basic cultural or economic structures of the capitalist system. RED focuses on capitalism and the individual consumer, instead of the collective and the state. The urgency of consumption is an antihorizon concept: instead of constantly receding into the future, it is reimagined as emergent and reiteratively re-presenting the present, the "now." To succeed, consumption must be insatiable. That this translates into notions of "sustainable funding" to combat HIV/AIDS, a disease of global excess, is more than ironic.

If reputable aid celebrities negotiate the interface between shopping and helping, it is also the pivotal role of the consumer that distinguishes Brand Aid from previous modalities of funding development assistance. Cooper argues that "whether flawed or not, the Product RED campaign illustrates how a new issue or practice is suddenly grabbed by celebrities" who act as mediators between mass society and elite-biased institutions (2008a, 127). Yet RED does not challenge elite bias along gender, ethnicity, or class divisions. Instead, the juxtaposition of "sexy" fashion models, worthy ARV recipients, and the most visible aid celebrity, Bono, reaffirms the power and privilege of private consumption.

With Brand Aid, consumers can position themselves as holding a status above everyone else with designer products that do not represent the exploitation of the most downtrodden—these products actually help them. Consumers are able to maintain distance and the illusion of proximity. Images of people suffering with AIDS substitute the images of workers suffering from labor exploitation. Bono is the totem of compassionate consumption, steering away attention from the causes of poverty, such as the inequities of systems of production and trade, by focusing on one of the outcomes, HIV/AIDS. The beauty of this celebrity simplification is that it provides the possibility that everyday people can engage in low-cost heroism. Brand Aid creates a world where it is possible to have as much as you want without depriving anyone else.

NOTES

PREFACE

1. See http://www212.americanexpress.com/.

INTRODUCTION

1. See the official RED Web site, http://www.joinred.com.

2. Ibid.

3. RED funding does not support programs in Africa that are struggling, or are even average, but out of the 140 countries in which the Fund operates, RED supports only those Global Fund country programs performing best in HIV/AIDS. This excludes both underperforming programs and successful smaller initiatives that are not up to the scale to meet the Global Fund's byzantine application and monitoring processes, which we will discuss in chapter 3. Thus, there is a built-in selection bias toward a record of good performance on a larger scale.

4. According to *Promo Magazine,* the Gap RED launch was planned in less than a month. Its event marketing agency, A Squared Group, spent over thirty-three hours in the snow and rain during three nights wrapping the Gap store in red vinyl and another sixty hours building displays inside. The launch campaign worked through negotiations with city hall and the "notoriously strict" Greater North Michigan Avenue Association. The launch plan included a celebrity fashion show, special displays for RED apparel, and three hundred clerks from local Gap stores to "seed" the crowd inside and outside the store ("The Gap Wrap," *Promo Magazine,* January 2007, 22).

5. See video at http://www.hiptobesquared.com.

6. See "Costly RED Campaign Reaps Meager $18 million," *Advertising Age,* 4 March 2007; "The Big Question: Does the Red Campaign Help Big Western Brands More than Africa?" *Independent,* 9 March 2007; and Bobby Shriver's rebuttal at http://www.joinred.com/archive/adage.

7. However, RED's inception may be less attributable to celebrity genius and more to advanced fundraising strategies. The Global Fund's marketing and media campaign that began in 2004 includes "co-branded product tie-ins" as part of a priority of "engaging consumer audiences in key donor markets" (see http://www.theglobalfund.org).

8. M. Bishop, "View from Davos: Bono Marketing His Red Badge of Virtue," *Daily Telegraph,* 27 January 2006, http://www.telegraph.co.uk/.

9. Ibid.

10. RED product launch at Davos, video, http://www.joinred.com/.

11. Ibid.

12. For example, Converse is owned by Nike, the company notorious for years of using sweatshop labor in the Third World and for sparking university activism against the brand.

13. T. Weber, "Bono Bets on Red to Battle Aids," *BBC News,* 26 January 2006, http://news.bbc.co.uk/.

14. Although its overhead costs are proportionally low, it seems to cost more to lead the Global Fund than its public/international counterparts. The reported salary in 2007 of the then executive director of the Global Fund was a tax-free $320,000 per year plus a housing subsidy, as compared to only $230,000 for the head of the Joint United Nations Programme on HIV/AIDS (UNAIDS), and $145,000 (minus taxes) for the head of the U.S. President's Emergency Plan for AIDS Relief (PEPFAR) (Global Fund Observer, "Newspaper Alleges Inappropriate Expenditure by Global Fund Executive Director," 70, 5 February 2007, http://www.aidspan.org/).

15. In 2002, Bono and Bobby Shriver set up DATA, which "leveraged investment from the public sector to the Global Fund, but a need remained for greater private sector funding" (see http://www.joinred.com/). From 2008, DATA merged with ONE, the campaign and advocacy organization "committed to the fight against extreme poverty and preventable disease, particularly in Africa." ONE was cofounded by Bono and Bobby Shriver (see http://www.one.org/).

16. The Global Fund, press release, 26 January 2006, http://www.theglobalfund.org/.

17. T. Darke, "The Sex Appeal of Red," *Sunday Times,* 26 February 2006, http://www.women.timesonline.co.uk/.

18. Ibid.

19. "The Business of HIV/AIDS," *Lancet* 368, no. 9534 (2006): 423.

20. For other examples of how large corporations and the wealthy can be saviors of the world, see Bishop and Green (2008); see also Kinsley 2008 for a spirited discussion on whether corporations should be involved in doing good at all.

21. Bono, commencement address, Harvard University, 2001, http://www.commencement.harvard.edu/.

22. See http://www.joinred.com/.

23. Cultural Christianity permeates even Bono's architectural apparatus. U2's recent 360 Degree tour is played in the round "under a claw-like, spired structure that's part insect, part spacecraft, part cathedral" according to the music review in the *New York Times:* J. Pareles, "U2 in the Round, Fun with a Mission," 24 September 2009, http://www.nytimes.com/.

24. See Jonathan Rauch, "This Is Not Charity," *The Atlantic* 300, no. 3 [the "values" issue] (October 2007), 64–76.

25. The array of documented "breast cancer awareness products" is remarkable and ranges from the Republic of Tea's "Sip for the Cure" to Breeder's Choice Pet Foods "Caring for Both Ends of the Leash" program (King 2006, 14).

26. See http://www.benetton.com/.

27. This is a simplification, as philanthropy is also evolving itself. For example, Google.org, the philanthropic arm of Google, is a business unit of the company rather than a separate foundation. For other examples, see Bishop and Green (2008); Frumkin (2006).

1. BAND AID TO BRAND AID

1. Colin Macilwain, "A Firm Response to AIDS: Product Red Is the Private Sector's Bid to Fight HIV. But Is It Too Little Too Late?" *Nature* 143 (19 October 2006), 738–39, http://www.nature.com.

2. *TIME* Global Health Summit, "Rock and Roll Philanthropy: How Can Mass Media Campaigns Make a Difference?" 1 November 2005, http://www.time.com/time/2005/globalhealth.

3. "Bono, Oprah, Kanye Converge Downtown to Launch Campaign," *Redeye,* 13 October 2006.

4. *TIME* Global Health Summit, "Rock and Roll Philanthropy."

5. See Look to the Stars, http://www.looktothestars.org/ (accessed 16 September 2010). Thanks to Joanna Hood for pointing this out to us.

6. Manzo (2008, 646); quoting D. McDougall, "Now Charity Staff Hit at Cult of Celebrity," *Observer,* 26 November 2006, 38.

7. Zine Magubane, "Africa Script Needs Rewrite," *Zeleza Post,* 13 June 2007, http://www.zeleza.com/.

8. Brendan O'Neill, "Brad, Angelina and the Rise of 'Celebrity Colonialism,'" *Spiked,* 30 May 2006, http://www.spiked-online.com/.

9. Zine Magubane, "Africa and the New Cult of Celebrity" *African Affairs,* 20 April 2007, http://www.zeleza.com/blogging/popular-culture/africa-and-new-cult-celebrity.

10. Ibid.

11. The marriage of branding and celebrity activism per se is not a new phenomenon. "Newman's Own" range of food products has been around for over twenty years, and its cumulative profits of over $300 million have been donated to charities.

12. See http://www.theglobalfund.org/ and http://www.earthinstitute.columbia.edu/. Perhaps this was both reflecting how critical it is that the Global Fund not be associated with any individual or partisan interest and a tacit acknowledgement that many noncelebrities worked hard to bring about this major institutional change.

13. We are not arguing here that Bono, Sachs, and Farmer alone were literally responsible for creating the Global Fund, but that they were the celebrities associated with this particular response to a large perception of institutional failure and to the exceptionalism of HIV/AIDS at the time. We discuss this further in chapter 3.

14. Interestingly, Sachs also credits Bono's "reading of scripture with Jesse Helms" and charismatic lobbying of the U.S. religious right for the introduction of PEPFAR (2005, 344). Jamie Drummond links his negotiations over a photograph of Bono with U.S. president Bush with agreement on the "terms of the deal . . . $15bn for Aids in Africa, which has risen to $20bn" (T. Adams, "Our Man in Africa," *The Observer,* 11 May 2008).

15. *TIME* Global Health Summit, "Rock and Roll Philanthropy."

16. D. DeLuka, "Being Hailed Here 'a Very Big Deal,'" *Philadelphia Inquirer,* 27 September 2007, http://www.philly.com/.

17. "O'Neill, Bono in Africa Focus on Money, Development and AIDS," http://www.usafricaonline.com/bonooneil.africa.html.

18. Associated Press, "Geldof, Bono Praise G-8 for Africa Aid," MSNBC, 8 July 2005, http://www.msnbc.msn.com/.

19. CBC News, "Harper Risks Tainting Legacy by Ignoring Africa: Bono," 18 June 2008, http://www.cbc.ca/.

20. See http://www.live8live.com/.

21. In this, RED is different from initiatives such as Lance Armstrong's wristbands. The main point of wearing these bands is not to appropriate their aesthetics—they only become "cool" through their association with the celebrity and his cause of funding cancer research. The co-branding of RED with established brands and products allows wearers/users both to make an aesthetic statement and to signal the "good" factor in ways that are more subtle to the public.

22. J. Busby, "Is There a Constituency for Global Poverty? Jubilee 2000 and the Future of Development Advocacy," Brookings Blum Roundtable, 1 August 2007, 2, http://www.brookings.edu/.

23. Adams "Our Man in Africa."

24. Jeffrey Sachs, speech to the University of Copenhagen attended by the authors, 11 September 2007.

25. Ibid.

26. Ibid.

27. Truthdig, "Professor for President?" 28 August 2006, http://www.truthdig.com/.

28. Nina Munk, "Jeffrey Sachs' $200 Billion Dream," *Vanity Fair,* July 2007, http://www.vanityfair.com/.

29. The Experts by G Monkey, "Bono Launches Product (Red) to Fund the Fight on AIDS and Poverty in Africa," 26 January 2006, http://gliving.tv/news/.

30. M. Satchell, "Wiping out TB and AIDS," *U.S. News and World Report,* 31 October 2005.

31. This story can be found in many sources, and the photographs at even more; one reference is http://www.who.int/3by5/treatmentworks/en/.

32. *TIME* Global Health Summit, "The Case for Optimism," 1 November 2005, http://www.time.com/time/2005/globalhealth/.

33. C. Kielburger and M. Kielburger, "The Good Doctor Prescribes Health Care for the World's Poor," *Huffington Post,* 3 October 2008, http://www.huffingtonpost.com/.

34. T. Tighe, "Paul Farmer and Thomas Tighe Discuss the Practical Ways to Cure the World," *Santa Barbara Independent,* 11 October 2007.

35. Ibid.

36. See http://www.joinred.com/.

37. Sammi Fredenburg, Blog in response to Bono's receipt of the NAACP Chairman's Award at the 38th NAACP Image Awards, comment posted 27 February 2007, http://joinred.blogspot.com/.

38. Marshall's book argues that public identities of leadership, including celebrity, have converged in capitalist democracies and that the management of affect supercedes that of rational debate in the context of leadership, i.e. in political campaigns (1997, part II).

39. Rojek uses "para-social interaction" as descriptive of a mass media–constructed social relationship that is of "second-order intimacy" because it is not based on face-to-face interaction (2001, 52).

40. Adams, "Our Man in Africa."

2. THE ROCK MAN'S BURDEN

1. The decade of the 1980s produced foundational scholarship on critical engagement with global media representations of AIDS. See, for example, Crimp 1988; Watney 1987; Patton 1990. Media reporting on African AIDS began to receive scrutiny in the 1990s. See Austin 1989–90; Johnson 2002; Patton 1992; Watney 1990.

2. O'Manique (2009) demonstrates how our gendered constructions of the "African woman" have limited the necessary multifaceted critique of structural power and how the governance of the global political economy has contributed to HIV and AIDS and its growing feminization.

3. R. Kipling, "The White Man's Burden," *McClure's* 12 (February 1899), 290.

4. In an interesting article, Zine Magubane argues that Bono himself references his history of oppression as an Irishman to claim a certain legitimacy in support of Africa, claiming to provide "good news from an Irishman" about "coming out from under the hoof of colonialism" (C. Cobb, "Rock Star Bono, US Secretary Plan Africa Tour," cited in Magubane 2008, 102.6). She notes that "at the time that Kipling penned the words 'half devil and half child' those words were frequently applied to Africans and the Irish" (ibid., 102.7). However, her analysis concludes that Bono's distancing from questions of race undermines his claim.

5. Commodity racism lies at the heart of the Victorian marketing spectacle that reinvented racial difference in ways that brought intimate, gendered life through signs of domesticity (women laced into corsets, children bathing,

maids scrubbing floors) into public space and signs of empire (black natives in need of cleansing) into every home (McClintock 1994).

6. In the same year as the Berlin Conference that carved up Africa for European consumption, the first wrapped soap was sold under a brand name. Soap was one of the first commodities to mark the shift in economic history from small businesses to imperial monopolies: hundreds of small soap companies negotiated the emerging market in the 1870s, but by the end of the century the trade was monopolized by only ten large companies who had mastered the craft of advertisement (McClintock 1994).

7. Bono, "Message 2U: Guest Editor's Letter," *Vanity Fair,* July 2007, 32.

8. Hintzen describes the advertisement that faces Bono's quote: "The advertisement features a photograph of a nude woman with her torso covered by a large upscale leather or crocodile bag (a signature feature of the company) hooked around her left shoulder. She is straddling a nude man with her naked legs around his naked thighs. His eyes are closed while she stares, with a sultry gaze, into the camera. A second, equally nude, man is straddling her back, upside down. The woman's head appears to be resting slightly on his naked thighs. The man's upper arm hides her nude buttocks. His elbow rests on the bag, and his lower arm touches almost the entire length of her leg. The man's face is seemingly positioned between her legs in a pose that suggests cunnilingus. Her arms are wrapped around the neck of the other male in the photograph. Both men are muscular with light brown bodies indicating racial ambiguity. The woman's eyes are blue and her body tanned" (2008, 78).

9. See Jungar and Salo (2008) for a comparison between RED's commercial campaign and the Treatment Action Campaign (TAC) activism.

10. Dr. Ryan Phelps, "Stories about Sipho, Part 1," comment posted 24 September 2007, http://joinred.blogspot.com/.

11. See Dr. Ryan Phelps, http://pediatrician-in-swaziland.blogspot.com/.

12. These are people or groups who have requested that their MySpace profiles be linked with RED's. These "friends" are permitted to leave comments for each other on the MySpace Web site.

13. Lizzie, comment on RED, MySpace comment posted 11:53 a.m., 28 July 2007. Cited in Anderson (2008, 45).

14. D. Hockney, "Pictures and Power: Whoever Controls Images Has Great Social Influence. Did the Camera Damage the Church's Popularity," *Guardian,* 27 March 2008, http://www.guardian.co.uk/.

15. Magubane, "Africa Script Needs Rewrite."

16. Curtin (1964, 325). Cited in Z. Magubane, "Oprah in South Africa:

The Politics of Coevalness and the Creation of a Black Public Sphere," *Zeleza Post*, 13 June 2007, http://www.zeleza.com/.

17. J. N. Pieterse describes how the missionary society tradition of buying children from slave markets to raise and baptize them was transformed postabolition into child-sponsorship schemes. Buyers could then purchase a "heathen child" that would entitle them to give the child a Christian baptismal name and in return they would receive their child's picture (1992, 72).

18. See Hunter (2002) for one of the best discussions of the materiality of sexual exchanges in Africa. This article avoids stereotypes of "sugar daddies" and "prostitutes" while maintaining a loyal and thorough material analysis of sexuality. See also Campbell, Nair, and Maimane (2006) for a frank and engaged discussion of these topics.

19. D. Carr, "Citizen Bono Brings Africa to Idle Rich," *New York Times*, 5 March 2007.

20. See the *Vanity Fair* Web site at http://www.vanityfair.com/.

21. See http://www.youtube.com/watch?v=D7srZjpCTaI.

22. See http://gawker.com/news/. There were no articles on the diamond trade in Africa, which might have been expected given Leonardo DiCaprio's embrace of the topic.

23. See G. Carter, "Annie Get Your Passport: Editor's Letter," *Vanity Fair*, July 2007, 28. The focus of the first column of the piece involves the earnestness of the work done by Graydon Carter, the magazine editor, and Bono, his guest editor for the Africa Issue. However, the piece details how the actual work seemed to have been done by "Aimee" and "Sheila" (no last names given), their respective deputies.

24. Yet the cultural angst of the West brought forth by 9/11 may have increased interest in Africa, both as an outlet for charitable impulses and as a preventive strategy against poverty-induced terrorism (Magubane, "Africa Script Needs Rewrite").

25. *Vanity Fair*, July 2007, 24.

26. "The Lazarus Effect," *Vanity Fair*, July 2007, 156–61. This is a biblical reference to the raising of the dead Lazarus of Bethany by Jesus in the New Testament.

27. Ibid., 160.

28. There is a tiny aerial shot of the "Mathare Valley Slum," but only rooftops are visible so one would have to know that this is the largest slum in Nairobi to have any sense that this photograph could represent suffering.

29. J. Ferguson's (1999) work on the abjection of Zambians from the promises of neoliberal modernity places insightful emphasis on how "expec-

tations of domesticity" left unfulfilled create particularly painful repercussions on familial and conjugal life.

30. Patton analyzes the categorization of "African AIDS" and points to the example of the South African campaigns from the 1980s in which the "white" campaign concerned itself with homosexual sex while the "black" campaign focused on the preservation of the family (2002, 80).

31. Alison Jackson's work shows images ranging from the British Queen on the loo to former U.S. president Bush appearing to struggle with a Rubik's Cube in the Oval Office; from Madonna changing the nappies of a little black baby to the family portrait of Princess Diana, Dodi, and their mixed-race baby; see http://www.alisonjackson.com/.

32. L. George, "In This Tabloid World," *Los Angeles Times,* 18 November 2007, http://www.alisonjackson.com/.

33. Playing up to the irony of perceptions of Africa and imagined realities, some of the top British celebrity do-gooders star in a short video for the British charity Comic Relief. In the video, Ricky Gervais fakes a report from Africa to raise money for a charity that plays on the perceptions of celebrity caring for Africa to promote products and celebrity image. The punch line of the video comes when Gervais, who is pretending to be in Kenya while really on a staged set, finds that the "African" he is interviewing is actually Bono in disguise. See http://www.metacafe.com/.

34. See http://www.youtube.com/, the fifteen-second version and the thirty-second version.

35. On 21 September 2007 *The Independent* published its second RED edition, this one edited by Giorgio Armani. It included articles by Leonardo DiCaprio, George Clooney, Bill Gates, and Beyoncé.

36. H. Pool, "Return to the Dark Ages," *Guardian,* 22 September 2006, http://www.guardian.co.uk/.

37. See Browning (1998) for a critique of any aesthetic representation of Africanness.

38. In her critique of the 1989 show at the Royal Ontario Museum called Into the Heart of Africa, Browning points out the desire to locate the "real Africa" in the midst of representations (1998, 56–59). She describes how picketers protested the show's repetition of stereotypical language and imagery— "it wasn't a problem of inability to see irony. The protesters 'argued that the subtleties of irony could not compete with the power of images of subjugation'" (ibid., 57).

39. "Kenyan Maasai 'Supermodel' Prefers Goat Herding to Stardom," *International Herald Tribune,* 22 March 2007, http://www.iht.com/.

40. Ibid.

41. Watson and Stratford (2008) argue that distance is central to the governance of public health representations of risk and that this "socio-spatial ordering" perpetuates gender biases in HIV preventative technologies as well.

42. In a provocative presentation, Kathryn Mathers argues that in fact, "saving Africa through tough love helps Americans to resolve the tensions between what they believe America to be about and what they experience" (2008, 2). Her other work examines popular humanitarianism in the American reality show *Survivor Africa* (Hubbard and Mathers 2008).

43. See http://www.joinred.com/news/17/news.htm.

44. M. Hume, "Africa: A Stage for Political Poseurs," *Spiked,* 19 June 2005, http://www.spiked-online.com/. Cited in Harrison (2006).

45. A. S. Woudstra, "Lazarus-like," The Micah Centre, King's University College, Canada, 2007, http://www.kingsu.ca/micah/.

3. SAVING AFRICA

1. Interestingly this is the same characterization given by U.S. congressman Everett Dirksen of aid to Europe after World War II; he termed the Marshall Plan "Operation Rat-Hole" in 1947 (Radelet and Levine 2008, 432).

2. Some of the more technical debates revolve around the minimum terms one might use to define "development"—how to use aid to increase economic growth. One position claims that there is no relation between aid and growth, and the relation between the two may even be negative (this is the position held by Easterly 2006 in particular, but see also Rajan and Subramanian 2005). The mechanisms that are thought to hinder aid from working positively for growth are many and diverse: aid can get wasted through corruption on government luxury consumption (i.e. presidential jets); it can keep bad governments in power; it cannot be absorbed because of limited capacity of governments; it reduces domestic savings; it undermines private-sector investment (aid tends to overvalue local currencies, making exports less competitive) (Radelet 2006). A second and more commonly held position is that there is a positive, if not completely understood, relation between aid and growth. Aid may spur growth by increasing savings and adding to capital available, by improving worker productivity via better health and education, and by helping the transfer of technology and knowledge. This is the position held by the main promoters of a "big push approach" to aid (especially Jeffrey Sachs). A related argument claims that there is a positive general relationship between aid and growth, but with diminishing returns (Radelet 2006; Radelet and Levine

2008). In other words, increases in aid finance do not translate in proportional increases in growth; the more aid is added, the lower the returns will be (Dalgaard, Hansen, and Tarp 2004). A very broad umbrella of scholars argues that aid helps growth only in certain conditions depending on the characteristics of the recipient country (Burnside and Dollar 2000), the type of aid, donor practices, and donor harmonization and coordination (Radelet and Levine 2008). Perhaps the most influential work within this camp in the last few years has been Paul Collier's (2007). According to Collier, aid should be targeted to the "bottom billion" instead of the other four billion that live in countries that are doing better. Note that for Collier, the bottom billion is not the poorest people on earth (as in Prahalad's four billion "Bottom of the Pyramid" markets), but the populations of "bottom billion countries" (that is, most of Africa plus a few more countries in Asia and Latin America). For Collier, these are countries that are stuck in one or more "traps" (conflict, natural resources, landlocked, and/or bad governance) or that have come unstuck from these traps too late (that is, after the 1980s). Most significant for RED, however, is the justification that emerges from these debates that supports the aid modality (and the target of HIV/AIDS) used by RED, regardless of the link between aid and growth. This position argues that, whatever the impact of aid is on growth, its positive impact on other development outcomes should not be discounted, especially in health (Levine, the What Works Working Group, with Kinder 2004). This allows for a seemingly apolitical, technical, and managerial solution to the problems that beset aid.

3. These debates aim at solving problems of efficiency and governance in international aid delivery. A common trend has been a clear movement toward funding toward support of "proven, developmental governments," and some donors have moved toward "common basket funds" or "sector investment programs" in an attempt to alleviate the negative impact of too many uncoordinated donor efforts on recipient countries' governance (Brautigam and Knack 2004, 277). At the same time, others have placed more emphasis on reverse conditionality, highlighting what recipient countries can do to make aid work for their own purposes, not the donors' (Whitfield 2009).

4. The Millennium Project was commissioned by the UN secretary-general in 2002 to develop a concrete action plan for the world to achieve the Millennium Development Goals (MDGs). In 2005, the independent advisory body, headed by Jeffrey Sachs, presented its final reports and recommendations for the achievement of the MDGs. The UN Millennium Project secretariat was later integrated into the UNDP; see http://www.unmillenniumproject.org/.

5. This argument is not new and tends to resurface regularly. The most prominent past holders of such a position were economists Milton Friedman (1958) and Peter Bauer (1972).

6. Of course such an extreme argument has met with criticism. A. G. Karnani (2006), for example, argues that only a few products that can be sold to BOP markets are attractive for MNCs. Instead of targeting BOP as consumers, MNCs should address BOP as *producers*—they should buy from them. Karnani and others also highlight that simply selling to the poor does not necessarily improve their welfare or reduce poverty (Jenkins 2005). Prahalad only includes success stories in his book, and it is not clear how BOP strategies address poverty—in only three cases out of twelve does there seem to be a positive impact on income (Crabtree 2007).

7. The U.S. MCA is the largest application of ex-post conditionality so far. Set up in 2004 independently from USAID and managed by the Millennium Challenge Corporation (MCC), MCA releases funds to countries that qualify according to a series of indicators grouped under the headings of "ruling justly," "investing in people," and "ensuring economic freedom." Countries that are improving policies but have not reached the required levels may qualify for a "threshold program." MCC has a small secretariat and limited presence in recipient countries and expects recipients to design their own programs for approval. As of November 2008, out of MCC's total of eighteen grants, also known as Millennium Challenge Compacts, eleven were with African countries. The total grants to African countries amounted to $4.5 billion or almost 75 percent of the total value of all MCC Compacts signed until then. Eight out of eighteen countries in the threshold program are African. MCA funds programs that specifically promote "sustainable economic growth"; see http://www.mcc.gov/.

8. ODA transfers from the United States are the largest among OECD members in absolute terms, but the smallest as a percentage of national income (Goldstein and Moss 2005, 1300).

9. Pressure from the Republican right wing on a few African causes, including their "recent conversion" in response to HIV and AIDS, is likely to have been the biggest factor in former president George W. Bush's "newfound enthusiasm" for African aid (Goldstein and Moss 2005, 1300). PEPFAR funds only selected countries and is administered through the U.S. Department of State, signalling its strategic importance in contrast to typical health-related initiatives. The initial PEPFAR was a $15 billion program over three years that is reported as having supported ARV treatment for over a million Africans; see http://www.pepfar.gov/.

10. "Debt Relief Is Down: Other ODA Rises Slightly," OECD, press release, 4 April 2008, http://www.oecd.org.

11. The disease burden of AIDS is 84.5 million compared to lower respiratory infections at 91.3 million. There is also an extensive overlap between diseases occurring in developing countries (Hotez et al. 2006, 102; see earlier analyses of coinfections of tropical diseases and HIV in Stillwaggon 2005; Harms and Feldmeier 2002.

12. See the Copenhagen Consensus of Economists Web site at http://www.copenhagenconsensus.com/.

13. See P. Piot, "Why AIDS Is Exceptional," speech, London School of Economics, 8 February 2005, http://data.unaids.org/Media/Speeches02/SP_Piot_LSE_08Feb05_en.pdf, for the UNAIDS argument for why AIDS should be exceptional.

14. These are variously also referred to as "global health programs" or "global public policy networks" and are characterized as "a blueprint for financing, resourcing, coordinating, and/or implementing disease control across at least several countries in more than one region of the world" (Hanefeld et al. 2007, 11).

15. See *TIME* Global Health Summit, http://www.time.com/time/2005/globalhealth/.

16. For arguments in favor of the privileged position of ARV provision, see Ventelou and Moatti (2008).

17. See the official RED Web site, http://www.joinred.com/.

18. UN Global Compact Learning Forum, "Instituting a Whistleblower Policy in the Global Fund to Fight Aids, Tuberculosis and Malaria," in *Business Fighting Corruption: Experiences from Africa Case Study Series,* South Africa: Pretoria, Global Compact Regional Learning Forum, http://www.unglobalcompact.org/.

19. Paul Farmer, Cofounder Partners In Health (Global Fund 2005, 23).

20. While the CCM is formally in charge of oversight of implementation, it is actually a local fund agent appointed by the Global Fund itself that, acting on the Fund's behalf, will verify that the funds are properly managed and spent.

21. A. Ingram and K. Peterson, "HIV/AIDS: Obama's Easy Win," Open Democracy News Analysis, 26 November 2008, http://www.opendemocracy.net/.

22. As of December 2010, RED had disbursed $160 million.

23. Global Fund, "The Global Fund to Fight AIDS, Tuberculosis and Malaria Launches Corporate Champions Program," press release, 21 January 2008, http://www.theglobalfund.org/.

24. See http://www.theglobalfund.org/en/partners/private/.

25. See http://www.theglobalfund.org/en/about/how/.

26. See http://www.theglobalfund.org/en/funds_raised/distribution/.

27. The four countries were Ghana, Lesotho, Rwanda, and Swaziland. South Africa and Zambia started receiving grants with RED financing only in 2010.

28. These are, of course, not the only areas of critique levied against the Global Fund, but they encompass the bulk of the issues raised in the current literature. For the most recent and in-depth look at both country-level and Fund-level problems, see Rivers (2008).

29. The "three ones" are one agreed HIV/AIDS Action Framework that provides the basis for coordinating the work of all partners; one National AIDS Coordinating Authority, with a broad-based multisectoral mandate; and one agreed country-level Monitoring and Evaluation System (see http://www.unaids.org/). The dynamics of aid harmonization vary significantly from country to country, but form part of the context in which the Global Fund operates.

30. Global Fund, "Confirmation of U.S. Pledge for 2004 Boosts Global Fund Resources for Fourth Proposal Round to $900 Million," press release, 26 February 2004, http://www.theglobalfund.org/.

31. See the PEPFAR Web site, http://www.pepfar.gov/.

32. UN Global Compact Learning Forum, "Instituting a Whistleblower Policy."

33. Ibid., 40.

34. Ibid., 54.

35. Editorial, "A Call for Transparency at the Global Fund," *Lancet* 368 (2006): 815. The *Lancet* goes on to note that the WHO bureaucracy can delay a new Global Fund appointment by up to six months, every travel request must go through "lumbering internal procedures," and the two organizations have a "dysfunctional dynamic surrounding technical advice" (ibid.).

36. See http://www.theglobalfund.org/.

37. M. Frazier, "Bono & Co. Spend up to $100 Million on Marketing, Incur Watchdogs' Wrath," *Advertising Age,* 5 March 2007, http://adage.com/.

38. See http://www.joinred.com/archive/adage/.

39. RED was not the first co-branding initiative to support the Global Fund, as the Fund itself was part of a co-branded marketing initiative in 2004 with VH-1, a U.S. music television channel that produced a series of HIV/AIDS public service announcements highlighting the Global Fund (Global

Fund, "Report of the Resource Mobilization and Communication Committee," Eighth Board Meeting, Geneva, 2004, http://www.theglobalfund.org/).

40. Global Fund, "Fifteenth Board Meeting Report," April 2007, 7, http://www.theglobalfund.org/.

41. *Global Social Policy Digest* 6.2 (August 2006), 232.

42. Global Fund Observer, "Interview: Michel Kazatchkine, the Fund's New Executive Director," 72, 1 March 2007, http://www.aidspan.org.

43. Global Fund, "Fifteenth Board Meeting Report," 27.

4. HARD COMMERCE

1. Converse, http://www.converse.com/#/products/shoes/red/108937.

2. See, among others, the special issues on CSR in *International Affairs* 81, no. 3 (2005), *Third World Quarterly* 28, no. 4 (2007), and *Development and Change* 39, no. 6 (2008).

3. RED impact calculator, http://www.joinred.com/Learn/Impact/Calculator.aspx.

4. See European Commission, http://ec.europa.eu/.

5. For example, the World Business Council for Sustainable Development uses the following definition: "Corporate Social Responsibility is the continuing commitment by business to behave ethically and contribute to economic development while improving the quality of life of the workforce and their families as well as of the local community and society at large" (Holmes and Watts 2000, 8).

6. According to Grahame Thompson, "corporate citizenship" is based on a "citizenship of acts," which stresses active involvement in the public sphere where agents can "pick and choose which aspects of citizenly behaviors they wish to uphold or stress" (2008, 2). Such an approach is in line with the voluntary nature of CSR, but tends to obfuscate another approach to citizenship, one based on "status" and highlighting "rights and obligations determined within the context of a definite polity" (ibid.). Lacking enforcement mechanisms and a clear legal basis, "corporate citizenship" is not exercised, but rather *performed*. Such performance takes place within the legitimizing boundaries of semi-institutionalized frameworks (the UN Global Compact, or the World Economic Forum, where RED was launched) and through enabling and learning networks (McIntosh, Waddock, and Kell 2004), such as CSR conferences, "how to" manuals, and with the engagement of specialized consultants (Thompson 2008).

7. McKinsey, "The State of Corporate Philanthropy: A McKinsey Global Survey," February 2008, http://www.mckinseyquarterly.com/.

8. Peter Frumkin makes an explicit distinction between charity and philanthropy. According to Frumkin, charity is "the uncomplicated and unconditional transfer of money or assistance to those in need with the intent of helping" (2006, 5). Philanthropy, instead, is based on the (very American) "principles of self-help and opportunity creation" (ibid., 6). On the basis of this distinction, Frumkin argues that charity has a much longer history than philanthropy, since in Christianity and other religions, charity and faith have gone hand in hand for a long time.

9. See Friedman (1962) and M. Friedman, "The Social Responsibility of Business Is to Increase Its Profits," *New York Times,* 13 September 1970.

10. The focus on the "business case" for CSR is not without its critics. Michael Jensen (2000) claims that CSR fails because it does not provide a "corporate objective function" of business, and provides too many variables for managers to juggle. A different criticism of the business case focuses on the willingness and eagerness of CSR discourse to adopt the language and stance of the business community. In this context, stakeholder theory can be seen as a way of replacing genuine social responsibility with simple profit calculation (Jenkins 2005; Newell 2005; Prieto-Carron et al. 2006).

11. Blowfield and Frynas (2005) point out that this approach among companies continues today.

12. American Express's campaign for the renovation of the Statue of Liberty in the early 1980s generated a 27 percent increase in card use and a 10 percent increase in new card membership applications, in addition to raising $1.7 million for the cause (King 2006, 11). To achieve this, American Express spent $6 million promoting its Statue of Liberty campaign and "announced its good works with authority and fanfare, making a break with the humbler philanthropy of the past, and in direct response to the public's raised consciousness. The genius of this campaign was recognizing that the marketplace would reward firms that acted in a socially responsible way and that assisted ordinary citizens to act responsibly too" (Berglind and Nakata 2005, 446).

13. This chapter is based on the analysis of the seven companies that were partners of RED as of December 2007 (American Express, Apple, Armani, Converse/Nike, Gap, Hallmark, and Motorola). Subsequently, Microsoft, Dell, Starbucks, and many others joined RED, while Motorola dropped out. We contacted both Motorola and RED to find out the reasons behind Motorola's abandonment, but were not able to get answers from either. Motorola (as of late 2008) still listed its RAZR (RED) on its Web site and included a link to the RED Web site, but the RED Web site had cleaned out all references (even historical ones) to Motorola's involvement.

14. Many corporations labeled as "manufacturers" do not actually manufacture anything, as they have outsourced part or all of their production functions to contractors, often in developing countries. They focus on brand design, marketing, financial management, and supply-chain management.

15. Thus these companies did not need to "save Africans" to justify their contributions to development in areas of greatest need. They actually depend on the workforce in other areas of the developing world, so their initiatives could have been engaged by improving their own ways of doing business while helping "others."

16. We owe this observation to Grahame Thompson.

17. B. Steverman, "Credit-Card Stocks Slug It Out," *Business Week,* 9 July 2007, http://www.businessweek.com/.

18. Apple's 30G iPod sells at $299, while its most expensive component (the hard drive) costs about $73. The next most costly components are the display module (about $20), the video/multimedia processor chip ($8), and the controller chip ($5). The estimated final assembly cost, done in China, is about $4 a unit (Hal R. Varian, "An iPod Has Global Value: Ask the (Many) Countries That Make It," *New York Times,* 28 June 2007, http://www.nytimes.com/).

19. Martyn Williams, "How Much Should an IPod Shuffle Cost?" *IDG News Service,* 24 February 2005, http://www.pcworld.com/.

20. An iSuppli teardown of the Mac Mini found the cost of material and manufacturing on that computer to be about $283, leaving a gross margin of 44 percent before marketing and distribution costs (A. Hesseldahl, "Unpeeling Apple's Nano," *Business Week,* 22 September 2005, http://www.businessweek.com/).

21. Beth Herskovits, "Product Red Initiative Draws Star, Brand Power," *PR Week,* 27 January 2006, http://www.prweek.com/uk/search/article/538407/.

22. Lauren Goldstein Crowe, "Luxury's Little Green Secret," *Financial Times,* "Business of Fashion" supplement, Spring 2007, 16–17.

23. P. L. Stepankowsky, "Converse Rebounds for Nike," *Seattle Times,* 12 September 2007, http://seattletimes.nwsource.com/.

24. Mindbranch Market Research, "Market Research Report: Greeting Cards," September 2007, http://www.mindbranch.com/.

25. Research and Markets, "Greeting Cards Market Report Plus 2006," September 2006, http://www.researchandmarkets.com/.

26. D. Frommer and B. Caulfield, "What Will Cure Motorola?" *Forbes,* 22 March 2007, http://www.forbes.com/.

27. R. O. Crockett, "Shifting Gears at Motorola," *Business Week,* 19 January 2007, http://www.businessweek.com/.

28. For individual CSR profiles of the RED companies, see Ponte, Richey, and Baab (2008).

29. For the methodology used in the *Business Ethics* magazine ranking, see http://www.business-ethics.com/BE100_all.

30. Microsoft and Dell joined RED in January 2008, while Starbucks joined in November 2008, and more companies joined in the following years; these companies are not covered in our analysis.

31. Similarly, Joss Stone also donated 100 percent profits of one of her music videos to RED.

32. Excluding the Hirst auction, RED raised $60 mllion in its first two years and another $60 million in the next three.

33. L. Story, "Want to Help Treat AIDS in Africa? Buy a Cellphone," *New York Times,* 4 October 2006, http://www.nytimes.com/.

34. Weber, "Bono Bets on Red to BATTLE Aids."

5. DOING GOOD BY SHOPPING WELL

1. See http://www.buylesscrap.org.

2. A. Kingston, "The Trouble with Buying for a Cause," *Maclean's Magazine,* 26 March 2007; see also Sarna-Wojcicki (2008).

3. See, among others, the special issue of *International Journal of Consumer Studies* 30, no. 5 (2006), on "Political and Ethical Consumerism around the World."

4. See Converse, "Make Mine (RED)," http://www.converse.com/#/products/shoes/converseOne/scratch.

5. The RED home page includes a section where readers can submit their own videos on "What does RED mean to me?" in the hope of being featured in a "video wall" of people, including celebrities, talking about what RED is. See http://www.joinred.com/you.asp.

6. "(RED)NIGHTS Hosts Star-Studded Concert at Carnegie Hall," http://blog.joinred.com/2009/09/rednights-hosts-star-studded-concert-at.html.

7. See Agritrade, "Coffee: Trade Issues for the ACP," http://agritrade.cta.int/en/Commodities/Coffee-sector/Executive-brief.

8. See, among many others, Gibbon and Ponte (2005), Gibbon, Ponte, and Lazaro (2010), and the research output of the "Regoverning Markets" project based at the International Institute for the Environment and Development (IIED), http://www.regoverningmarkets.org/.

9. In organic coffee, producers may pay for certification (directly, or indirectly through pricing arrangements with an exporter holding the certification), but often not in full—in many schemes, governments and aid agencies heavily subsidize the cost (Gibbon 2006).

10. N. Koehn, "Respected Harvard Business School Professor and Author Nancy Koehn Speaks Out on Managing Brands," *Interbrand, Best Global Brands* (2008), http://www.interbrand.com/.

11. For the methodology used in the Interbrand valuation, see http://www.interbrand.com/.

12. If one considers the brands that joined RED during 2008 (Microsoft, Dell, and Starbucks), the total is seven out of ten RED brands in the top one hundred.

13. See Interbrand, Best Global Brands 2008 ranking, http://www.interbrand.com.sg/.

14. See http://www.starbucks.com/.

CONCLUSION

1. D. Carr, "Citizen Bono Brings Africa to Idle Rich," *New York Times,* 5 March 2007, http://www.nytimes.com/.

2. *Sunday Times,* "Shop with Bono," 26 February 2006, http://women.timesonline.co.uk.

3. See the Newman's Own Web site at http://www.newmansown.com/.

4. RED product launch at Davos, video, http://www.joinred.com/.

5. J. Erwing, "For Bono, Star Power with Purpose," *Business Week,* 27 January 2006, http://www.businessweek.com/.

6. See http://joinred.blogspot.com.

7. Paradoxically, by following this line of argument, one could see RED as a better initiative than mainstream sustainability labels and certifications. At least RED does not impose any extra costs on producers, but it does not improve social and environmental conditions either.

8. RED product launch at Davos, video.

WORKS CITED

Adorno, T. 1991. *The Culture Industry: Selected Essays on Mass Culture.* London: Routledge.

Agenor, P.-R., N. Bayraktar, E. P. Moreira, and K. El. Aynaoui. 2005. "Achieving the Millennium Development Goals in Sub-Saharan Africa: A Macroeconomic Monitoring Framework." World Bank Policy Research Working Paper 3750. World Bank, Washington, D.C.

Aglietta, M. 1979. *A Theory of Capitalist Regulation: The US Experience.* London: New Left Books.

Alberoni, F. 1972. "The Powerless Elite: Theory and Sociological Research on the Phenomenon of the Stars." In *Sociology of Mass Communications,* ed. Denis McQuail, 75–98. Harmondsworth: Penguin.

Aldridge, A. 2003. *Consumption.* Cambridge: Polity.

Allen, P., and M. Kovach. 2000. "The Capitalist Composition of Organic: The Potential of Markets in Fulfilling the Promise of Organic Agriculture." *Agriculture and Human Values* 17(3): 221–32.

Anderson, N. 2008. "Shoppers of the World Unite: (RED)'s Message and Morality in the Fight Against African AIDS." *Journal of Pan African Studies* 2(6): 32–54.

Andreasson, S. 2005. "Orientalism and African Development Studies: The 'Reductive Repetition' Motif in Theories of African Underdevelopment." *Third World Quarterly* 26(6): 971–86.

Appadurai, A. 1986. "Introduction: Commodities and the Politics of Value." In *The Social Life of Things: Commodities in Cultural Perspective,* ed. A. Appadurai, 3–64. Cambridge: Cambridge University Press.

Arvidsson, A. 2007. "The Logic of the Brand." *Quaderno* 36 (May).

Assayas, M. 2005. *Bono: In Conversation with Michka Assayas.* New York: Riverhead.

Austin, S. B. 1989–90. "AIDS and Africa: United States Media and Racist Fantasy." *Cultural Critique* (Winter): 129–52.

Bancroft, A. 2001. "Globalisation and HIV/AIDS: Inequality and the Boundaries of a Symbolic Epidemic." *Health, Risk and Society* 3(1): 89–98.

Banet-Weiser, S., and C. Lapsansky. 2008. "RED Is the New Black: Brand Culture, Consumer Citizenship and Political Possibility." *International Journal of Communication* 2:1248–68.

Baudrillard, J. 1998. *The Consumer Society: Myth and Structures.* London: Sage.

Bauer, P. 1972. *Dissent on Development.* Cambridge, Mass.: Harvard University Press.

Bauman, Z. 1991. *Modernity and Ambivalence.* London: Polity.

———. 2005. *Liquid Life.* London: Polity.

Bayart, J.-F. 2000. "Africa in the World: A History of Extraversion." *African Affairs* 99:217–67.

Beck, U. 1992. *Risk Society: Towards a New Modernity.* London: Sage.

Berglind, M., and C. Nakata. 2005. "Cause-Related Marketing: More Buck Than Bang?" *Business Horizons* 48(3): 443–53.

Biehl, J. 2007. "Pharmaceuticalization: AIDS Treatment and Global Health Politics." *Anthropological Quarterly* 8(4): 1083–1126.

Bishop, M., and M. Green. 2008. *Philanthrocapitalism: How the Rich Can Save the World.* New York: St. Martin's Press.

Bleiker, R., and A. Kay. 2007. "Representing HIV/AIDS in Africa: Pluralist Photography and Local Empowerment." *International Studies Quarterly* 51(1): 139–63.

Blowfield, M. 2007. "Reasons to Be Cheerful? What We Know about CSR's Impact." *Third World Quarterly* 28(4): 683–95.

Blowfield, M., and J. G. Frynas. 2005. "Setting New Agendas: Critical Perspectives on Corporate Social Responsibility in the Developing World." *International Affairs* 81(3): 499–513.

Boltanski, L. 1993. *La souffrance a distance.* Paris: Métailié.

Boltanski, L., and E. Chiapello. 1999. *Le nouvel esprit du capitalisme.* Paris: Gallimard.

Boltanski, L., and L. Thévenot. 1991. *De la justification: Les economies de la grandeur.* Paris: Gallimard.

Bonanno, A., L. Busch, W. Friedland, L. Gouveia, and E. Mingione. 1994. *From Columbus to ConAgra: The Globalization of Agriculture and Food.* Lawrence: University of Kansas Press.

Boorstin, D. J. 1971. *The Image: A Guide to Pseudo-Events in America*. New York: Atheneum. Originally published as Daniel J. Boorstin, *The Image, or What Happened to the American Dream* (London: Weidenfeld and Nicolson, 1961).

Bourdieu, P. 1976. *Distinction: A Social Critique of the Judgement of Taste*. Cambridge: Cambridge University Press.

Brautigam, D. A., and S. Knack. 2004. "Foreign Aid, Institutions, and Governance in Sub-Saharan Africa." *Economic Development and Cultural Change* 52(2): 255–85.

Brockington, D. 2009. *Celebrity and the Environment: Fame, Wealth and Power in Conservation*. London: Zed.

Browning, B. 1998. *Infectious Rhythm: Metaphors of Contagion and the Spread of African Culture*. New York: Routledge.

Brugha, R. 2005. *Global Fund Tracking Study: A Cross-Country Comparative Analysis*. Final Draft (2 August). http://www.theglobalfund.org/.

Bryman, A. 1999. "The Disneyization of Society." *Sociological Review* 47(1): 25–47.

Burman, E. 1994. "Innocents Abroad: Western Fantasies of Childhood and the Iconography of Emergencies." *Disasters* 18(3): 238–53.

Burnside, C., and D. Dollar. 2000. "Aid, Policies and Growth." *American Economic Review* 90(4): 847–68.

Butt, L. 2002. "The Suffering Stranger: Medical Anthropology and International Morality." *Medical Anthropology* 21(1): 1–24.

Calderisi, R. 2006. *The Trouble with Africa: Why Foreign Aid Isn't Working*. New York: Palgrave.

Calhoun, C. 2008. "The Imperative to Reduce Sufering: Charity, Progress, and Emergencies in the Field of Humanitarian Action." In *Humanitarianism in Question: Power, Politics, Ethics*, ed. M. Barnett and T. G. Weiss. Ithaca, N.Y.: Cornell University Press.

Callon, M., C. Méadel, and V. Rabeharisoa. 2002. "The Economy of Qualities." *Economy and Society* 31(2): 194–217.

Cameron, J., and A. Haanstra. 2008. "Development Made Sexy: How It Happened and What It Means." *Third World Quarterly* 29(8): 1475–89.

Campbell, D. 2004. "Horrific Blindness: Images of Death in Contemporary Media." *Journal for Cultural Research* 8(1): 55–74.

Campbell, D., Y. Nair, and S. Maimane. 2006. "AIDS Stigma, Sexual Moralities and the Policing of Women and Youth in South Africa." *Feminist Review* 83:132–38.

Carrier, J. G. 1998. "Introduction." In *Virtualism: A New Political Economy*, ed. J. G. Carrier and D. Miller, 1–24. Oxford: Berg.

Carrier, J. G., and D. Miller, eds. 1998. *Virtualism: A New Political Economy.* Oxford: Berg.

Carroll, A. B. 1999. "Corporate Social Responsibility: Evolution of a Definitional Construct." *Business and Society* 38(3): 268–95.

Cela Díaz, F. 2005. "An Integrative Framework for Architecting Supply Chains." PhD diss., MIT.

Chesler, E. 2005. "Introduction." In *Where Human Rights Begin: Health, Sexuality and Women in the New Millennium,* ed. W. Chavkin and E. Chesler, 1–34. New Brunswick, N.J.: Rutgers University Press.

Cohen, S. 2001. *States of Denial: Knowing about Atrocities and Suffering.* Cambridge: Polity.

Cole, K., ed. 2008. *Awearness: Inspiring Stories on How to Make a Difference.* New York: Melcher Media.

Collier, P. 2007. *The Bottom Billion: Why the Poorest Countries Are Failing and What Can Be Done about It.* Oxford: Oxford University Press.

Collins, J. L., M. di Leonardo, and B. Williams, eds. 2008. *New Landscapes of Inequality: Neoliberalism and the Erosion of Democracy in America.* Santa Fe, N.M.: School for Advanced Research Press.

Comaroff, J. 2007. "Beyond Bare Life: AIDS, (Bio)Politics, and the Neoliberal Order." *Public Culture* 19(1): 197–220.

Conroy, M. E. 2007. *Branded! How the "Certification Revolution" Is Transforming Global Corporations.* Gabriola Island, B.C.: New Society.

Cook, I., and P. Crang. 1996. "The World on a Plate: Culinary Culture, Displacement, and Geographical Knowledges." *Journal of Material Culture* 1:131–53.

Cooper, A. F. 2008a. *Celebrity Diplomacy.* Boulder, Colo.: Paradigm.

———. 2008b. "Beyond One Image Fits All: Bono and the Complexity of Celebrity Diplomacy." *Global Governance* 14:265–72.

———. 2008c. "Beyond the Boardroom: 'Multilocation' and the Business Face of Celebrity Diplomacy." Paper presented at the International Studies Association Meeting, San Francisco, March.

Crabtree, A. 2007. "Evaluating 'The Bottom of the Pyramid' from a Fundamental Capabilities Perspective." CBDS working paper, Copenhagen Business School, Centre for Business and Development.

Crimp, D. 1988. *AIDS: Cultural Analysis/Cultural Activism.* Boston: MIT Press.

Curtin, P. D. 1964. *The Image of Africa: British Ideas and Action, 1780–1850.* Vol. 1. Madison: University of Wisconsin Press.

Dalgaard, C.-J., H. Hansen, and F. Tarp. 2004. "On the Empirics of Foreign Aid and Growth." *Economic Journal* 114(496): 191–216.

Daviron, B., and S. Ponte. 2005. *The Coffee Paradox: Global Markets, Commodity Trade, and the Elusive Promise of Development.* London: Zed.

de Janvry, A., and E. Sadoulet. 2004. "Beyond Bono: Making Foreign Aid More Efficient." Working Paper 982, University of California, Berkeley.

de Soto, H. 2000. *The Mystery of Capital: Why Capitalism Triumphs in the West and Fails Everywhere Else.* New York: Basic Books.

de Waal, A. 2008. "The Humanitarian Carnival." *World Affairs,* Fall: 43–55.

Debord, G. 1967. *La société du spectacle.* Paris: Buchet-Chastel.

di Leonardo, M. 2008. "Introduction: New Global and American Landscapes of Inequality." In *New Landscapes of Inequality: Neoliberalism and the Erosion of Democracy in America,* ed. J. L. Collins, M. di Leonardo, and B. Williams. Santa Fe, N.M.: School for Advanced Research Press.

Dieter, H., and R. Kumar. 2008. "The Downside of Celebrity Diplomacy: The Neglected Complexity of Development." *Global Governance* 14:259–64.

Douglas, M., and B. Isherwood. 1980. *The World of Goods: Towards an Anthropology of Consumption.* Harmondsworth: Penguin.

DuPuis, M. 2000. "Not in My Body: BGH and the Rise of Organic Milk." *Agriculture and Human Values* 17(3): 285–95.

Durkheim, E. 1915. *The Elementary Forms of Religious Life.* London: Allen and Unwin.

Dyer, R. 1979. *Stars.* London: BFI.

Dyer-Witheford, N. 2001. "Empire, Immaterial Labor, the New Combinations, and the Global Worker." *Rethinking Marxism* 13, nos. 3–4 (Fall): 70–80.

Easterly, W. 2006. *The White Man's Burden: Why the West's Efforts to Aid the Rest Have Done So Much Ill and So Little Good.* New York: Penguin.

———, ed. 2008a. *Reinventing Foreign Aid.* Cambridge, Mass.: MIT Press.

———. 2008b. "Introduction: Can't Take It Anymore?" In *Reinventing Foreign Aid,* ed. W. Easterly. Cambridge, Mass.: MIT Press.

Edwards, M. 2008. *Just Another Emperor? The Myths and Realities of Philanthrocapitalism.* New York: Demos and the Young Foundation.

England, R. 2008. "The Writing Is on the Wall for UNAIDS." *British Medical Journal* 336 (10 May): 1072.

Fadlalla, A. H. 2008. "The Neoliberalization of Compassion: Darfur and the Mediation of American Faith, Fear and Terror." In *New Landscapes of Inequality: Neoliberalism, and the Erosion of Democracy in America,* ed. J. L. Collins, M. di Leonardo, and B. Williams, 209–28. Santa Fe, N.M.: School for Advanced Research Press.

Farmer, P. 1992. *AIDS and Accusation: Haiti and the Geography of Blame.* Berkeley: University of California Press.

———. 1999. *Infections and Inequalities: The Modern Plagues.* Berkeley: University of California Press.

———. 2003. *Pathologies of Power: Health, Human Rights, and the New War on the Poor.* 1st ed. Berkeley: University of California Press.

Fassin, D. 2007. *When Bodies Remember: Experiences and Politics of AIDS in South Africa.* Berkeley: University of California Press.

Featherstone, M. 1987. "Lifestyle and Consumer Culture." *Theory, Culture and Society* 4(1): 55–70.

———. 1991. *Consuming Culture and Postmodernism.* London: Sage.

Ferguson, J. 1999. *Expectations of Modernity: Myths and Meanings of Urban Life on the Zambian Copperbelt.* Berkeley: University of California Press.

———. 2006. *Global Shadows: Africa in the Neoliberal World Order.* Durham, N.C.: Duke University Press.

———. 2009. "The Uses of Neoliberalism." *Antipode* 41(51): 166–84.

Ferguson, N. 2009. "Foreword." In D. Moyo, *Dead Aid: Why Aid Is Not Working and How There Is Another Way for Africa.* London: Allen Lane.

Fine, B. 2002. *The World of Consumption: The Material and Cultural Revisited.* 2nd ed. London: Routledge.

Finkelstein, J. 1989. *Dining Out: A Sociology of Modern Manners.* Cambridge: Polity.

Flint, J., and A. de Waal. 2005. *Darfur: A Short History of a Long War.* London: Zed.

Freeman, R. E. 1984. *Strategic Management: A Stakeholder Approach.* Boston: Pitman/Ballinger.

Freeman, R. E., and J. Liedtka. 1991. "Corporate Social Responsibility: A Critical Approach—Corporate Social Responsibility No Longer a Useful Concept." *Business Horizons* 34(4): 92–98.

Freidberg, S. 2003. "Cleaning Up Down South: Supermarkets, Ethical Trade and African Horticulture." *Social and Cultural Geography* 4(1): 27–43.

———. 2004. *French Beans and Food Scares: Culture and Commerce in an Anxious Age.* New York: Oxford University Press.

Friedman, M. 1958. "Foreign Economic Aid." *Yale Review* 47(4): 501–16.

———. 1962. *Capitalism and Freedom.* Chicago: University of Chicago Press.

Frumkin, P. 2006. *Strategic Giving: The Art and Science of Philanthropy.* Chicago: University of Chicago Press.

Gabriel, Y., and T. Lang. 1995. *The Unmanageable Consumer: Contemporary Consumption and Its Fragmentation.* London: Sage.

Gamson, J. 1994. *Claims to Fame: Celebrity in Contemporary America.* Berkeley: University of California Press.

Gibbon, P. 2006. "An Overview of the Certified Organic Export Sector in Uganda." DIIS Working Paper 13, Danish Institute for International Studies, Copenhagen.

———. 2008. "An Analysis of Standards-Based Regulation in the EU Organic Sector, 1991–2007." *Journal of Agrarian Change* 8(4): 553–82.

Gibbon, P., and S. Ponte. 2005. *Trading Down: Africa, Value Chains and the Global Economy.* Philadelphia: Temple University Press.

———. 2008. "Global Value Chains: From Governance to Governmentality?" *Economy and Society* 37(3): 365–92.

Gibbon, P., S. Ponte, and E. Lazaro. 2010. *Global Agro-Food Trade and Standards: Challenges for Africa.* Basingstoke: Palgrave.

Giovannucci, D., and S. Ponte. 2005. "Standards as a New Form of Social Contract? Sustainability Initiatives in the Coffee Industry." *Food Policy* 30(3): 284–301.

Giovannucci, D., P. Liu, and A. Byers. 2008. "Adding Value: Certified Coffee Trade in North America." In *Value-Adding Standards in the North American Food Market: Trade Opportunities in Certified Products for Developing Countries,* ed. P. Liu. Rome: FAO.

Gitlin, T. 1980. *The Whole World Is Watching: Mass Media in the Making and Unmaking of the New Left.* Berkeley: University of California Press.

Gledhill, C. 1991. *Stardom: Industry of Desire.* London: Routledge.

Global Fund. 2001–9. *The Global Fund to Fight AIDS, Tuberculosis and Malaria.* Geneva: Global Fund.

———. 2005. *Annual Report, Haiti, Operations and Results.* Geneva: Global Fund. http://www.theglobalfund.org/.

———. 2007a. *Report of the Global Fund Task Team on Resource Mobilization.* Geneva: Global Fund.

———. 2007b. *Special Consolidated Report: Report of the Executive Director and Secretariat Update.* http://www.theglobalfund.org/.

Goldstein, M. P., and T. J. Moss. 2005. "Compassionate Conservatives or Conservative Compassionates? US Political Parties and Bilateral Foreign Assistance to Africa." *Journal of Development Studies* 41(7): 1288–1302.

Goodman, D. 2004. "Rural Europe Redux? Reflections on Alternative Agro-Food Networks and Paradigm Change." *Sociologia Ruralis* 44(1): 3–16.

Gopal, P. 2006. "The Moral Empire: Africa, Globalization and the Politics of Conscience." *New Formations* 59:81–97.

Grossberg, L. 1992. *We Gotta Get Out of This Place: Popular Conservatism and Postmodern Culture.* London: Routledge.

Gurevich, M., C. M. M. Mathieson, J. Bower, and B. Dhayanandhan. 2007.

"Disciplining Bodies, Desires and Subjectivities: Sexuality and HIV-Positive Women." *Feminism and Psychology* 17(1): 9–38.

Guthman, J. 2002. "Commodified Meanings, Meaningful Commodities: Re-thinking Production-Consumption Links through the Organic System of Provision." *Sociologia Ruralis* 42(4): 295–311.

———. 2003. "Fast Food/Organic Food: Reflexive Tastes and the Making of 'Yuppie Chow.'" *Social and Cultural Geography* 4(1): 45–58.

Haakonsson, S. J., and L. A. Richey. 2007. "TRIPS and Public Health: The Doha Declaration and Africa." *Development Policy Review* 25(1): 71–90.

Hanataka, M., C. Bain, and L. Busch. 2005. "Third-Party Certification in the Global Agrifood System." *Food Policy* 30(3): 354–69.

Hanefeld, J., N. Spicer, R. Brugha, and G. Walt. 2007. "How Have Global Health Initiatives Impacted on Health Equity?" Commissioned by the Health Systems Knowledge Network, WHO Commission on the Social Determinants of Health.

Harding, J., and E. D. Pribram. 2004. "Losing Our Cool? Following Williams and Grossberg on Emotions." *Cultural Studies* 18(6): 863–83.

Hardt, M., and A. Negri. 2000. *Empire*. Cambridge, Mass.: Harvard University Press.

Harms, G., and H. Feldmeier. 2002. "Review: HIV Infection and Tropical Parasitic Diseases—Deleterious Interactions in Both Directions?" *Tropical Medicine and International Health* 7(6): 479–88.

Harrison, G. 2006. "Sovereignty, Poverty, History: 2005 and Western Moralities of Intervention." Paper presented at the African Studies Association of the United Kingdom, 11–13 September, London.

Hartwick, E. 1998. "Geographies of Consumption: A Commodity Chain Approach." *Environment and Planning D: Society and Space* 16:423–37.

Heidegger, M. 1977. "The Age of the World Picture." In *The Question concerning Technology,* trans. William Lovitt, 116–54. New York: Harper and Row.

Hintzen, P. C. 2008. "Desire and the Enrapture of Capitalist Consumption: Product Red, Africa, and the Crisis of Sustainability." *Journal of Pan African Studies* 2(6): 77–91.

Hirst, P., and G. Thompson. 1999. *Globalization in Question: The International Economy and the Possibilities of Governance*. London: Polity.

Hoffman, K. 2008. "Placing Enterprise and Business Thinking at the Heart of the War on Poverty." In *Reinventing Foreign Aid,* ed. W. Easterly, 485–502. Cambridge, Mass.: MIT Press.

Holmes, R., and P. Watts. 2000. *Corporate Social Responsibility: Making*

Good Business Sense. Geneva: World Business Council for Sustainable Development.

Holt, D. B. 2004. *How Brands Become Icons: The Principles of Cultural Branding.* Cambridge, Mass.: Harvard Business School Press.

Holtzer, B. 2006. "Political Consumerism between Individual Choice and Collective Action: Social Movements, Role Mobilization and Signalling." *International Journal of Consumer Studies* 30(5): 405–15.

Hood, J. 2009. "Celebrity Philanthropy: The Cultivation of China's HIV/AIDS Heroes." In *Celebrity in China,* ed. L. Edwards and E. Jeffreys. Hong Kong: Hong Kong University Press.

Hotez, P., D. H. Molyneux, A. Fenwick, E. Ottesen, S. E. Sachs, and J. D. Sachs. 2006. "Incorporating a Rapid-Impact Package for Neglected Tropical Diseases with Programs for HIV/AIDS, Tuberculosis, and Malaria." *PLoS Medicine* 3(5): 102.

Hubbard, L., and K. Mathers. 2008. "Surviving American Empire in Africa: The Anthropology of Reality Television." *International Journal of Cultural Studies* 7(4): 441–59.

Huddart, S. 2005. *Do We Need Another Hero? Understanding Celebrities' Roles in Advancing Social Causes.* Mimeo. Montreal: McGill University.

Hudson Institute. 2008. *The Index of Global Philanthropy.* Washington, D.C.: Center for Global Prosperity.

Hunter, M. 2002. "The Materiality of Everyday Sex: Thinking beyond Prostitution." *African Studies* 61(1): 99–120.

ICRW. 2004. *Civil Society Participation in Global Fund Governance: What Difference Does It Make?* Geneva: Global Fund.

Igoe, J., K. Neves, and D. Brockington. 2010. "A Spectacular Eco-Tour around the Historic Bloc: Theorising the Convergence of Biodiversity Conservation and Capitalist Expansion." *Antipode* 42(3): 486–512.

Jenkins, R. 2005. "Globalization, Corporate Social Responsibility and Poverty." *International Affairs* 81(3): 525–40.

Jensen, M. 2000. "Value Maximization and the Corporate Objective Function." HBS Working Paper 00-058, Harvard Business School, Cambridge, Mass.

Johnson, K. E. 2002. "AIDS as a US National Security Threat: Media Effects and Geographical Imaginations." *Feminist Media Studies* 2(1): 81–96.

Jones, S. 2009. "Alternative Development Financing Mechanisms: Pre-crisis Trends and Post-crisis Outlook." DIIS Report 11, Danish Institute for International Studies, Copenhagen.

Jungar, K., and E. Salo. 2008. "Shop and Do Good?" *Journal of Pan African Studies* 2(6): 92–102.

Karnani, A. G. 2006. "Fortune at the Bottom of the Pyramid: A Mirage." Paper 1035, University of Michigan, Ross School of Business.

Kates, J., J. S. Morrison, and E. Lief. 2006. "Global Health Funding: A Glass Half Full?" *Lancet* 368(9531): 187–88.

Kidder, T. 2003. *Mountains beyond Mountains: The Quest of Dr. Paul Farmer, a Man Who Would Cure the World.* New York: Random House.

King, S. 2006. *Pink Ribbons, Inc.: Breast Cancer and the Politics of Philanthropy.* Minneapolis: University of Minnesota Press.

Kinsley, M. 2008. *Creative Capitalism.* New York: Simon and Schuster.

Kitzinger, J., and D. Miller. 1992. "'African AIDS': The Media and Audience Beliefs." In *AIDS: Rights, Risk and Reason,* ed. P. Aggleton, P. Davies, and G. Hart, 28–52. London: Falmer.

Klein, N. 2000. *No Logo.* New York: Picador.

Kleinman, A., and J. Kleinman. 1996. "The Appeal of Experience; The Dismay of Images: Cultural Appropriations of Suffering in Our Times." *Daedalus,* Winter, 1–24.

Klooster, D. 2005. "Environmental Certification of Forests: The Evolution of Environmental Governance in a Commodity Network." *Journal of Rural Studies* 21(4): 403–17.

Lantos, G. P. 2001. "The Boundaries of Strategic Corporate Social Responsibility." *Journal of Consumer Marketing* 18(7): 595–632.

Lazzarato, M., and T. Negri. 1991. "Travail immatériel et subjectivité." *Futur Antérieur* 6 (Summer).

Levine, R., and What Works Working Group, with M. Kinder. 2004. *Millions Saved: Proven Successes in Global Health.* Washington, D.C.: Center for Global Development.

Levitt, T. 1958. "The Dangers of Social Responsibility." *Harvard Business Review* 36(5): 41–50.

Littler, J. 2008. "'I feel your pain': Cosmopolitan Charity and the Public Fashioning of the Celebrity Soul." *Social Semiotics* 18(2): 237–51.

Locke, R. M. 2002. "The Promise and Perils of Globalization: The Case of Nike." Working Paper Series 02-007, MIT-Industrial Performance Center.

Lyon, A. 2005. "Misrepresentations of Missing Women in the U.S. Press: The Rhetorical Uses of Disgust, Pity, and Compassion." In *Just Advocacy? Women's Human Rights, Transnational Feminisms, and the Politics of Representation,* ed. W. S. Hesford and W. Kozol, 173–95. New Brunswick, N.J.: Rutgers University Press.

MacKellar, L. 2005. "Priorities in Global Assistance for Health, AIDS, and Population." *Population and Development Review* 31(2): 293–312.

Magubane, Z. 2008. "The (Product) Red Man's Burden: Charity, Celebrity and the Contradictions of Coevalness." *Journal of Pan African Studies* 2(6): 102.1–102.25.

Mandelbaum, M. 1996. "Foreign Policy as Social Work." *Foreign Affairs* (January/February). http://www.foreignaffairs.com/.

Manzo, K. 2008. "Imaging Humanitarianism: NGO Identity and the Iconography of Childhood." *Antipode* 40(4): 632–57.

Marcuse, H. 1973 (1969). *An Essay on Liberation.* Harmondsworth: Penguin.

Marks, M. P., and Z. M. Fischer. 2002. "The King's New Bodies: Simulating Consent in the Age of Celebrity." *New Political Science* 24(3): 371–94.

Marsden, T., A. Flynn, and M. Harrison. 2000. *Consuming Interests: The Social Provision of Foods.* London: UCL Press.

Marshall, P. D. 1997. *Celebrity and Power: Fame in Contemporary Culture.* Minneapolis: University of Minnesota Press.

Marx, K. 1976. *Capital.* Vol. 1. London: Penguin.

Mathers, K. 2008. "Finding Yourself in Africa: How Oprah (and Americans) Find Their 'True North' in Africa." Berkeley Tourism Colloquium Presentation, 25 August.

Mbembe, A. 2001. *On the Postcolony.* Berkeley: University of California Press.

Mbembe, A., and S. Nuttall. 2004. "Writing the World from an African Metropolis." *Public Culture* 16(3): 347–72.

McClintock, A. 1994. "Soft-Soaping Empire: Commodity Racism and Imperial Advertising." In *Travellers' Tales: Narratives of Home and Displacement,* ed. G. Robertson, M. Mash, L. Tickner, J. Bird, B. Curtis, and T. Putnam, 131–54. London: Routledge.

McCord, G., J. Sachs, and W. T. Woo. 2005. "Understanding African Poverty: Beyond the Washington Consensus to the Millennium Development Goals Approach." Paper presented at the conference on "Africa in the Global Economy: External Constraints, Regional Integration, and the Role of the State in Development and Finance" held at the South African Reserve Bank, Pretoria, 13–14 June 2005.

McIntosh, M., S. Waddock, and G. Kell. 2004. *Learning to Talk: Corporate Citizenship and the Development of the UN Global Compact.* Sheffield: Greenleaf.

Milberg, W. 2008. "Shifting Sources and Uses of Profits: Sustaining US Financialization with Global Value Chains." *Economy and Society* 37(3): 420–51.

Miller, D. 1998. "A Theory of Virtualism." In *Virtualism: A New Political Economy*, ed. J. G. Carrier and D. Miller. Oxford: Berg.

———. 2001. *The Dialectics of Shopping*. Chicago: University of Chicago Press.

Mitchell, W. J. T. 2005. *What Do Pictures Want? The Lives and Loves of Images*. Chicago: University of Chicago Press.

Moeller, S. 1999. *Compassion Fatigue: How the Media Sell Disease, Famine, War and Death*. London: Routledge.

Morris, M., and N. Dunne. 2004. "Driving Environmental Certification: Its Impact on the Furniture and Timber Products Value Chain in South Africa." *Geoforum* 35:251–66.

Moyo, D. 2009. *Dead Aid: Why Aid Is Not Working and How There Is Another Way for Africa*. London: Allen Lane.

Muradian, R., and W. Pelupessy. 2005. "Governing the Coffee Chain: The Role of Voluntary Regulatory Systems." *World Development* 33(12): 2029–44.

Mutersbaugh, T. 2005. "Fighting Standards with Standards: Harmonization, Rents, and Social Accountability in Certified Agrofood Networks." *Environment and Planning* 37(11): 2033–51.

Narayan, U. 1997. *Dislocating Cultures: Identities, Tradition and Third World Feminism*. New York: Taylor and Francis.

Nelson, J. 2008. "Effecting Aid through Accountable Channels." In *Global Development 2.0: Can Philanthropists, the Public, and the Poor Make Poverty History?* ed. L. Brainard and D. Chollet, 149–86. Washington, D.C.: Brookings Institution Press.

Newell, P. 2005. "Citizenship, Accountability, and Community: The Limits of the CSR Agenda." *International Affairs* 81(3): 541–57.

———. 2008. "CSR and the Limits of Capital." *Development and Change* 39(6): 1063–78.

Newell, P., and J. G. Frynas. 2007. "Beyond CSR? Business, Poverty and Social Justice: An Introduction." *Third World Quarterly* 28(4): 669–81.

O'Manique, C. 2004. *Neoliberalism and AIDS Crisis in Sub-Saharan Africa: Globalization's Pandemic*. Basingstoke: Palgrave-MacMillan.

———. 2009. "The Global Risk Culture: Gendered Vulnerabilities to HIV/AIDS in Sub-Saharan Africa." In *The Fourth Wave: Violence, Gender, Culture, and HIV in the 21st Century*, ed. J. Klot and V.-K. Nguyen. New York: Social Science Research Council.

Oomman, N., M. Bernstein, and S. Rosenzweig. 2007. *Following the Funding for HIV/AIDS: A Comparative Analysis of the Funding Practices of PEPFAR*.

The Global Fund and World Bank MAP in Mozambique, Uganda and Zambia: HIV/AIDS Monitor and Center for Global Development.

Ooms, G. 2008. "The Right to Health and the Sustainability of Health Care: Why a New Global Health Aid Paradigm Is Needed." PhD Thesis, Ghent University, Faculty of Medicine and Health Sciences.

Pattberg, P. 2006. "Private Governance and the South: Lessons from Global Forest Politics." *Third World Quarterly* 27(4): 579–93.

Patton, C. 1990. *Inventing AIDS.* New York: Routledge.

———. 1992. "From Nation to Family: Containing 'African AIDS.'" In *Nationalisms and Sexualities,* ed. A. Parker, M. Russo, D. Sommer, and P. Yaeger, 218–34. New York: Routledge.

———. 1996. *Fatal Advice: How Safe-Sex Education Went Wrong.* Durham, N.C.: Duke University Press.

———. 2002. *Globalizing AIDS.* Minneapolis: University of Minnesota Press.

Pieterse, J. N. 1992. *White on Black: Images of Africa and Blacks in Western Popular Culture.* New Haven: Yale University Press.

Polanyi, K. 1957. "Aristotle Discovers the Economy." In *Trade and Market in Early Empires: Economies in History and Theory,* ed. K. Polanyi, C. M. Arensberg, and H. W. Pearson, 64–94. Glencoe, Ill.: Free Press.

Ponte, S. 2002. *Farmers and Markets in Tanzania: How Policy Reforms Affect Rural Livelihoods in Africa.* Oxford: James Currey; Dar es Salaam: Mkuki na Nyota; and Portsmouth, N.H.: Heinemann.

———. 2007. "Bans, Tests and Alchemy: Food Safety Regulation and the Uganda Fish Export Industry." *Agriculture and Human Values* 27(2): 179–93.

———. 2008. "Greener than Thou: The Political Economy of Fish Ecolabeling and Its Local Manifestations in South Africa." *World Development* 36(1): 159–75.

Ponte, S., L. A. Richey, and M. Baab. 2008. "Bono's Product (RED) Initiative: Wedding Hard Commerce and Corporate Social Responsibility," DIIS Working Paper 2008/13, Danish Institute for International Studies, Copenhagen.

Power, M. 1997. *The Audit Society: Rituals of Verification.* Oxford: Oxford University Press.

Prahalad, C. K. 2005. *The Fortune at the Bottom of the Pyramid: Eradicating Poverty through Profits.* Upper Saddle River, N.J.: Wharton School.

Prieto-Carron, M., P. Lund-Thomsen, A. Chan, A. Muro, and C. Bhushan. 2006. "Critical Perspectives on CSR and Development: What We Know,

What We Don't Know, and What We Need to Know." *International Affairs* 82(5): 977–87.

Rachman, G. 2007. "The Aid Crusade and Bono's Brigade." *Financial Times*, 30 October.

Radelet, S. 2006. "A Primer on Foreign Aid." Working Paper 92, Center for Global Development, Washington, D.C.

Radelet, S., and R. Levine. 2008. "Can We Build a Better Mousetrap? Three New Institutions Designed to Improve Aid Effectiveness." In *Reinventing Foreign Aid,* ed. W. Easterly, 431–60. Cambridge, Mass.: MIT Press.

Rajan, R. G., and A. Subramanian. 2005. "Aid and Growth: What Does the Cross-Country Evidence Really Show?" IMF Working Paper 05/127, International Monetary Fund, Washington, D.C.

Raynolds, L. T. 2002. "Consumer/Producer Links in Fair Trade Coffee Networks." *Sociologia Ruralis* 42(4): 404–24.

———. 2004. "The Globalization of Organic Agro-Food Networks." *World Development* 32(5): 725–43.

Raynolds, L. T., D. Murray, and P. L. Taylor. 2004. "Fair Trade Coffee: Building Producer Capacity via Global Networks." *Journal of International Development* 16:1109–21.

Richey, L. A. 2008. *Population Politics and Development: From the Policies to the Clinics.* New York: Palgrave MacMillan.

———. 2011. *Gendering the Therapeutic Citizen in Reproduction, Globalization and the State,* ed. C. H. Browner and C. F. Sargent. Durham, N.C.: Duke University Press.

Richey, L. A., and S. Ponte. 2006. "Better RED™ than Dead: 'Brand Aid,' Celebrities and the New Frontier of Development Assistance." DIIS Working Paper 2006/26, Danish Institute for International Studies, Copenhagen.

Ritzer, G. 1996. *The McDonaldization of Society: An Investigation in the Changing Character of Contemporary Social Life.* London: Sage.

Rivers, B. 2008. "Scaling Up to Meet the Need: Overcoming Barriers to the Development of Bold Global Fund–Financed Programs." Aidspan White Paper, Aidspan, Nairobi, Kenya.

Rojek, C. 1985. *Capitalism and Leisure Theory.* London: Methuen.

———. 2001. *Celebrity.* London: Reaktion.

Sachs, J. D. 2005. *The End of Poverty: Economic Possibilities of Our Time.* London: Allen Lane.

———. 2008. "On Carrying Each Other." In *Awearness: Inspiring Stories on How to Make a Difference,* ed. K. Cole. New York: Melcher Media.

Sarna-Wojcicki, M. 2008. "Refigu(red): Talking Africa and Aids in 'Causumer' Culture." *Journal of Pan African Studies* 2(6): 14–31.

Seckinelgin, H. 2005. "A Global Disease and Its Governance: HIV/AIDS in Sub-Saharan Africa and the Agency of NGOs." *Global Governance* 11:351–68.

———. 2008. *The International Politics of HIV/AIDS: Global Disease-Local Pain.* London: Routledge.

Shadlen, K. C. 2007. "The Political Economy of AIDS Treatment: Intellectual Property and the Transformation of Generic Supply." *International Studies Quarterly* 51(3): 559–81.

Simmel, G. 1930. *The Philosophy of Money.* London: Routledge and Kegan Paul.

Slater, D. 1997. *Consumer Culture and Modernity.* London: Polity.

Smith, D. J., and B. C. Mbakwem. 2007. "Life Projects and Therapeutic Itineraries: Marriage, Fertility, and Antiretroviral Therapy in Nigeria." *AIDS* 21, suppl. 5: S37–41.

Sontag, S. 2003. *Regarding the Pain of Others.* New York: Farar, Straus, and Giroux.

Spivak, G. 1985. "Can the Subaltern Speak? Speculations on Widow Sacrifice." *Wedge* 7–8:120–30.

Steiner-Khamsi, G. 2008. "Donor Logic in the Era of Gates, Buffet and Soros." *Current Issues in Comparative Education* 10(1/2): 10–15.

Stillwaggon, E. 2003. "Racial Metaphors: Interpreting Sex and AIDS in Africa." *Development and Change* 34(5): 809–32.

———. 2005. *AIDS and the Ecology of Poverty.* Oxford: Oxford University Press.

Strathern, M. 2000. *Audit Cultures: Anthropological Studies in Accountability, Ethics and the Academy.* London: Routledge.

Taylor, P. L. 2005. "In the Market but Not of It: Fair Trade Coffee and Forest Stewardship Council Certification as Market-Based Social Change." *World Development* 33(1): 129–47.

Therkildsen, O. 2005. "Major Additional Funding for the MDGs: A Mixed Blessing for Capacity Development." *IDS Bulletin* 36(3): 28–39.

Thomas, K. 2008. "Selling Sorrow: Testimony, Representation and Images of HIV-Positive South African Women." *Social Dynamics* 34(2): 216–26.

Thompson, G. 2008. *Tracking Global Corporate Citizenship: Some Reflections on "Lovesick" Companies.* Mimeo. Copenhagen: Copenhagen Business School.

Treichler, P. A. 1999. *How to Have Theory in an Epidemic.* Durham, N.C.: Duke University Press.

Trentmann, F. 2006. "An Introduction: Knowing Consumers—Histories, Identities, Practices." In *The Making of the Consumer: Knowledge, Power and Identity in the Modern World*, ed. F. Trentmann. Oxford: Berg.

Turner, G. 2004. *Understanding Celebrity*. London: Sage.

Turner, S. P. 2003. *Liberal Democracy 3.0: Civil Society in an Age of Experts*. Thousand Oaks, Calif.: Sage.

UN. 2008. *Declaration of Commitment on HIV/AIDS and Political Declaration on HIV/AIDS: Midway to the Millennium Development Goals*. Report of the Secretary. New York: UN.

UNAIDS. 2008. *Report on the Global HIV/AIDS Epidemic 2008*. Geneva: UNAIDS.

van Dalen, H. P., and M. Reuser. 2005. "Assessing Size and Structure of Worldwide Funds for Population and AIDS Activities." NIDI report, 9 May, Netherlands Interdisciplinary Demographic Institute.

Van Der Gaag, N., and C. Nash. 1987. *Images of Africa: The UK Report*. Oxford: Oxfam.

Vavrus, F., and L. A. Richey, eds. 2003. "Women and Development: Rethinking Policy and Reconceptualizing Practice." Special issue, *Women's Studies Quarterly* 31.

Veblen, T. 1912. *The Theory of the Leisure Class: An Economic Study of Institutions*. New York: B. W. Huebsch.

Ventelou, B., and J. P. Moatti. 2008. "Bigger Is Better: Scaling-Up Antiretroviral Policies in Sub-Saharan Africa." *Future HIV Therapy* 2(4): 297–98.

Virno, P., and M. Hardt, eds. 1996. *Radical Thought in Italy: A Potential Politics*. Minneapolis: University of Minnesota Press.

Ward, M. C. 1993. "A Different Disease: HIV/AIDS and Health Care for Women in Poverty." *Culture, Medicine and Psychiatry* 17:413–30.

Warde, A. 1997. *Consumption, Food and Taste: Culinary Antinomies and Commodity Culture*. London: Sage.

Wartick, S. L., and P. L. Cochran. 1985. "The Evolution of the Corporate Social Performance Model." *Academy of Management Review* 10(4): 758–69.

Watney, S. 1987. *Policing Desire: Pornography, AIDS and the Media*. London: Methuen.

———. 1990. "Missionary Positions: AIDS, 'Africa,' and Race." In *Out There: Marginalization and Contemporary Cultures*, ed. R. Fertuson, M. Gever, T. Minh-ha, and C. West, 89–106. New York: New Museum of Contemporary Art.

Watson, D. B., and E. Stratford. 2008. "Feminizing Risk at a Distance: Critical Observations on the Constitution of a Preventive Technology for HIV/AIDS." *Social and Cultural Geography* 9(5): 353–71.

Weber, M. 1968. *On Charisma and Institution Building,* ed. S. N. Eisenstadt, Heritage of Sociology Series. Chicago: University of Chicago Press.

Welsh, J. C. 1999. "Good Cause, Good Business." *Harvard Business Review* 77(1): 1–3.

Whitfield, L. 2009. *The Politics of Aid: African Strategies for Dealing with Donors.* Oxford: Oxford University Press.

Wilde, J., and E. de Haan. 2006. *The High Cost of Calling: Critical Issues in the Mobile Phone Industry.* Amsterdam: Centre for Research on Multinational Corporations.

World Bank. 2003a. *Strengthening Implementation of Corporate Social Responsibility in Global Supply Chains.* Washington, D.C.: World Bank.

———. 2003b. "Supporting Sound Policies with Adequate and Appropriate Financing." Report prepared for the meeting of the Development Committee, 22 September, Document No. DC2003-00.

———. 2005. "Food Safety and Agricultural Health Standards: Challenges and Opportunities for Developing Country Exports." Report No. 31207, World Bank, Washington, D.C., Poverty Reduction and Economic Management Trade Unit, and Agriculture and Rural Development Department.

Wrigley, N., and M. Lowe. 2002. *Reading Retail: A Geographical Perspective on Retailing and Consumption Spaces.* London: Arnold.

INDEX